EMPOWERING PANCHAYATS
Handbook for Master Trainers

About the Rajiv Gandhi Foundation

The Rajiv Gandhi Foundation as a registered Trust was set up in 1991 to commemorate Rajiv Gandhi's contributions to the building of a modern India and to realise his vision most important being decentralised democracy, literacy, application of science and technology, concern for the deprived and the under-privileged, peace and international cooperation, disarmament and total destruction of nuclear weapons etc. For special emphasis on decentralised governance, the Foundation set up a Task Force on Panchayati Raj in 1993. This handbook is one of the outputs of the Task Force.

About the Authors

***D. Bandyopadhyay**, IAS (Retd.) was the Secretary, Ministry of Rural Development and Secretary (Revenue), Ministry of Finance, Government of India; Executive Director, Asian Development Bank; and is presently connected in different senior capacities with various States and Cenral organisations as also civil society organisations.*

***Dr. Amitava Mukherjee** is the Executive Director of Development Tracks, New Delhi, a knowledge company and is currently Master Trainer, with the United Nations, Economic and Social Council for Asia and The Pacific, Bangkok. He was earlier Professor of Economics and Planning, Lal Bahadur Shastri National Academy of Administration, Mussoorie and Consultant to various UN Agencies and International Organisations. He has written extensively on decentralisation, poverty and hunger, with over two dozen books and numerous papers to his credit.*

***Smt. Mitali Sen Gavai** is an IAS officer of the Maharashtra cadre. She has held important positions in the Government of Maharashtra including those of Sub-Divisional Magistrate, Jalgaon; Collector & District Magistrate, Osmanabad; Chief Executive Officer, Zila Parishad, Thane and Deputy Director-General, YASHADA (State Training Institute, Pune). She has vast experience in rural development and Panchayati Raj.*

EMPOWERING PANCHAYATS
Handbook for Master Trainers
(Using Participatory Approach)

D. BANDYOPADHYAY
AMITAVA MUKHERJEE
MITALI SEN GAVAI

Published for
Task Force On Panchayati Raj
RAJIV GANDHI FOUNDATION
by
CONCEPT PUBLISHING COMPANY, NEW DELHI-110059

ISBN 81-8069-041-5

First Published 2003

Published and Printed by
Ashok Kumar Mittal
Concept Publishing Company
A/15-16, Commercial Block, Mohan Garden
New Delhi-110059 (INDIA)

Phones : 25351460, 25351794
Fax : 091-11-25357103
Email : publishing@conceptpub.com

Preface

It was a massive exercise involving 10 academic, research and activist institutions. With a plethora of training programmes going on for Panchayat members from 1993, one felt a bit uneasy to embark upon this enterprise. But it was felt that nowhere was there any handbook of training evolved through Participatory Learning and Action Process where the actual or potential trainees could express their views and where the master trainers could identify the strength and weakness of the training processes somehow going on.

We went about it systematically, starting from making a Directory of Training institutions, their training methodologies and their training infrastructure by a survey. A paper on training methodology based on the survey was prepared and tested in the National Workshop where over 80 experts participated. Generic training modules prepared on the basis of recommendations were tested by a workshop of master trainers from State Resource Institutions. Then state specific training modules were prepared, tested and evaluated locally. Inputs received went into updating generic modules. These were then again tested at Lal Bahadur Shastri National Academy of Administration (LBSNAA), Mussoorie, by the participating institutions and experts. All these were taken into account to prepare the final set, which we believe will require continuous updating as the democracy at the grassroots marches on.

Camp: New Delhi
November, 2002

D. Bandyopadhyay
Amitava Mukherjee
Mitali Sen Gavai

Acknowledgements

The Rajiv Gandhi Foundation is thankful to the following persons and institutions who greatly helped in the preparation of this book:

1. Directors and Faculty of the following institutions:
   (i) Kerala Institute of Local Administration (KILA), Thrissur, (Kerala);
   (ii) Centre for Youth and Social Development (CYSD), Bhubaneshwar, (Orissa);
   (iii) Department of Political Science, Mohan Lal Sukhadia University (MLSU), Udaipur, (Rajasthan);
   (iv) Omeo Kumar Das Institute of Social Change and Development (OKDISCD), Guwahati, (Assam);
   (v) Gandhigram Rural Institute, Gandhigram, (Tamil Nadu);
   (vi) Madhya Pradesh Institute of Social Science Research (MPISSR), Ujjain;
   (vii) Lal Bahadur Shastri National Academy of Administration (LBSNAA), Mussoorie, (Uttranchal);
   (viii) Andhra Pradesh Academy of Rural Development (APARD), Hyderabad;
   (ix) Abdul Nazir Sab State Institute of Rural Development (ANSSIRD), Mysore, (Karnataka); and
   (x) Haryana Institute of Public Administration (HIPA), Gurgaon.

2. Task Force Members: Shri L.C. Jain, Dr. C.H. Hanumantha Rao, Dr. M. Shiviah, Dr. V.A. Pai Panandikar, Shri Mani Shankar Aiyar, Prof. B.K. Chandrashekar, Dr. Y.K. Alagh, Dr. (Mrs.) Kumud Sharma, Prof. M. Aslam, Dr. Ghanshyam Shah, Mrs. Jarjum Ete, Mrs. Nirmala Buch, Dr. Revathi Narayanan, Shri V. Ramachandran and Shri C. Narayana Swamy.

3. Participants of various workshops and seminars, particularly the evaluators and participants of Training of Trainers (ToT) Programme and those who tested the state specific modules.
4. Shri Wajahat Habibullah, Director; Professors and Staff of Lal Bahadur Shastri National Academy of Administration (LBSNAA) for co-hosting the National Workshop held in Mussoorie on 22-23 March, 2002.
5. Ford Foundation for generous grant which made this publication and the preparation of other modules possible.
6. Shri Manmohan Malhoutra, Secretary-General, Rajiv Gandhi Foundation; Shri O.P. Rehan, Coordinator; Ms. Kavita Sharma and Shri Vinod Kumar Verma.

We are also thankful to numerous other individuals who helped us in this endeavour in different ways. For shortage of space it is not possible to spell out all the names.

Contents

Appendices

List of Figures

Chapter I

Prelude

I. INTRODUCTION

Initially, it was a journey into the unknown. The Task Force on Panchayati Raj of the Rajiv Gandhi Foundation began its activities from March 1993 soon after Parliament passed the 73rd Constitutional Amendment. It was to act as a catalyst to make panchayats "genuine institutions of self government". To find out what was happening at the ground level, the Task Force organised 46 Sub-Regional Workshops at the district level and below, 10 Regional and five National level Workshops/Seminars involving hundreds of elected panchayat representatives at local and state level government officials, academia, representatives of NGOs and panchayat friendly persons. Newly elected panchayat representatives, both men and women, expressed their views, aspirations, fears, frustration, hope and despair in their own immutable language and style. One could discover an emerging pattern of reinforcing the existing bureaucratic administration set-up instead of empowering the panchayats.

II. THE PROBLEMATIQUE

It was noticed that the elected panchayat functionaries felt that they were being stymied, obstructed, hindered and prevented from discharging their constitutional role by the bureaucracy and the MLAs and MPs. They were being looked down upon. They were not being taken seriously. They were not being given powers, functions, finance and functionaries to make panchayats effective institutions of self-government as mandated by the Constitution. There were attempts to make them feel as a bunch of ineffective and incompetent women and men incapable of fulfilling the desires and aspirations of their constituents. There were attempts to denigrate them and to lower their self-esteem, particularly in respect of elected women members.

The Task Force undertook highly innovative dialogical sessions with three major players in democratic decentralisation : (i) elected panchayat members, (ii) MLAs and MPs, and (iii) members of the bureaucracy. Members of the academia and representatives of NGOs were in attendance. In a way, it was not only novel but a daring exercise in behavioural dynamics. No one else in India did it before. Conflict of ego and interest came out in the fore. It did not solve the problem but initiated a process of awakening.

One of the issues that came out sharply through all these exercises was the need for capacity building for the members and elected functionaries of panchayats. Simultaneously, there was a felt necessity for attitudinal and behavioural change among members of the bureaucracy and MLAs/MPs.

Long ago Socrates, in one of his dialogues, had said, "There is only one good, knowledge, and one evil, ignorance". Without appearing to be presumptuous, we may state that the vision of this current exercise of developing an appropriate training strategy and training modules for the master trainers is to stimulate the yearning and passion for knowledge of the elected panchayat members and functionaries, imparting some basic skills necessary for ensuring good governance, generating their appreciation of the basic philosophy of autonomy and self-governance and building up their self-esteem and confidence.

Every five years, there would be panchayat elections for electing little over three million members and functionaries all over the country. At least half of these three million elected members would be newcomers. More than one million would be women, many of whom would be coming out of their homes for the first time in public life. They would face formidable impediments and road blocks when they would try to be autonomous decision makers.

III. WHY AND WHAT IS THIS HANDBOOK?

The aim of this strategy and the handbook is to aid these millions of elected members, mostly newcomers, and lakhs of women functionaries who would step out of their homes for the first time in public life, to realise their inherent potential as the repository of people's power and confidence to ensure responsiveness, accountability, transparency, autonomy, fair deal and other ingredients of good governance. There are modules already in existence but there are none which give a systems' approach to capacity building of PRI functionaries and for all stakeholders both primary and secondary. Secondly, the existing literature on capacity building does not use or suggest the use of Participatory Learning and Action methods, right from training needs assessment, political orientation to planning orientation of the PRI functionaries. Thirdly, the thrust of the system of training for PRI suggested in the handbook is always inducing the PRI functionaries to be conscious of their rights and obligations and seek those to empower themselves, instead of looking upto some faceless entity for the enhancement of their capacity. The handbook attempts, as it were, a rights-based approach to capacity building of PRI functionaries. Finally, the design of the handbook itself is unique, in terms of its contents: modules and an andragogy of training which have been widely tested, content flow, session plans, games, steps for conducting the sessions, further reading and notes to trainers.

We are not suggesting in this handbook a straitjacketed manual for regimental training. We are all for variety and diversity to take care of the multiplicity of situation prevailing in the country. Our emphasis would be on the metaphysics of justice — social, economic, political, gender and environmental as well as on the nitty-gritty of daily administration and proper management practices. After developing the philosophy of training strategy, the handbook contains generic modules of training for the master trainers. The whole exercise has been built on the methodology of participatory learning and action — a new attempt in the field of empowering the functionaries of the panchayati raj institutions in India.

It needs to be mentioned that though the handbook, deals with only one set of modules, it has been germane to several state specific modules as well. The base modules were first developed at the RGF and a network of collaborating institutions was established. The institutions of this network adapted the base modules to state specific situations and developed state specific modules for Andhra Pradesh, Assam, Kerala, Karnataka, Madhya Pradesh, Orissa, Rajasthan, Tamil Nadu, Uttranchal and Tripura. A special module was also developed for tribal women Sarpanches of Rajasthan.

IV. CREDITS AND DISCLAIMERS

The project was conceived and co-ordinated by Prof. M. Aslam. He conducted a survey of the institutions (both in the governmental and the non-governmental sectors) throughout India imparting training in capacity building and published the Directory of Institutions engaged in training PRI functionaries. Prof. Aslam was also responsible for holding a series of meetings as well as a national workshop on building capacity of panchayati raj institutions, from which valuable lessons were culled out for prosecuting the project objectives. He made very valuable contributions in taking forward the project.

From May 2001, Dr. Amitava Mukherjee took over the task of co-ordinating the project. He developed the eleven modules along with the training methodology for the functionaries of the panchayati raj institutions, by adapting methods from "tool box" of Participatory Learning and Action (PLA). He worked out in detail which PLA "tool" or "method" was to be used for which topic, like use of Historical Transect to raise awareness of PRI functionaries about evolution of panchayats, etc. A Consultative Workshop of collaborating institutions from different states in the country was held on 18th and 19th July 2001, where the modules and the new methodology suggested by Dr. Mukherjee were discussed. The meeting, while fully endorsing the modules and methodology, felt that since use of PLA methods in training panchayati raj institution functionaries, on such areas as functions and powers of PRIs, management, gender, political and legal dimensions of panchayats and paradigms of development was novel, there was a critical need to conduct a Training of Trainers' Programme for the participating institutions. Pursuant to the decision of the meeting, Dr. Mukherjee designed and conducted a Training of Trainers' Programme in September 2001, at the Haryana Institute of Public Administration, Gurgaon, Haryana, for key trainers from the collaborating institutions. He also oversaw both the adoption of the methodology by the collaborating institutions and development of state specific modules. The brief strategy for utilizing the modules was also developed by Dr. Mukherjee based on feedback provided from various quarters.

Mrs. Mitali Sen Gavai, an officer of the Indian Administrative Service, joined as Senior Research Fellow in October 2001, on leave of absence from the Government of Maharashtra. She along with Dr. Mukherjee supervised the successful testing of the modules by the collaborating institutions in different parts of the country, evaluating them and developing the session plans, encapsulated in the base module. Mrs. Gavai has also worked out a detailed document for follow up measures that need to be initiated for completing some of the unfinished agenda of this project, viz., catering to the special capability building of the women PRI functionaries and creating a social capital in which they will be comfortable in operating, together with improvement of the training-ware of the state level institutions who would take forward the bulk of the responsibility of the capability enhancement of the women PRI functionaries.

Mrs. Kumud Sharma, Mrs. Nirmala Buch, Prof. Ghanashyam Shah, Dr. Y.K. Alagh, Mr. Wajahat Habibullah, Shri L.C. Jain and

Mr. V. Ramachandran provided valuable comments on the earlier drafts of the modules which have greatly enhanced their value. The state resource institutions and their staff/faculty have tested the modules and carried out innovations in the state specific modules. These institutions are: Kerala Institute of Local Administration (KILA), Thrissur, (Kerala); Centre for Youth and Social Development (CYSD), Bhubaneshwar, (Orissa); Department of Political Science, Mohan Lal Sukhadia University (MLSU), Udaipur, (Rajasthan); Omeo Kumar Das Institute of Social Change and Development (OKDISCD), Guwahati, (Assam); Gandhigram Rural Institute, Gandhigram, (Tamil Nadu); Madhya Pradesh Institute of Social Science Research (MPISSR), Ujjain; Lal Bahadur Shastri National Academy of Administration (LBSNAA), Mussoorie, (Uttranchal); Andhra Pradesh Academy of Rural Development (APARD), Hyderabad; Abdul Nazir Sab State Institute of Rural Development (ANSSIRD), Mysore, (Karnataka); and Haryana Institute of Public Administration (HIPA), Gurgaon.

Since training needs of all evolving institutions are dynamic and the PRIs are still evolving, the training interventions cannot be cast in stone. These modules are, therefore, expected to be updated and changed by the users, trainers and training institutions. The methodology adopted will concurrently, it is expected, be changed and improved upon. The Handbook is also expected to trigger new thinking on how to meet the constant challenge of training thousands of PRI functionaries, many of whom will be neo-literates and semi-literates, in the art of governance, planning and bringing about social justice and gender equity. It is recognized that this Handbook does not specifically deal with the capacity building of women functionaries, though gender equity has been made one of the principal areas of focus. The need for developing a training system for women functionaries of the panchayati raj institutions will have to be met in a future venture. The sooner it is done, the better.

Shri Manmohan Malhoutra, Secretary-General of the Rajiv Gandhi Foundation, extended his full support and cooperation throughout the project. Valuable assistance was received from Shri O.P. Rehan, Coordinator, Panchayati Raj Unit, RGF during this period. The project was undertaken with generous funding provided by the Ford Foundation, New Delhi.

Chapter II

Training for Empowerment *A Recital*

I. INTRODUCTION

The Seventy-third Constitutional Amendment Act of 1993 and the consequent conformity Acts enacted by the states have opened the floodgates of political participation to the rural masses through the panchayati raj institutions (PRIs). There are more than 3 million members who have been elected to the different tiers of the PRIs in the elections held in accordance with the conformity Acts. The spectrum of elected members has been considerably broadened and diversified in the post-Amendment period. It now includes literates, neo-literates, illiterates, women, scheduled castes, scheduled tribes and other marginalized groups.

In many states, sizeable proportions of the elected members are first or second generation entrants into the arena of panchayati raj politics. Notwithstanding their enthusiasm to participate in the affairs of the PRIs, large number of them are inhibited by lack of an understanding of the art of governance. Given the complexities of the tasks before them, many PRI functionaries have not been able to make much headway in the discharge of their functions. The reasons for this situation are many, like the inadequate devolution and delegation of powers and authority to them by the state governments and their own lack of awareness about their rights, in local governance. The elected women members are additionally disadvantaged because they face the *double jeopardy* of having to overcome their own political innocence and the traditional patriarchal dispositions of rural communities, given that the PRIs have been historically male bastions of power. Similarly, the scheduled caste and scheduled tribe members have to face many challenges as the PRIs have also been traditional bastions of upper-castes.

II. THREE TRAINING QUESTIONS AND THEIR ANSWERS

For analyzing the context of training and the spectrum of training needs of the members and functionaries of the PRIs, we have to address three key questions:

(a) Why is a special training regime required to be planned for this audience?
(b) What is the problem that the training regime hopes to address?
(c) Can development training best solve the problem in this context?

The answers are discussed below:

(a) Why is a special training regime required to be planned for this audience?

The spectrum of training needs of this kind of audience is determined by several considerations. As mentioned earlier, many of the elected members and the government functionaries have expertise in their own fields of experience and are also in a manner of speaking *specialists*. They need to know more about the specifics of community development management and grassroots self-government. These training needs flow from the fact that the members and the functionaries of the PRIs are required to carry out a total of twenty-nine tasks that have been outlined in the Eleventh Schedule to the Constitution. These tasks encompass almost the entire gamut of development architecture and development engineering in this country. The plethora of present-day development programmes, that conceptually fall within the domain of the PRIs, is mind-boggling in its variety, beneficiaries, basket of services and delivery rules. Consequently, the members and the functionaries of the PRIs need to possess an incredible amount of expertise in diverse fields. The members, especially, have to live up to the expectations that their communities have reposed in them and the faith that the constitution has reposed in them. To this end, they need to comprehend their rights, duties, the limits of their domains, jurisdiction, authority, and the principles of democratic decentralization and self-government that underpin the creation of the PRIs.

Take for instance the situation of the *Sarpanch* of a typical village panchayat. The *Sarpanch* along with the *Gramsevak* is expected to manage the village panchayat professionally like a corporate entity. This pair has to negotiate hand-in-hand (and very artfully at that) the everyday twists and turns of village panchayat governance. This pair has to oversee the management of the rural development programmes in their village. The *Sarpanch* is also expected to possess the qualities and vision of a leader. And that too after having been fortunate enough to have attended a few local-level training programmes. The oft-berated government functionaries of the panchayati raj institutions have also to accomplish many difficult development tasks. The *Gramsevak,* who is the secretary to the village panchayat, in fact plays no less a role than the *Sarpanch.* In some states, the *Gramsevak* attends a foundational training course of about three months, with a two-week refresher course thrown in at some point in his career. In-service training opportunities are otherwise very few and far apart. Although this government functionary is at the very bottom rung of the bureaucratic ladder, he is expected to be literally a jack of all trades. The *Sarpanch* and the *Gramsevak* together share the onus of implementing development programmes at the very cutting edge of the development process. They undoubtedly need a very strong grounding in the disciplines of village panchayat governance and community development. The same is also true for the elected members and functionaries of the two upper rungs of the PRIs. The training regime suggested in this Handbook has been informed by these considerations.

The shifting of the mechanistic development paradigm to an organic, people-centred one has added to the list of desired capabilities of the members and the functionaries. The new generation of *Sarpanches* (and *Gramsevaks*) has to possess appropriate attitudes and display behaviour, best described as humanistic. They have to be gravely concerned and committed about the development of the vulnerables in their village, particularly the SCs/STs and woman. They have to elicit the development participation of her community. They are also is also expected to follow a certain code of development ethics based upon the principles of equity, responsiveness, transparency, accountability, participation, etc. Thus, the capacity building of the elected members also includes a process of confidence building, reinforcing/injecting self-esteem, proactive behaviour modelling, inculcating leadership qualities and an ability to envision village development in its entirety. These are some of the other imperative training needs of the audience that are being addressed through the Handbook.

(b) What is the problem that the training regime hopes to address?

The basic problem that confronts the nation today is that despite the constitutional creation of a third tier of self-government in the PRIs, this tier has been largely relegated to the background. It is functioning at best as an implementing agency of the line departments of the government. In effect, the fundamental logic underlying the creation of the PRIs of giving power to the people to govern themselves for achieving economic development, gender and social equity has been jeopardised. As a result, *a culture of silence* or of maintaining *status quo,* amongst the PRI functionaries, has grown in as much as they do not ask for the rights that rightfully belong to the PRIs. The general perception is that barring a few exceptions, most of them lack the required enthusiasm and attitude for making the PRIs true units of self-government. The *culture of silence*, as it were, has been, in part fostered by an inadequate appreciation of the logic behind the creation of the PRIs and in part because they lack the necessary wherewithal to handle the subjects enjoined in the Eleventh Schedule to the Constitution. It is this problem of breaking the *culture of silence* which is sought to be addressed through this training regime, where the focus deliberately concentrated on making the PRI functionaries alive of their rights, duties and obligations.

(c) Can development training best solve the problem in this context?

There are two alternatives to breaking the *culture of silence* that have set in and enthusing the PRI functionaries. One, a change in the attitudes and approaches of the States so that they embark on a programme of devolution and delegation of functions, finances and functionaries to the PRIs with regard to the twenty-nine subjects listed in the Eleventh Schedule to the Constitution. This is the "top-down" approach, in consonance with the process followed in amending the Constitution to create the PRIs. Second, a change in the attitudes and approach of the PRI functionaries themselves in the way they conduct the affairs of the panchayats. Instead of relying on the higher echelons of the government to devolve power upon the PRIs, they have to become proactive in seeking to exercise effective jurisdiction of the subjects specified in the Schedule and proactively seek to exercise the right to govern that belongs to them. This is the "bottom-up" approach which is believed to be the better of the two alternatives because it would be grounded in demands from the people who matter. Since by this approach thousands of PRIs will seek to act on issues that affect the lives of the poor and common men, it will create a momentum and grounds well of its own to change the way the PRIs currently function, and such a momentum may not be dependent upon the discretion of the bureaucracy and politicians.

The second approach is best achieved through a *Training System* consisting of structured training events addressing the different kinds of training needs of different sections of the audience. This will raise the awareness of the PRI functionaries, that is, create an urge in them to play the role assigned to them and make them alive of their rights and obligations, which, in turn, would break the *culture of silence* prevailing amongst the PRI members. The PRIs are still perceived as a direct challenge to the political and administrative bureaucracy. There is no need to labour the point that in the Constitution, the PRIs are conceived as "autonomous", in the sense that they are units of self-government not dependent upon any line department for their operation. Nevertheless, the PRIs will have to operate within the political and bureaucratic environment that has been nurtured on the "blue-print" supply-driven approach, keen to reach targets. At the same time, the PRIs have to nurture a bottom-up approach to deliver the development thrust stemming from a demand-driven approach.

III. THE CHALLENGES BEFORE DEVELOPMENT TRAINERS

The capacity building of the members and functionaries of the PRIs is of great significance in the wake of the Amendment Act. The trainer-fraternity is playing a key role in initiating members, especially the first generation ones into the multifaceted discipline of panchayati raj governance. Their efforts to train the members have picked up momentum in all the states, with trainers from both the government and NGO sectors joining hands. But they are facing many challenges in their task. Though there are a number of training institutions proactive in the field, they have not as yet been able to generate the kind of synergy among the PRIs that is essential to enable them to redeem substantially the faith and trust reposed in them by village communities at large. Many of these training events are often unstructured and discontinuous. Their quality is affected from the lack of funds and the availability of core training modules. Even almost a decade after the Amendment Act, the trainer-fraternity acutely feels the absence of need-specific modules for conducting targeted training interventions. The trainers do not have sufficient learning and networking opportunities, either.

The elected members of the PRIs are adult learners, many of whom are illiterate and neo-literate. There are several methodological issues related to training which need to be addressed in this context. What should be the nature of the training methodology for motivating these adult learners? This is the question which is uppermost in the minds of the trainers since the choice of methodology is crucial for inducing learner participation. Many of the members have not been present in a formal learning environment before, and the training event may be the first such opportunity for them. They may be seeing the precincts of a classroom for the first time. The audience includes many socially deprived members, like the women whose motivation to learn is usually thwarted by their low social status. The biggest challenge before development trainers is, therefore, to increase the *learner valence* of the audience. This is defined as the *motivation to learn* which a learner may possess. This may be described as *positive* when the learner is eager to participate in the learning process and negative when the learner is hesitant. The *valence* may vary for a particular learner in the course of the training event because of a host of factors related to the training contents of different sessions, trainer-attitudes, methodology, etc. The challenge before trainers is to increase the *learner valence* and sustain it at a positive count throughout the training programme. This is possible by adopting a training methodology, which uses the tools and methods of Participatory Learning and Action, and involving the participants throughout the training programmes.

So while the *Sarpanch* and the *Gramsevak* are expected to be people-centred in their attitudes, their trainers have to take up a learner-centric position. In terms of adult learning models, the trainers have to shift from their previous trainer-centric model and abandon their age-old didactic attitudes towards their learners. The trainers must move from "what is known" to the unknown. Thus, the training of the elected members of the PRIs calls for methodological shift in the training paradigm. It requires a learner-centric training model that uses participatory training methodology whereby the participant assumes a dominant stance vis-à-vis the trainer. The PRI members have to be empowered through the training process to function as the agents of social change at the grassroots. This prescribes a training process which is by itself an empowering one and conscientises the *oppressed* learners like the first time elected members, especially the women members and members belonging to SC/ST communities. We thus enter the realm of Paulo Freire and his *praxis* cycles. The training process should ideally be able to generate at the participant-level a *praxis* behavioural mode or a series of continuous action-reflection-action cycles. In functional terms, the training methodology should enable the PRI members to *assess* and *analyze* their village-level realities and plan proactive *actions* for village development.

The training methodology developed is based on the instruments provided by a genre of methods labelled as "Participatory Learning and Action". These methods have been used in generating plans, developing projects, monitoring evaluations and research in diverse fields. They have now been adopted for the first time in this book as training methodology for PRI functionaries in different aspects having bearing on PRIs such as politico-legal orientation, management orientation and role orientation of PRI functionaries.

IV. TRAINING GOAL AND OBJECTIVES OF THE PROPOSED TRAINING SYSTEM

Keeping these deliberations in mind, this Handbook has attempted to design a ***Training System*** which would serve the cause of the empowerment of the members and the functionaries of the PRIs. It spells out the ***Training Vision*** before development trainers working in the arena of panchayati raj training as:

"To break the culture of silence prevailing amongst the members of the PRIs by conscientising them about their rights and duties and empowering them to exercise those rights to their truest extent and to discharge their duties fully and fairly."

The ***Training System*** designed in the context of this ***Vision*** would have manifold ***Objectives*** like:

- Rekindling the vision, mission and values that were at the heart of the process that led to the formation of PRIs, and imploring the PRI functionaries to seek their rights and responsibilities to govern.
- Sensitizing all stakeholders within the interactive domain of the PRIs such as the political executives, bureaucracies, line departments, civil society actors and the media about the concepts underlying the PRIs and the need to allow them to exercise their powers and functions.
- Attempting to emphasize the right attitudes and behaviours in PRI functionaries, so that they come out of the culture of *status quo*.
- Building capacity in developing grassroots level development plans for social justice and gender equity, through participatory methods and tools
- Building confidence in the members and functionaries of the PRIs and establishing a network of major development actors and training institutions to take forward the agenda of capacity building in this sector.
- Creating a cadre of master trainers in different training institutions for the capacity building of the members and functionaries of the PRIs, with requisite aids, training materials and access to information that are necessary prerequisites for carrying out the tasks assigned to them.
- Resolving conflicts amongst all stakeholders associated with the PRIs and creating an enabling environment for the PRIs to function as effective institutions of self-government at the local level for promoting social justice and gender equity.

V. THE AUDIENCE OF THE TRAINING SYSTEM: WHOM TO TRAIN?

The principal audience for the training events outlined in the Handbook consists of the elected members of the three tiers of the PRIs. However, there are several other stakeholders who can either impede or facilitate the functioning of the PRIs as institutions of self-government for promoting social justice and gender equity. The targeted audience for this Training

System, therefore, consists of the elected members of the PRIs and other associated functionaries or "significants". The Training System suggested in this Handbook is directed towards the capacity building of the following stakeholder-groups:

- All members of the three tiers of the PRIs;
- All officials of the three tiers of the PRIs;
- All CEOs of the three tiers of the PRIs;
- Key officials at the state level;
- Chairpersons of the Zilla Parishad, Pramukhs and Up-Pramukhs of the Panchayat Samities and Sarpanches of the Village Panchayats;
- All district officers;
- Members of the Advisory Committees and Taluka/Village Committees;
- Bank Managers;
- NGOs, Self-Help Groups and other voluntary agencies.

VI. THE TRAINING AUDIENCE

The modules in this Handbook have thus been designed to address a combined audience of elected members, government functionaries, bank officials, NGOs, etc. The rationale behind having a mixed training audience, *albeit* of many conflicting interests is that they should learn together. The training methodology suggested for use promotes participatory learning and expectedly a degree of bonding amongst learner-groups which may be of a permanent or semi-permanent nature. This may or may not resolve the inter-group and inter-personal conflicts that are prevailing in the field. But it definitely makes the expertise of the elected members complementary to that of the parallel non-elected functionaries, the two arms that are together responsible for managing the PRIs. The elected members thus become less vulnerable to the dictates of the government functionaries. It is also likely that both the groups would become more accountable to each other after having experienced a common learning process which includes a strong content on social audit and the roles and responsibilities of different development actors. The interconnectivities amongst these actors influence the nature of the development process at the village level. It is, therefore, necessary that the network of their relationships be synergistic. A combined training initiative for all these development actors, especially those whose methodology positively enhances their group dynamics, can greatly influence this network of relationships and development outcomes.

It may be added here that the government functionaries and the extension agents of the PRIs constitute an important section of the training audience addressed by the modules. They are expected to be specialists in their own work domain and their in-service training is geared to equip them. For this reason, their work expertise may not be that much of a contentious issue, but their attitudes and behaviours certainly are. With the shifting of the mechanistic development paradigm to an organic, people-centred one, the government functionaries are also expected to adopt suitable patterns of behaviours that would facilitate participatory development. This is a definite departure from their previous roles as *benefactors* and as directors of the process of development of the so-called *beneficiaries*. But sadly, in many instances, the desired attitudinal change in the functionaries have been, as all other such changes usually are, very slow. This has definitely hindered the handing over of the locus of control over the development process to the poor stakeholders.

It may be underscored that training events of different kinds, intensities and durations have been designed for the different participant-groups. While operational or foundational training programmes have been proposed for some of them, others will be targeted through awareness building exercises and specialised courses to equip them with the desired skills and attitudes.

VII. THE TRAINING HORIZON OF THE TRAINING SYSTEM

Training is not a single shot event, but a process of continuous learning. The training of the members and functionaries of the PRIs will not only be a vehicle for imparting appropriate skills and knowledge and inculcating attitudes and behaviours, but will also act as a problem solving and continuous reinforcing mechanism. The training regime should be a nested approach where one training event feeds into another for generating a cumulative learning process. Some of the training events would help the participants to gain skills and knowledge required to deal with the subjects laid down in the Eleventh Schedule of the Constitution. Others would generate an enabling environment for them to seek their rights and space to work as units of self-government for promoting economic development, social justice and gender equity.

The ***Training System*** has been designed for eliminating the *cascading effect* of training. It has been the fate of many training regimes whereby large and considerable resources and time are invested in training the upper echelons of the organization which is targeted first. Much less effort and resources are spent in training the functionaries at the cutting edge-level. Concomitantly, the supervision and care in training the functionaries at the cutting edge diminishes, though the size of the training audience is larger (see the diagram given hereunder). This blunts the effectiveness of the training system. Therefore, the proposed ***Training System*** has taken special care to eliminate such costly miscalculations by focusing on the members and the functionaries of the village panchayat as one of the most important sections of the training audience.

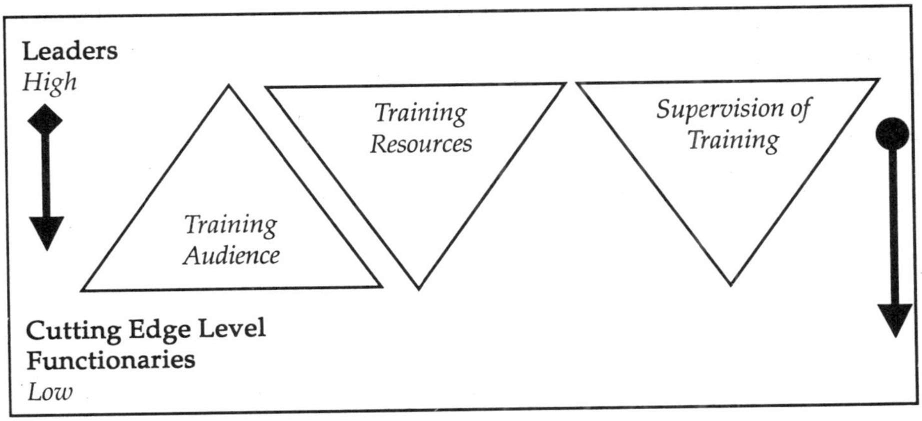

VIII. ANDRAGOGY OF THE PROPOSED TRAINING REGIME

The principal vehicles for imparting the training inputs will be through Participatory Learning and Action methods, which include, though not restricted to, workshops, role playing, drama, experience sharing, group discussions, story telling, case study method, buzz group sessions, listing and structured hands-on exercises in real life situations. To this end in designing the training modules and in customizing the course contents in the training modules, the Andragogy of input delivery has been worked out based upon the following three principles:

- The principle of transiting from the *known to unknown*, drawing upon the knowledge and skill base of the members and functionaries of the PRIs.
- The principle of *cumulative learning*, where the participants successively learn and assimilate, leading to action planning.
- The principle of *reinforced learning*, where institutional training about a specialized subject-matter is backed by on-the-job/ attachment in a good practice or best problem situation.

IX. ACCESSIBILITY OF TRAININGS: WHERE?

It is true that the participant's access to training is often affected by his/ her work schedule and daily/seasonal routine. An important inhibiting factor cutting into the efficacy of any training regime is the participant's lack of time to avail of the training opportunity that is afforded because of different kinds of reasons. For example, in a training audience consisting of the elected members of the village panchayat, it is often seen that women cannot be present in sizeable numbers because of their household related responsibilities or the social taboo against stepping outside their village. Often, they attend training programmes accompanied by their husbands or some other escorts. Training venues will, therefore, have to be chosen keeping considerations related to both convenience and costs in mind. Lengthy and ambitious training programmes away from the village would otherwise remain thinly attended.

X. LOCATIONAL ACCESSIBILITY

The institutional training programmes can ideally be held in the extension training centres in the state or in nearby states. These centres also have residential accommodation with separate living quarters for women participants. The sensitization and awareness camps can be organized at the district headquarters. Specialized courses, if necessary, could be held at institutions of specialization both inside and outside the state.

XI. PSYCHOLOGICAL ACCESSIBILITY

The first element in increasing the *psychological accessibility* of the participants will be trying to limit the programme to a week's duration and the Andragogy of training should scrupulously follow the dictum of *training without tears*. The second element in increasing psychological accessibility is quality management of the training that is delivered. A training programme of poor quality or a good quality training programme that is poorly delivered drastically reduces the psychological accessibility of the participants. Therefore, the training content has to be based upon a rigorous training needs analysis of the targeted audience. Continuous modifications and improvements in the training regime will have to be made continuously in the training design based upon participant feedback.

XII. THE TRAINERS: WHO/WHICH?

The choice of the trainers and training institutions has to be based on the criteria of maturity, experience and ability to meet deadlines. It is important that they have both subject matter knowledge and participatory facilitation skills to handle a wide spectrum of participants who have their fair share of knowledge (and hence arrogance), ego, inflexibility and hardened attitudes. Sensitivity to gender and other forms of exclusion is critical in order to encourage self-respect and understanding among the participants. The training regime should ideally use both governmental training institutions, NGOs, universities and involve attachments to a whole range of field experiments and experiences of civil society actors.

Entrusting the task of implementing the training regime to a single institution is disfavoured. Instead, the strengths of each institution should be fully utilized, without carrying the baggage of their weaknesses, since all institutions have their strengths. Ideally, the endeavour should be to tie up with one or two institutions to provide the training inputs of a particular nature. Thus, there will be a network of institutions for the empowerment of the PRI functionaries and other *'significants'* who interface with the PRIs. This would also help in better co-ordination of inputs, cost effectiveness and continuity in all follow-up measures required. Where, however, enlisting the services of more than two institutions becomes unavoidable, the trainers of such institutions should attend common workshops. This would be critical to arrive at an accepted course design, methodology and Andragogy, so that inputs to the trainers are uniform. Though this may lead to some loss in diversity, this has its own advantages and the unique strengths of each institution/individual could be built into the training programmes through the consultation workshops that are held.

XIII. TRAINING METHODOLOGY

The guiding principle being "training without tears", efforts will be made to make the training programmes consistent with the aims, values and principles of participatory development. That is, for the most part they will be participative using Participatory Learning and Action oriented training methods. The training methods will, as far as possible, be participatory and experiential. More specifically, they would include, but not restricted to:

- Awareness generation;
- Experimental Learning;
- Institutional training, principally in functional and foundational areas;
- Through participatory workshops; and
- Field immersion programmes.

XIV. THE TRAINING SYSTEM

Against this backdrop, a ***Training System*** has been designed for the members and government functionaries of the different tiers of the PRIs, which is encapsulated in 11 training modules. These modules vary in terms of both horizontal reach and vertical intensity. The modules have been so designed that a balanced mix of the two is achieved. The functions of the institutions of the village panchayat, intermediate panchayat and the Zilla Parishad have been kept in mind for the purpose of developing the ***Training System***. Since it was neither possible nor necessary to draw from the provisions of the different state panchayat Acts, the Act of Karnataka State has been taken as a reference point for evolving the ***Training System***. Additionally, the provisions of Article 243 of the Constitution have also been kept in view.

The ***Training System*** outlined in this Handbook consists of the 11 Training Modules listed below:

1. *The Base Module:* Operational Training for the Members and Government Functionaries of the Village Panchayat.
2. *Module 1*: Introductory Training for the Members and Government Functionaries of the Village Panchayat.
3. *Module 2:* Introductory Training for the Members and Officers of the Intermediate Panchayat.
4. *Module 3:* Training-cum-Awareness Camp for the Zilla Parishad Members and Officers.
5. *Module 4:* Training-cum-Awareness Camp for the Key Zilla Parishad Office Bearers.
6. *Module 5:* Operational Training for the Members and Officers of the Zilla Parishad.
7. *Module 6:* Operational Training for the Members and Officers of the Intermediate Panchayat.
8. *Module 7:* Mass Awareness cum Motivation Camps for the Members and Officers of the Panchayati Raj Institutions.
9. *Module 8:* Training cum Motivation Camps for the Members of the Gram Sabha.
10. *Module 9:* Mass Awareness Camps about Panchayati Raj.
11. *Module 10:* Awareness Camps for the Media About Panchayati Raj.

The session plans for the ***Base Module*** have been designed with step-by-step details of the training methodology to be followed. The other modules follow the pattern of this Module. It is expected that the trainer will use the ***Base Module*** to gain suitable training expertise and conduct the other modules only thereafter. The trainer is encouraged to innovate and improvise wherever possible, keeping in mind the overall training context and the emphasis on using participatory training methodology.

The ***Training System*** pertains to the training of the members and government functionaries of the PRIs. It presumes that the trainers will be proficient in the subject-matter of the modules and possess the necessary expertise in the use of participatory training methods and group facilitation. No training module has been included in the Handbook for the training of trainers. Training of trainers should be dealt with separately with special emphasis on the Andragogy of training, methodologies and delivery of the training inputs.

The training modules are of two categories. The Training Modules 1 to 4 and from 7 to 10 are introductory (not elementary) in nature and are to create an awareness about the rights of the PRIs, particularly about the principles underlying the formation of the PRIs as institutions of local government. This is expected to create an enabling environment for the PRIs to function properly for bringing about social justice and gender equity. The Base Module and Training programmes 5 and 6 have been developed as professional courses to equip the PRI functionaries to discharge their functions effectively for social development and gender equity. These courses will be building the capability of the PRIs to be effective institutions of local government.

It has to be recognized that the needs of the PRIs will be different in different states and even vary across the three tiers within the state as well. There will be a need for conducting Training Needs Assessment (TNA) in the state for the stakeholders of the PRIs and then customize the training modules to the findings of the TNA exercise. Also, the training modules of the Handbook, that will be used, will depend on these findings. It is not envisioned that there will be a need to run all the modules. It should be remembered that imparting training over extended periods degenerates into "picnics" and it is difficult for the trainers, howsoever skilful, to hold the interest of adults for long periods of time. That is, the participants will be first imparted the introductory modules and then will return to their places of work and reassemble after a period of time. This is the "sandwiched" approach. This approach has its pitfalls, prominent amongst which is that in the second round some of the earlier participants might have dropped out and new faces appear. Nevertheless, there is no escape from this.

XV. CREDITS AND DISCLAIMERS

In developing these training modules, given in the Handbook, different kinds of ideas and concepts have been drawn from different sources, wherever possible, to avoid the pitfall of reinventing the wheel where a wheel already exists and has the potential of serving our purposes well, when suitably used.

Chapter III

The Base Module

Operational Training for the Members and Government Functionaries of the Village Panchayat

Profile of the Base Module

Operational Training for the Members and Government Functionaries of the Village Panchayat

Objectives

- To empower the elected members and officials of the Village Panchayat to realise their true roles and responsibilities and seek their rights to act to their full potential as members of the institution of self government.
- To empower them for realising their true roles and responsibilities for social and economic development and for bringing about gender and social justice.
- To acquaint them with knowledge about the structure of the PRIs in the light of the Constitutional provisions, State Government Acts, Rules and Executive orders.
- To help them acquire knowledge and the necessary skills in preparing and implementing development programmes with special reference to gender justice and social equity.

Participants

- Village Panchayat Sarpanches.
- Chairperson of Village Panchayat Standing Committees.
- Elected members of the Village Panchayat.
- Gram Sevaks.
- Development professionals, para-professionals, extension agents and other kinds of community development functionaries.

Trainer Profile

- Elected Members of PRIs/Government Officers/Faculty of Extension Training Institutions.
- Well grounded in the subject areas covered in the Module.
- Believes in the Participatory Training Model for Adult Learning.
- Skilful in using Participatory Learning and Action Methods and facilitating learner groups.

Contents

Section I: General Orientation
Section II: Politico-Legal Orientation
Section III: Management Orientation
Section IV: Role Orientation
Section V: Micro-level Planning Orientation
Section VI: Field Immersion

Training Methodology

- Participatory Learning and Action Methods
- Lectures restricted to a minimum
- Simulation Games
- Field Visits/Demonstrations
- Case Studies
- Experience Sharing
- Role Play/Drama
- Film Show

Number of Sessions : *19*

Suggested Venue : Intermix of classroom and village locales

Seating Arrangements

Participants and trainers sit/stand on the ground in a circle for the group work and move around for the games and other activities

Number of Trainees : *30*

Duration : *days*

Note: This will be a purely professional training.

DETAILED CONTENT FLOW IN THE BASE MODULE

OPERATIONAL TRAINING FOR THE MEMBERS AND FUNCTIONARIES OF THE VILLAGE PANCHAYAT

Section I: General Orientation

(a) Democratic Decentralization: its true meaning; the underlying concepts and philosophy.
(b) What are the factors that make democratic decentralisation work?
(c) The fundamental basis of PRIs: self government with the attendant responsibilities, transparency and accountability.
(d) Changes in development paradigm and the consistency of current state of decentralisation in India with the changing paradigm.
(e) Neglect of gender and social justice and explore ways and means to rectify the situation.
(f) Different approaches to development and the approach most appropriate for development for India at its current juncture in its development history.
(g) State of development in the country and the state in the context of the different approaches to development, including the state of gender equity and social justice.
(h) Ways and means to improve the state of development of the country.
(i) Development Programmes and ways and means to improve their efficiency.

Section II: Politico-Legal Orientation

(a) Panchayati Raj: Concept and Status.
(b) Self -governance and institution of self-government in the context of PRIs: Concepts and framework, implications and frame of action for economic development, gender equity and social justice.
(c) What was the original intention of the legislatures and protagonists of the movement?
(d) What happened to the original ideas and justification for the PRIs?
(e) Salient Features of 73rd Constitution Amendment Act and the State Conformity Acts.
(f) Salient Features of Panchayati Raj structure in the concerned State-Gram Sabha, Village Panchayat, Panchayat Samity and Zilla Parishad.

(g) *De facto* functions of the Village Panchayat.

(h) *De Jure* functions of Village Panchayats with particular reference to:

- Raising of resources in the Village Panchayat.
- Powers of taxation and borrowing within the Village Panchayat.
- Planning for social development at the Panchayat level.
- Bringing about gender and social justice.
- Implementation of plans for social and economic development at the Panchayat level.
- Management of Rural Development Schemes.
- Monitoring and evaluation.

Section III: Management Orientation

(a) Administrative management of programmes in the Village Panchayat.

(b) Role of Panchayats in planning and development.

(c) Maintenance of records.

(d) Preparation of village plans with special reference to problems of women, Scheduled Castes and Scheduled Tribes and other marginalised groups.

(e) Implementation of village plans.

(f) Monitoring of village level development programmes.

(g) Carrying out gender audit of village development programmes.

(h) Implementation of Special Programmes.

(i) State Government agencies operating at the Block Level and Village Panchayat.

(j) Development agencies operating within the Village Panchayat like Banks/NGOs.

(k) Protection and management of common property resources.

(l) Management of Primary schools.

(m) Governance Issues in the Village Panchayat:

- Conduct of Business
- Resolution
- No Confidence in Sarpanch or Upa Sarpanch
- Administration of Affairs of Village Panchayat
- Duties of the Sarpanch of Village Panchayat
- Powers of the Sarpanch and Upa Sarpanch
- Establishment
- Imposition of Taxes etc. by Gram Panchayat
- Fees for Inspection of Records and for Obtaining Certified Copies

- Panchayat Fund.
- Maintenance of accounts, audit and budget
- Budget
- Supervision of Panchayats
- Immovable Properties
- Execution of Works
- Administration Report Gram Panchayat Administration
- Registers and Records

Section IV: Role Orientation

A. Behavioural Aspects

(a) Roles and responsibilities of elected members as facilitators of the process of development at the grass-roots level.
(b) Roles and responsibilities of elected members as facilitators of the process of attaining gender and social justice at the grass-roots level.
(c) Roles and responsibilities of elected members as facilitators of the process of social and economic development at the grass-roots level.
(d) Roles and responsibilities of elected members as regulators being units of self government at the village level.
(e) Roles and responsibilities of elected members as custodians of public property at the village level.
(f) Roles and responsibilities of officials as facilitators of the process of development; as regulators and as custodians of public property, being parts of the institution of self government.
(g) Roles and responsibilities of elected members as facilitators of the process of bringing about social justice with special reference to management of conflict and conflict resolution.
(h) Relationship between officials and elected members at different levels.
(i) Roles and responsibilities of officials at village level.
(j) Roles of Village Panchayat members in development of collective leadership.
(k) Roles of Village Panchayat members enlisting and valuing people's participation in the political and economic governance.
(l) Developing accountability (both performance and financial) and transparency in the functioning of Village Panchayat.

B. Attitudes and Behaviour

(a) Eschewing Dominance.

(b) Shedding Arrogance.
(c) Embracing Errors.
(d) Valuing accountability (both performance and financial) and transparency.
(e) Team Building.
(f) Eliminating biases.
(g) Seeking Diversity.
(h) Respecting other's views.
(i) Believing that people know their problems and are capable of suggesting solutions.
(j) The reality of the people count.
(k) People's analysis, people's criteria, people's monitoring, people's evaluation, people's views and people's knowledge counts. Not ours.

Section V: Micro-Level Planning Orientation

A. Planning for Development: On-Farm Livelihoods

- Agriculture, including agricultural extension.
- Land improvement, implementation of agrarian reforms and soil conservation.
- Management of water resources and watershed development.
- Regulation of manure pits in public places.

B. Planning for Development: Off-Farm Livelihoods

- Animal husbandry, dairying, poultry and fisheries.
- Minor forest produce.
- Khadi, village and cottage industries.
- Artisans.

C. Planning for Development of Physical Capital

- Social forestry and farm forestry.
- Management of common property resources.
- Rural housing.
- Drinking water, fuel and fodder.
- Roads, culverts, bridges, ferries and other means of transportation.
- Non-conventional energy sources.
- Maintenance of community assets.
- Construction and maintenance of Dharmashalas/shelters and similar institutions.

- Construction and maintenance of Cattle Sheds, Ponds and Cart Stands.
- Construction and maintenance of Slaughter Houses.
- Maintenance of public parks, playgrounds, etc.
- Removal of encroachments on public properties.
- Organising voluntary labour and contribution for community works.
- Poverty alleviation programme.

D. Planning for Development of Human Capital

- Education with special reference to education of the girl child, including primary and secondary schools.
- Adult and non-formal education.
- Markets and fairs.
- Family welfare, health, sanitation, primary health centres and dispensaries.
- Women and child development.
- Social Welfare, including welfare of those physically and mentally challenged.
- Welfare of the weaker sections, and in particular, of women, Scheduled Castes and Scheduled Tribes.
- Public distribution system.
- Immediate and mid-term response to natural disaster/natural calamities.
- Maintenance of essential statistics of the villages.

Section VI: Field Immersion

The objectives of the field immersion are primarily to expose the participants to successful projects and help them internalise the lessons from this experience. Visits may be arranged to model Panchayats, individuals/social workers who have helped bring about social change, Cooperative Banks and Non-Governmental Organisations who have done innovative work. Visits may also be arranged to an agricultural research programme like a seed multiplication farm, dairy farm, cattle and poultry farms, afforestation sites, etc. In all cases the visit will be structured and there will be facilitators to help the participants process the information that they assimilate. This will help the participants to internalise the experience so that they can use it when they return to their Zilla Parishads.

SESSION-WISE CONTENTS OF THE BASE MODULE

NOTE TO THE TRAINERS ON CHAPTER III

I. HOW ADULTS LEARN

A trainer has to know how adults learn.

Unlike children, adults do not learn on the basis of a "belief system". Adults learn

- If they want and need to learn;
- By rechecking their learning with their past or present experience;
- By practising what they have learnt in training sessions;
- With help and guidance from 'outsiders'; and
- Where the environment for learning is informal and non-threatening.

These five characteristics of adult learning make training different from teaching. The trainer should always bear in mind this fundamental difference between training and teaching while planning delivery of training input to functionaries of PRIs.

II. SPEED/PREFERENCES OF THE HUMAN BRAIN

The medium of training also has a strong bearing on adult learning.

Neurologits have in their experiments shown that:

- The average participant in a training programme can think on an average at 800 words per minute but the average trainer can only talk approximately at 120 words per minute. So trainers must give their participants something interesting to do with their spare "mental capacity" (as it were) of 680 words per minute.
- The lecture method does not work very well in a training context as the brain goes into 'auto shut-off' after only 10 minutes of lecturing if it is not given something to stimulate it. Thus trainers, especially in case of training of neo-literates, must vary the media and give multi-channel messages such as visuals (slides, overheads, power-point, presentation pictures, posters etc.) and feeling messages (such as smell, touch etc.).
- It may be mentioned that if a message is given once, the brain remembers only 10 per cent of it one year later and when the same

message is given six times in a year, the brain remembers 90 per cent of it. Hence trainers must repeat, recap and review the training messages several times over. Reference is invited to Figure 1A which is self explanatory. A system of training must, therefore, have an in-built mechanism by which training messages are repeated several times over a year (such as handouts, pictures, short refresher courses etc.).

- The trainer must also bear in mind that the brain prefers rounded diagrams and figures to square ones; it prefers "Times" and "Helvetica" typefaces and dark letters on light background. Hence all visuals prepared by the trainer should be informed of these features of the brain. This is also one of the reasons why in the seating arrangement for participatory session a circular seating arrangement is strongly recommended.

III. RECALL: 5 MAIN FACTORS

Training impart skills and knowledge to be applied by the participants in their work situation.

The trainers have to alive of the facts that:

- Participants are more likely to remember the beginning of events or the first in a series of events.
- The brain's recall falls rapidly after 24 hours without review. Hence recap and review, after regular intervals, of training input is strongly recommended.
- We remember unusual things exceedingly well such as death type experiences, winning a lottery ticket etc. This is the reason why when a person narrates his "life-history" over a period of time, only major events come to her/his mind. Thus first day in school, last day in the college, date of marriage, birth of the children, death of a "near and dear" one, first day in employment and such other events are recalled very easily.
- Recall is high for things which are linked by mnemonics or analogy such as 'Sen', where "S" stands for somebody "e" for everybody and "n" for nobody.
- We are more likely to remember the end of events or the last in a series of events.

IV. HOW TO ACTIVATE THE WHOLE BRAIN

A successful trainer must be able to activate the whole brain of the participants. Where the whole brain is activated both absorption of inputs and contribution to the training programme by the participants improve significantly.

The brain has two parts, the left and the right, as it is called.

Left part of the brain deals with logical aspects of activity of the brain, as under:

- Speaking
- Calculating
- Intellectually analysing
- Reading
- Writing
- Naming
- Ordering
- Sequencing
- Critiquing
- Evaluating
- Logic

The right part of the brain deals with the creative aspects of cerebral activity as under:

- Creativity (new combinations)
- Artistic activity
- Musical ability/rhythm
- Emotions
- Recognition
- Comprehension
- Perception of abstract patterns
- Spatial abilities
- Facial expressions
- Holistic ability
- Intuition
- Images
- Colour

The trainer must, therefore, attempt all the time in the training at stimulating both "parts" of the brain in all training programmes. Professional trainers encourage participants to use both sides of the brain by organising training activity which induces participants to think logically and at once be creative. The trainer must, however, remember that experiments have shown that:

- Participants, who have been trained traditionally to use only one side of the brain more than the other (accountants, engineers, musicians), find it difficult to 'switch' when necessary. Thus a musician finds it difficult to follow a "manual" on how to compose a piece. Similarly, chartered accountants find it difficult not to follow the set rules.

- When the weaker side of the brain is stimulated and encouraged to co-operate with the stronger side of the brain, there is a greater synergy. There are however participants who have both sides of their brains strong and keep them activated.

It is believed that Newton understood the theory of gravity while day-dreaming. Thus the trainers should combine analytical exercises with creative, expressive activities during the training sessions, to activate both sides of the brain.

To help participants use both sides of the brain the trainers should also be cognizant of the act that information is stored in the brain with Very High Frequency, in VHF form, where 'V' stands for visual, 'H' stands for hearing and 'F' stands for feeling.

(i) *Examples of Visual are*:
pictures, scenes, images, logos, diagrams, graphs, charts, photographs and painting/posters.

(ii) *Examples of Hearing are*:
words, music, sounds, accents, conversations/discussions, debates, etc.

(iii) *Examples of Feeling are*:
smells, tastes, tactile experiments, pain/comfort, pleasure, anger, grief, affection, love, etc.

It is important to reiterate that experiments show that, when tested after 24 hours, participants' recall of a "visual" message is 80 per cent correct answers and a "feeling" message leads to 79 per cent correct answers. This is almost twice as good as their recall of a "hearing" message which hovers around 45 per cent correct answers. *(See figure-1A* and *1B).*

Therefore, because participants will store information in the left and the right brain in the form of pictures (**V**), words (**H**) or sensations and feelings (**F**), trainers are well advised to use visuals, words and feelings to provide training inputs, so that multi-channel messages are sent out in training sessions. Thus, lectures, pictures, exercises like mapping and modelling, and actual experience of reality through games and exposure visits have all to be combined for a good training. This also means giving colourful visual back up to our verbal messages at the same time as appealing to trainees' emotions and senses. Thus, for example, when the

Figure: 1 A Learning Theory

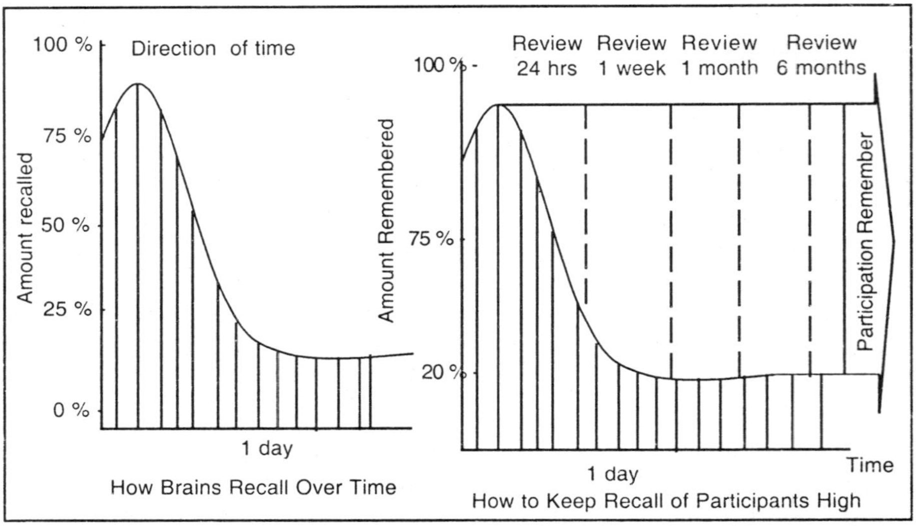

Figure: 1 B Seating Arrangements

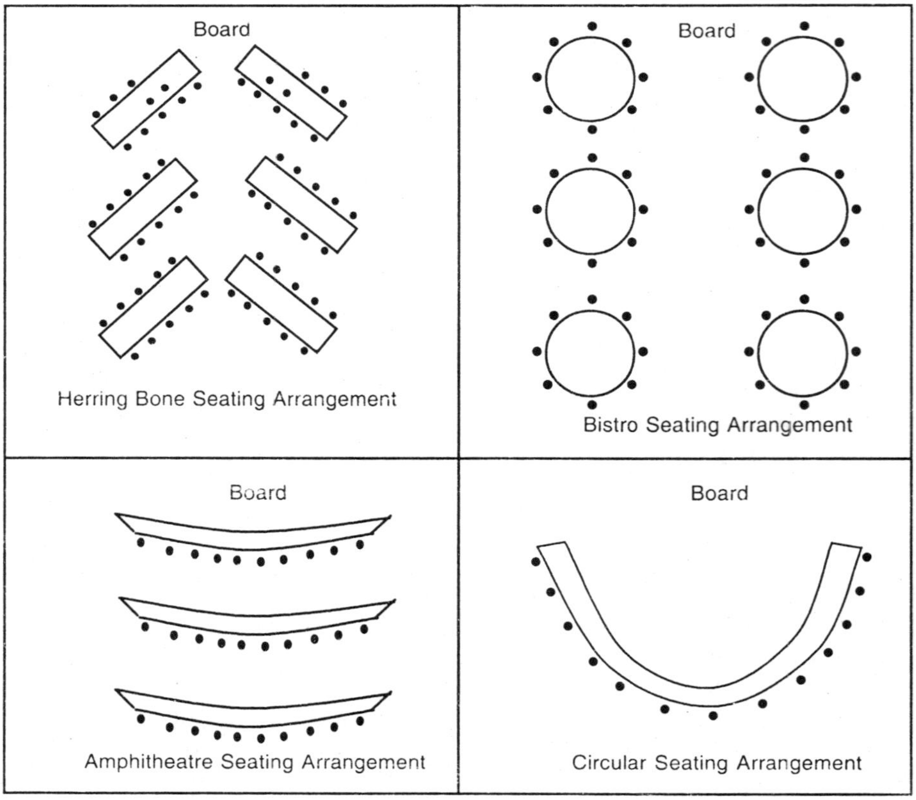

trainer wants to impress upon the participants the 29 items covered under the Eleventh Schedule of the Constitution, each item while spoken of, is also shown by a picture. That is why posters have been provided with this handbook. The messages when so delivered, by a combination of visual and verbal modes of delivery, will be stored simultaneously in several parts of the left and right brain of the participants, and therefore, the chances of recall are greater.

V. SEATING PATTERNS

Seating patterns have a strong impact on both the level of participation of the trainees and their reception. There are basically seven types of seating pattern as under:

1. 'U' Shaped Seating Arrangement

The advantages of 'U' shaped seating arrangement are:

- It is a business like seating arrangement.
- Trainer can walk into 'U' and contact the trainers.
- Generally such an arrangement provides good participant visibility.
- It is a standard seating arrangement and is therefore non-threatening for trainees.

But the disadvantages of a 'U' shaped arrangement are also significant:

- It is a somewhat formal arrangement and hence needs ice-breaking.
- Some participants often get masked by audio visual equipment.
- The participants seated in the front of the 'U' have to constantly have their head at 60-90° which can cause neck ache and distract from learning.
- Rear participants are far from screen/flip chart or board and may have difficulty in viewing writings on the board or transparencies or pictures in slides etc., and may, therefore, receive poor visual messages.
- The eye contact of the participants seated at the corners with those at the front is limited.

2. 'V' Shaped Seating Pattern

The advantages of 'V' shaped seating arrangement are:

- It is the best pattern for visibility and problems of neck ache syndrome is eliminated.

- It affords optimum trainer and participant contact usually and it is easier for the trainer to use his/her "lighthouse".
- It is a less formal seating arrangement than the 'U' shaped one and hence it is intimidating than 'U' shaped seating pattern.

However, the disadvantages are:

- Space requirements of a V shaped seating arrangement are very large.
- It is suited only for small groups. If the number of participants is very large, those seated near the vertex of the 'V' will be too far from the screen etc. and hence may impair learning as visual messages may be poorly received.
- The eye contact between participants *inter se* on each flank of the 'V' is low, though the eye contact between trainer and the trainees is high.

3. Herring Bone Seating Arrangement

The advantages of the Herring Bone (*see Figure 1B*) seating arrangement are as follows:

- Space is used very effectively for large groups of trainees.
- All participants are seated at good angle to screen/flip chart/board, etc. and hence the problems associated with the 'neck ache' syndrome are eliminated.
- The trainer can walk down the 'spine' of the seating arrangement and maintain eye contact with the participants very easily.

However, the disadvantages of Herring Bone seating arrangement are:

- Several participants are masked by other participants.
- It is reminiscent of seating arrangement in schools and hence may hinder adult learning.
- It may encourage dysfunctional groupings amongst participants seated on separated tables and hamper learnings through cross fertilisation and impair the overall training environment.
- Participants at the rear rows/tables are far from screen/flip chart,board etc. and hence may be poor recipient of visual messages, which may hinder learning.
- The participants and trainer contact is relatively poor, especially those seated on the outer-fringes of the tables. Hence the trainer cannot use his "lighthouse" properly.

4. 'Bistro' Pattern of Seating Arrangement

Bistro pattern has several advantages such as:

- It is ideal for 'teambuilding' sessions and small group workshops/ sessions and for small group exercises.
- It is an informal seating pattern and hence encourages maximum trainee participation, identification and bonding.
- It brings out the originality, encourages creativity and open-mindedness amongst the participants.
- The contact between the participants and the trainer is good because the trainer can 'circulate' between participants and groups.

But the disadvantages are also not insignificant:

- Some participants have poor visibility of the screen, flip charts or boards or may be constantly at an angle to screen/flip chart and hence not suitable for plenary work. It also has the problems associated with the 'neck-ache' syndrome.
- The seating arrangement fosters lack of attention and encourages side conversations amongst the small groups (or what may be called, generate "whisperers" and "whisperees").
- Encourages splinter group identification, i.e., each group around a table becomes a sub-group and gets isolated from the others. This has consequences similar to formation of dysfunctional groups in Herring Bone seating pattern.

5. Amphitheatre Seating Arrangement

In Amphitheatre seating, the participants are seated in rows facing the screen as in a theatre (and hence the name).

The advantages of this arrangement are:

- If room is well designed, excellent visibility of the screen, flip charts and board is ensured and acoustics.
- It is a very space-effective as a large number of participants can be accommodated in a relatively small space.
- It is suitable for lecture-type presentations and briefing sessions, where interaction between the participants *inter se* or between the participants and the trainer is limited.

Disadvantages of Amphitheatre seating pattern are:

- It allows very poor trainer and participant contact and the trainer can hardly use "lighthouse" (eye contact) beyond the second row.
- Difficult to set up unless room is designed with permanent seating arrangement with "steps", otherwise those seated at the back cannot see or even hear what is going on in the front.
- Very university-like seating and hence reminiscent of "school-type" learning which may hinder adult learning.
- It can encourage formation of dysfunctional groups and/or "whisperers-whisperees" in the back-rows.

6. Circular Seating Arrangement

Here the participants sit in a circle, with a space at one end of the circle for the trainer to enter the circle to interact with the participants.

The advantages of the arrangement are:

- It is ideal for participatory sessions where participant involvement has to be very high.
- The trainer has excellent contact with the participants and the participants inter-se have lot of eye contact.
- The participants are focused, have little scope for side conversation, and possibility of formation of dysfunctional groups is eliminated.
- There is lot of bonding between the participants.

The disadvantages of circular seating are:

- It is not easy to find tables which can be set up in a circular formation. Hence most of the time participants end up seating without tables.
- If the participants are seated without tables, then they may have difficulty in writing/doing individual assignments, and feel exposed.
- Participants when seated in a circle without tables may feel unnecessarily exposed.

All the seating arrangements may be necessary for the training programme. For participatory sessions the circular seating arrangement is the best, for it allows maximum participation and participant-trainer eye contact. For break away group work, the "Bistro" is the best or alternatively the Herring Bone. For guest speakers *or* distinguished speakers the 'Amphitheatre' is recommended. For plenary presentation of group work 'V' or 'U' shape has been found to be useful. In training programme, it is best to have one large room for plenary and more than one small room group work, where different seating arrangements could be made.

In making seating arrangement the trainer must bear in mind the PSYCHOLOGY of the participants, namely:

- Distance reduces participation — trainees in back rows are less likely to participate than those in front. The trainer should keep social distance between herself/himself and the trainee.
- Any kind of 'row' reduces interaction between the participants *inter se*. Because it is difficult for those seated in the back row to have eye contact with those in the front row(s) and hear contributors from participants seated in the front rows and for those seated in the front row to twist round to interact with participants seated behind them.
- Changes in seating patterns from one session of a training programme to another can be psychologically upsetting for participants but at times such changes may help add variety, wake participants out of slumber and break "whisperer-whisperee" combination. Use best judgement. Hence care has to be taken to manage such disturbance.
- In a long to medium duration training programme, at repetitive sessions in the same room, participants will invariably sit in the same place and form some sub-groups. It is best to rotate people around once in a while both within the room and the rooms themselves.
- Angry or cynical participants will attempt to move away from a group seating pattern.

VII. STRUCTURE

Recap is very important for retention and recall of training inputs. Hence a trainer should:

- Review all learning points at end of each module (or beginning of next); use "VHF" support for better impact.
- Action Plan as a follow up is an excellent way to ensure retention of inputs.
- The trainer and the participants should agree on an action plan for the transfer of new skills or knowledge to real life and if necessary (and possible) have a written group promise.

- Follow up action including a refresher course should be worked out.
- The trainer and the participants should agree on any follow-up action or refresher to increase recall. Refer to figure-1A and 1B earlier.

Always finish a session with a succinct and provocative encapsulation of the learning experience of the session.

In structuring the training sessions, the trainer should keep in mind the effectiveness of different methods that are used in training. It is given below:

Ranking of Methods Depending on Teaching Goals (1 = high, 8 = low)

Method	*Knowledge Acquisition*	*Attitude Change*	*Problem Solving Skills*	*Inter-personal Skills*	*Participant Acceptance*	*Knowledge Retention*
Case Study	4	5	1	5	1	4
Workshop	1	3	4	4	5	2
Lecture	8	7	7	8	7	3
Games	5	4	2	3	2	7
Films	6	6	8	6	4	5
Programmed Instr.	3	8	6	7	8	1
Role-playing	2	2	3	1	3	6

Source: J. Newstrom "Evaluating Effectiveness of Training Methods.

We have thus suggested a combination of different methods of training in the Handbook, keeping the foregoing table in mind. We encourage the trainers to change the methods as they think best, depending on what they wish to achieve and how the trainees are responding.

VIII. TRAINING DELIVERY

Training delivery is a critical variable for success of a training. Remember the following points:

(a) Communication is the first golden rule

The trainer must be careful in her/his communication. She/he has to communicate well.

When a trainer gives a spoken message, the participants' understanding and judgment of that message come from three sources: Words, Paralinguistics and Facial Expressions.

- Words are only lables and listeners put their own interpretation on speakers' words. They convey only 7 per cent of the message that a trainer may wish to convey.
- Paralinguistics is the way in which the trainer says something (i.e., accent, tone, inflection, etc). Paralinguistics is very important to a trainer and trainee for communicating and for understanding respectively of the message being communicated. Paralinguistics communicate 38 per cent of the message.
- Facial expression is what a trainer looks like while delivering a message. Facial expressions affect the participants' understanding most and convey 55 per cent of the message that a trainer may wish to convey.

(b) Trainer's demeanour has a great impact on the participants

The trainer must be enthusiastic about his/her work.

- If the trainer is not enthusiastic about the training, how can the participants be expected to be enthusiastic.
- The trainer should consciously use her/his eyes and eyebrows to communicate enthusiasm.
- The trainer must always keep a sparkle in her/his voice.
- The trainer must fight boredom of repetitive sessions by introducing new anecdotes, examples, games, ice-breakers etc, or by changing lesson structure or methods given in the previous section.

(c) Mannerisms of the trainer can make or mar a training session

The trainer must, therefore, be careful about her/his mannerisms. There are certain tips that come in handy, as under:

- The trainer should not be tempted by or play around with what is called "manual props" such as pens, pencils, pointers, spectacles, key chains, etc. during a training session.
- If the trainer is a male make sure that he keeps no loose change in his pocket and fiddle around with them during a training session.
- The trainer should be aware of her/his verbal tics and work on eliminating them (i.e: 'OK'! — 'You know' — 'and so forth' — 'Now....')
- The trainer should avoid 'closed' or tense body positions such as clasped hands and crossed arms. She/he should be confident and open. Have open arms.

- The trainer need not worry about pacing, leaning, etc during the training sessions.
- The trainer should check her/his hair and dress before entering the class/workshop room. A neatly dressed trainer is well received just as a neatly organised data is well used.

(d) Dress

In dressing, it is important to be careful. Generally it helps trainers:

- It is best if the trainer avoids dressing in black and white and other strongly contrasting colours, for it will distract the attention of the trainees.
- The trainer should wear comfortable, loose-fitting clothes, especially in participatory sessions where body movement is very frequent and essential.
- Where the trainer cannot make up her/his mind, she/he wears something not loud so that at least her/his clothes would not detract from the message that she/he would be delivering.
- The trainer should try and dress one step above the audience, but should never be in loud or ceremonial dress.

IX. TEN TIPS FOR TRAINERS

- The trainer should never be late for her/his session.
- The trainer should never keep his/her eyes on his/her notes.
- She/he must never read out anything except quotations from a text.
- The trainer should exaggerate body movements and verbal emphasis, because paralinguistics and facial expressions convey more than words do.
- The trainer must perform; he should not act.
- The trainer should often pause remembering that silence is much longer for the trainers than for the participants.
- The trainer should use humour in the presentation; "a laugh is worth a thousand frowns".
- The trainer must be enthusiastic about the training. If the trainer is not enthusiastic about the session why should the participants be enthusiastic at all?
- The trainer should not try for technical accuracy to the last detail.
- The trainer should keep the training sessions simple.

Base Module: Section I
GENERAL ORIENTATION

CONTENT FLOW IN GENERAL ORIENTATION BASE MODULE: AT A GLANCE

Day 1		*Day 2*	
Time in min.	*Session No. and Name*	*Time in min.*	*Session No. and Name*
FORENOON			
80	1: Introductions and Icebreaking	105	4: People-Centred Community Development
20	*Break for Tea*	20	*Break for Tea*
130	2: Principles of Panchayati Raj Governance	135	4: People-Centred Community Development (continued)
60	*Break for Lunch*	60	*Break for Lunch*
AFTERNOON			
60	2: Principles of Panchayati Raj Governance (continued)		
60	*Break for Tea*		
165	3: Gender and Social Justice		
435	*Total Duration of Training*	240	*Total Duration of Training*

DETAILED CONTENT FLOW IN BASE MODULE, GENERAL ORIENTATION SECTION

Day 1 (Time in minutes)	Day 2 (Time in minutes)
FORENOON **Session 1: Introductions and Icebreaking (Duration: 80)** 1. **Content:** Welcoming the Participants **Training Method:** Talk by Trainer **Duration:** 10 2. **Content:** Game for Introductions and Icebreaking **Training Method:** Seed Game **Duration:** 20 3. **Content:** Overview of Training Goal, Content, Methodology and Scope **Training Method:** Visual **Duration:** 20 4. **Content:** Expectations of Participants from the Training Programme **Training Method:** Ranking Method **Duration:** 30 *Break for Tea (20)* **Session 2: Principles of Panchayati Raj Governance (Duration: 190)** 1. **Content:** *Name Game* for Introductions and Icebreaking: **Duration:** 15 2. **Content:** (a) To emphasise what the participants know about PRIs is of value; (b) History of the Evolution of PRIs **Training Methods:** Johari's Window and Timeline **Duration:** 70 3. **Content:** Democratic Decentralisation **Training Methods:** Brainstorming and Delphi Technique **Duration:** 45 *Break for Lunch (60)*	*FORENOON* **Session 4: People-Centred Community Development (Duration: 240)** 1. **Content:** (a) Changes in the Development Paradigm; (b) The consistency of the status of decentralization in India with the development paradigm **Training Methods:** Historical Transect and Lecture **Duration:** 60 2. **Content:** Different Approaches to Development **Training Method:** Matching Game **Duration:** 45 *Break for Tea (20)* 3. **Content:** (a) State of village development in India; (b) status of gender equity and social justice in this context **Training Method:** Pictures **Duration:** 30 4. **Content:** Ways and Means to improve the status of village development in India **Training Method:** Ranking and Scoring **Duration:** 45 5. **Content:** Development Programmes **Training Methods:** Pie Charts, Ranking and Scoring **Duration:** 45 6. **Content:** Synthesis by Trainer/ Participants **Training Method:** Visual **Duration:** 15 *Break for Lunch (60)*

Day 1 (Time in minutes)	Day 1 (Time in minutes)
AFTERNOON 3. **Content:** Democratic Decentralisation **Training Methods:** Listing, Sorting and Matrix Scoring **Duration:** 45 4. **Content:** Synthesis by Trainer/ Participants **Training Method:** Visual **Duration:** 15 *Break for Tea (20)* **Session 3: Gender and Social Justice (Duration: 165)** 1. **Content:** Energizing Game: *Who are We?* **Duration:** 15 2. **Content:** Concept of Gender, Differences between sexuality and gender **Training Method:** Pictures **Duration:** 45 3. **Content:** Neglect of gender and social justice **Training Method:** Gendered Resource Mapping **Duration:** 45 4. **Content:** Explore ways and means to rectify the situation **Training Method:** Access Social Mapping and Solution Tree **Duration:** 45 5. **Content:** Synthesis by Trainer/ Participants **Training Method:** Visual **Duration:** 15	*BEGIN SECTION:POLITICO-LEGAL ORIENTATION*
Total duration of Training: 435 minutes (7 Hours and 15 minutes)	Total duration of Training: 240 minutes (4 Hours)

NOTE TO TRAINERS FOR USING SECTION 1: GENERAL ORIENTATION

1. INTRODUCTION

Section I of the Module is designed to orient the participants with the fundamental concepts related to Panchayati Raj Governance. Its contents include the evolution of PRIs, the concept of democratic decentralisation, the shifts in the development paradigm and development approaches and concerns related to gender and social justice. It familiarizes the participants with the two-dimensional role of PRIs as institutions of self-government and agents of community development. This Section especially focuses upon the neglect of gender interests in the development process and the issues related to social justice and social exclusion. The Section, therefore, serves to sensitise the participants with their social roles and obligations and generate in them the urge to seek what is their right in the realm of local self governance.

2. TRAINING OBJECTIVES

These are stated as follows:

- To create an urge amongst the participants and trainers to seek their rights "guaranteed" by the Constitution of India.
- To expand the conceptual understanding of the participants about the basic principles of Panchayati Raj Governance and people-centred community development.
- To conscientise the participants about the social concerns related to gender, social justice and social exclusion.

3. SESSIONS, THEIR TRAINING OBJECTIVES AND EXPECTED LEARNING OUTCOMES

This Section has four sessions. Their contents have been designed to fulfil the stated training objectives. The introductory session for icebreaking, mixed with the energizing games in the other sessions and the group-work based upon PLA methods serve to promote positive group dynamics among the participants. For each session, the *Expected Learning Outcomes* at the end of the session that would demonstrate the fulfilment of the corresponding training objective, at the levels of both the individual participants and group are given in the Table 1.

Table 1

Session No.	*Session Description*	*Training Objective*	*Expected Learning Outcomes*
1	Introductions and Icebreaking	To create a feeling of comradeship amongst participants and trainers	(a) The participants and trainers are acquainted with each other and begin to form a sympathetic group (b) The participants understand the training design, purpose and methodology (c) The trainer becomes aware of the expectations of the participants from the training programme
2	Principles of Panchayati Raj Governance	To expand the conceptual understanding of the participants about the basic principles of Panchayati Raj Governance	The participants have increased understanding of the philosophy of self government, the concept and principles underlying PRIs. They are made aware of their rights and duties.
3	Gender and Social Justice	To conscientise the participants about issues related to gender, social justice and social exclusion	(a) The participants understand the issues related to gender and social exclusion that are prevalent in village-level society (b) They become aware of the duty of the Village Panchayat for promoting social justice through both its governance and development related functions
4	People-Centred Community Development	To expand the conceptual understanding of the participants about the basic principles of people-centred community development	(a) The participants get acquainted with the different approaches and programmes for village development (b) They are able to appreciate the philosophy of people-centred community development

4. SESSION 1: INTRODUCTIONS AND ICEBREAKING

The introductory session is in the nature of an icebreaker, which aims at establishing solidarity among the participants. Any hierarchical lines that usually exist among the trainers and participants and the participants themselves need to be gradually flattened to facilitate group learning. This also supports the subsequent group learning process. An overview of the training goal, design and methodology is done. The trainer explains that the training will involve active participation of each participant and also voices an expectation that the participants will join the group work readily. This session sets the overall tenor of training for participatory training.

5. SESSION 2: PRINCIPLES OF PANCHAYATI RAJ GOVERNANCE

We begin the formal coverage of the subject matter of training from the second session. The use of the Johari's Window emphasises the fact that we value the existing knowledge of the participants about PRIs. This is in keeping with the overall philosophy of participatory training, which believes in the underlying tenet that 'they know'The participants are first oriented with the basic principles of Panchayati Raj governance and democratic decentralisation. This orientation is achieved through experiential group learning, by relating the village level changes in governance structures as perceived and experienced by the participants to the gradual evolution of the PRIs. In this way, the participants transit from "known to the unknown" in terms of knowledge areas. There is great scope for cross learning during this session, but its degree essentially rests upon the facilitation skills of the trainer.

6. SESSION 3: GENDER AND SOCIAL JUSTICE

The third session initiates a discussion about issues related to gender and social justice. The purpose of introducing these issues at the very onset of training is to emphasise the centrality of the role played by gender in Panchayati Raj governance and development. The discussions in this session would sensitise the participants to the phenomenon of social exclusion whereby certain groups for reasons of gender, caste, ethnicity, age group, lack of control over resources and other factors are excluded from participating in the activities and benefits of development. The obligations of the PRIs for promoting social justice including gender equity through their local governance and village development related functions are focused upon in the context of the phenomenon of social exclusion.

7. SESSION 4: PEOPLE-CENTRED COMMUNITY DEVELOPMENT

The fourth session deals with the evolution of the development paradigm. It sets the present day development context for the PRIs in the country. It discusses the different development approaches and programmes which the participants assess in terms of consensual criteria determined by playing the *'matching game'*.

8. TRAINING METHODOLOGY

The training methodology suggested in this Section is predominantly based upon Participatory Learning and Action Methods and involves the participants in active group work leading to the construction of social realities in the training sessions. The use of PLA methods is best suited to adult learning and generates empathy among the participants. The less motivated and timid participants also learn with less effort through this group learning process.

9. DURATION OF TRAINING

The Section requires about one and a half training days. The total duration of training is estimated to be 650 minutes, which is 10 hours and 50 minutes.

Base Module *Session 1* — Section I General Orientation

Session Theme	INTRODUCTIONS AND ICEBREAKING
Duration	80 minutes
Venue	Classroom without fixed furnitures
Seating	Sit and stand on the floor forming a circle; move around the room for the game; sit in circles for the Ranking Method
Session Objective	*To create a feeling of comradeship amongst participants and trainers*

Expected Learning Outcomes

- The participants and trainers are acquainted with each other and begin to form a sympathetic group.
- The participants understand the training design, purpose and methodology.
- The trainer becomes aware of the expectations of the participants from the training programme.

Content Flow and Training Methodology

Sr. No.	*Content*	*Training Methodology*	*Training Aids*	*Duration (in minutes)*
1.	Welcoming the Participants	**Step 1** Talk by the Trainer	As desired by the trainer[1]	10
2.	Game for Introductions and Icebreaking	**Step 2** Seed Game	Seeds of various kinds	20
3.	Overview of training goal, content, methodology and scope	**Step 3** Visual Method	Posters and Slides	20
4.	Expectations of participants from the training	**Step 4** Ranking Method	Flash cards, flip charts and marker pens, seeds/ pebbles	30

1. Use as many visual aids as possible.

THE METHODOLOGICAL STEPS FOR SESSION 1

1. The Trainer welcomes the Participants

This introductory session is crucial for creating the desired ambience for the adult learning process to begin. It also sets the stage for the use of PLA- based training methodology. It creates a feeling of comradeship amongst the participants and the trainers. This *espirit de corps* or solidarity promotes group learning more effectively. The trainer is urged to keep the introductory session informal, open, semi-structured and of good humour. This will serve to induct everybody into a participatory mood and training environment.

In **Step 1**, it is suggested that heavy, didactic and literary introductory speeches be avoided, since this will not be congruent with the participatory training that follows. The participants should feel that this training is different from any other previous training. It is important to remember that the session has been designed to facilitate the opening up of lines of communication among the participants *inter se* and among the participants and the trainers present in the classroom.

2. *Play the Seed Game for making introductions and icebreaking with the participants*

In **Step 2**, the **Seed Game** is played for helping the participants know each other and icebreaking. The objective of the game is to introduce the participants to each other and to begin the training on an informal note that would encourage learner participation in the future. The steps for playing the game are given below:

2.1 This game is suitable for a group of 20-25 participants. Keep four to five kinds of seeds in sufficient numbers on a table. Each participant picks up a number of seeds that is equal to the number of participants. Each participant picks up only one kind of seed and keeps all the seeds in the left hand.

2.2 The participants then go around the room introducing themselves to each other and the trainers. Each time a participant introduces herself to another, she gives away one seed to the person she introduces herself to and gets one seed from that person in return. She keeps the seeds received in this way in her right hand.

2.3 Then at the end of the game, the participant should have no seeds left in her left hand and as many seeds, but of different varieties collected in her right hand, if she has met all the participants. Each participant thus personally introduces herself to the others. This provides a personal touch to these introductions and also for participant-bonding.

---

3. Visual Overview of training design, content, methodology and scope

---

In **Step 3**, posters and or flip charts and slides are used for the overview of the training design. This has a greater impact upon the participants, especially on the neo-literates/semi-literates who usually form a major party of such training audiences. The trainer is encouraged to create her own posters flip charts, and slides for introducing the training goal, design and methodology. The trainer must especially inform the participants about the participatory nature of training and express the hope that they will be whole-heartedly involved.

---

4. Catalogue and prioritise the expectations of the participants from the training programme

---

In **Step 4**, we use the **Ranking Method**, the steps for which are described below:

4.1 The participants are provided with flash cards and marker pens with a request to catalogue their expectations and write down one expectation on each flash card. But they can have as many flash cards as they may wish to have. After about five minutes, they are encouraged to place their cards on the floor.

4.2 The expectations are then classified into clusters wherever such classification is possible. For example, expectations of the participants can be to learn negotiation skills, nitty-gritty of Panchayati Raj working, experience sharing, etc. These expectations can be classified under several heads: inter-personal relationships, functional skills, knowledge about structure and role of PRIs, how to conduct the business of the Village Panchayat, information about development programmes and so on.

4.3 The participants are now encouraged to club together common or similar expectations, if any. Usually, there are several in each cluster. Once the common expectations are clubbed, there will be a single list of expectations under each category.

4.4 The lists are then examined and discussed. It may not be possible to fulfil some of the expectations through training because of resource or other constraints. The situation may be explained to the participants and such expectations may be thereafter discarded by consensus.

4.5 If the number of expectations is too large, there may be a need to prioritise them. For this purpose, **Scoring** may be used. Scoring can be of three kinds: **Free Scoring**[2], **Fixed Scoring**[3] **and Vector Scoring**[4].

4.6 Use any of the **Scoring Methods** for this exercise by taking up each expectation and asking the participants to give it a score using flexible material like seeds, pebbles etc. considering its importance.

4.7 Allow participants enough time to reflect. Give them some key questions as pointers to think.

4.8 Once the prioritisation is over, with the consent of the participants, the top ten expectations may be retained as those that are the most important. This number could vary according to the judgment of the facilitator.

4.9 Cards depicting the chosen expectations are then pasted on flip charts and displayed till the end of training. Recall the relevant expectations whenever they are being fulfilled in the course of the training. The trainer may keep a checklist for self-assessment vis-à-vis the list of expectations. The list is also useful for designing future training interventions.

---

2. Scoring is free when the participants score by placing seeds, etc. in ascending or descending quantities, with no upper limit on the number or amount of seeds placed.
3. In Fixed Scoring, scores are given to each item, where the maximum that an item can get will be equal to the number of items.
4. In Vector Scoring places, the scores are allotted on a scale chosen by the participants themselves on say a scale of 0-10 or 0-5 or 1-100 and so on.

Base Module Section I
Session 2 General Orientation

Session Theme	PRINCIPLES OF PANCHAYATI RAJ GOVERNANCE
Duration	190 minutes
Venue	Classroom without fixed furnitures
Seating	Sit and stand on the floor forming circles for the group work; move around the room for the games.
Session Objective	*To expand the conceptual understanding of the participants about the basic principles of Panchayati Raj Governance*

Expected Learning Outcomes

- The participants have an increased understanding of the philosophy of self government, the concept and principles underlying PRIs the participants become aware of their rights.

Content Flow and Training Methodology

Sr. No.	*Content*	*Training Methodology*	*Training Aids*	*Duration (in minutes)*
1.	Game for Introductions and Icebreaking	**Step 1** Name Game	None	15
2.	(a) To emphasise that what the participants know about Panchayati Raj Institutions is of value (b) History of the evolution of Panchayati Raj Institutions	**Step 2** Johari's Window **Step 3** Timeline to trace the Evolution of the PRIs and the underlying motive for setting up the PRI system	Flip charts, flash cards and marker pens	70[5] minutes

5. It is suggested that the duration indicated for the sessions that use PLA based training methods may be factored thus: preparation time: 50 minutes, presentation and Discussion time: 20 minutes, total: 70 minutes. However, this is only a suggested time. The trainer is free to modify these limites using his best judgment.

Sr. No.	*Content*	*Training Methodology*	*Training Aids*	*Duration (in minutes)*
3.	Democratic Decentralization (a) Its true meaning; underlying concepts and philosophy (b) Factors that make democratic decentralisation work (c) The fundamental basis of PRIs: self government with the attendant responsibilities, transparency and accountability	**Step 4** Brainstorming **Step 5** Delphi Technique **Step 6** Listing, Sorting and Matrix Scoring	Cards, marker pens, Flip charts and seeds of different varieties for the scoring/ sorting exercise	45 minutes 45 minutes
4.	Synthesis of learning points by Trainer/Participants	**Step 7** Visual Method	Overhead slides, Flip Charts, cards prepared by the participants	15 minutes

THE METHODOLOGICAL STEPS FOR SESSION 2

1. Play the Name Game to get to know each other better

In **Step 1**, the **Name Game**[6] has been suggested for which the steps are as follows:

1.1 The objectives of the game are to speed up the process of becoming acquainted and to help everyone learn the names of the other participants.

6. Adapted from Pretty *et al.*, 1995

1.2 Introduce and explain the exercise to the participants. Start the first round in which everybody carefully says his/her name. This is done slowly so that others have time to repeat it and find a way to link the name to that participant. Write the unusual names on the board.

1.3 When this round is completed, then the trainer says, 'My name is ....' points out another participant (B), says B's name and asks B to look for a person C, giving C's name, and so on. For example, the trainer says: 'My name is Vijaya, your name is Meena. Meena, Will you please find Amrita?' The trainer should not look at Amrita herself. Also, ask the rest of the group not to help.

1.4 Continue until everyone has had a turn.

1.5 This is a simple and effective exercise, which works well in new groups. This will also strengthen the introductions already made in the previous session and help facilitate the group dynamics.

1.6 Finally ask participants to say all the names in the group in the order in which they are seated. The participants may be asked to exchange chairs to cross-check whether each participant knows the names of the others.

---

2. *Use the Johari's Window to emphasise that the participants know about Panchayati Raj Institutions*

Step 2: The **Johari's Window** provides the starting point for beginning the discussion on the subject of Panchayati Raj Institutions in the training programme. The use of the Window will tell the participants that there is a lot to learn from each other. Thus, there is a lot to learn from people. This also helps to establish the need for participatory learning, planning, monitoring, evaluation and capacity building. The Window is explained below:

JOHARI'S WINDOW

	We Know	We do not Know	
They Know	1	2	
They do not Know	3	4	

In this exercise, we start from Box 1 of the Window this box indicates that there is knowledge which is *known to both them (insiders/villager) and us (outsiders)*. Then we move to Box 2 *which indicates that there is knowledge which they know and we do not know.* Then in the third stage, we move to Box 3, which indicates that there is some knowledge which is known to us but *they do not know.* Then attention is focussed on Box 4, which indicates that some knowledge is unknown to both them and us. Each Box is explored in the context of the evolution of the PRIs. This exercise emphasises the point that people know and their knowledge is to be sought and respected.

2.1 The **Johari's Window**[7] is further illustrated below:

Box 1: Open Knowledge What we know and what they know	*Box 2: Hidden Knowledge* What they know and we do not know
Box 3: Blindness What we know and they do not know	*Box 4: Knowledge that will be revealed* What we do not know and they do not know

3. Trace the evolution of the Panchayati Raj Institutions by drawing a Timeline

In **Step 3**, the participants draw a **Timeline** that traces the evolution of the PRIs. The **Timeline** traces the evolution of the Panchayati Raj Institutions and visualises the gradual changes that have occurred in village level power structures. It initiates a process of group learning. An example of a **Timeline** of a PRIs in India prepared in a different context, is given in *Figure 2.* The steps in doing the **Timeline** are described below:

3.1 Identify a group of persons and request them to talk about the history of their village. Initiate a discussion about the history of their Village Panchayat. Alternatively, an elderly person of villager may be engaged in this activity.

3.2 Some suggested key questions are:
- When was the Village Panchayat established?
- What are the important events in the history of the Village Panchayat?
- What major changes took place?
- What are the reasons for these changes?
- How have these changes affected the community?

---

7. Adapted from Pretty *et al.*, 1995

Figure 2: Time Line — Decentralization and Local Governance in India

Year	*Major Events*
1952	Community Development and Sahakari Samaj
1957	Balwantrai Mehta Committee
1958-1959	State Government enacting Panchayat Acts.
1959	Jawaharlal Nehru inaugurating the first generation Panchayats in Rajasthan (Nagaur)
1962	ZP Act of UP
1964-1977	Decline of First Generation of PR
1966-1967	Ministry of Community Development became a department under Ministry of Food & Agriculture
1977	Tribal sub plan in Tribal Area commenced
1977	Asoka Mehta Committee
1978	Asoka Mehta Committee Report Submitted
1978	West Bengal Panchayat elections on Political party lines. The beginning of Second generation PR
1978	Zinabhai Darj Committee on Social Justice/Orient elections
1983	Karnataka Government following West Bengal Panchayat Act, ushers in PR
1985	Andhra Pradesh followed suit
1980's	Idea of district Government especially the writings of Nirmal Mukharji came top be recognized
1988	Parliament Consultative Committee under P.K. Thungan made its recommendations
1989 May 15	63th Constitutional Amendment Bill introduced in Parliament
1989 Oct. 15	The 63th Constitutional Amendment Bill was defeated in Rajya Sabha
1990 Sep. 7	64th Constitutional Amendment Bill introduced in Parliament
1990	Panchayats were brought under Administrators in Karnataka
1991 Sep.	72nd (Panchayats) and 73rd (Nagarpalika) Amendments introduced in Parliament Referred to Joint Select Committee of Parliament
1992 Dec. 22	Lok Sabha passed the Bills (as 73rd and 74th Amendments) on Panchayats and Nagarpalikas
1992 Dec. 23	Rajya Sabha passed the Bills
1993 April 24	The 73rd Amendment Act was brought into force
May 30	The 74th Amendment Act was brought in force
1994 May 30	Madhya Pradesh was the First State to hold the Panchayat Elections under the new dispensation
1996 Dec.	The 73rd Amendment was extended to Scheduled Areas
1996	Kerala launched People's Plan Campaign a unique experiment under the new Panchayati Raj lauded nationally and internationally
2001	Bihar was the last state to hold the first election (after 23 years) under the new system

3.3 Ask one of the participants to note down the major events briefly on cards in bold letters. If the participants are unable to do so, one of the facilitators can help.
3.4 Once the participants feel the list of events is more or less complete, ask them to keep the cards in a chronological order — the earlier events on the top and the later events lower down. Request them to read out the events and ask them whether they are happy with the order or if they would like to modify it.
3.5 Add years to the left side of the events. Failure of memory and not using their system of calendar may come as a big block for the participants in getting the exact years. Use the best judgement to arrive at the years.
3.6 Now initiate a discussion on the Timeline to help the participants analyze and reflect on it. Interview the Timeline by asking open-ended questions to clarify doubts or to get an in-depth understanding about the evolution of the Village Panchayat.
3.7 The trainer may fill in any gaps as and when required, but record what gaps the trainer is filling.
3.8 Then request them to relate these events to years. If years cannot be recalled ask them to associate the events to major happenings such as a war, flood, drought, death of a national figure and so on. Then locate the year of occurrence, according to the major happenings.

---

4. Brainstorm to catalogue the concepts and philosophy of Panchayati Raj Governance

---

In **Step 4**, use **Brainstorming**, for which the process is described below:

4.1 The objective of the Brainstorming exercise is to catalogue the concepts and philosophy of Panchayati Raj Governance. This provides a valuable starting point for discussing about the fundamentals of the PRI system. The list of the concepts developed through this exercise is based upon the collective insights of the participant-group. It forms the basis for further discussion, grouping, sorting, prioritization and problem solving.
4.2 Ask the participants to nominate a facilitator who will not participate, but merely record the ideas.
4.3 Ask the group to think of the concepts and philosophy of PRIs based upon their own experience.
4.4 Encourage all the participants to think adventurously. Emphasize the number rather than the quality of ideas.

4.5 Let the ideas flow freely without any comments or evaluation being made.
4.6 The facilitator writes each idea on a flash card. All the flash cards are laid on the floor of the classroom in one column or row.
4.7 Evaluate the list after the **Brainstorming** is over.

5. Next cluster the brainstormed ideas by the Delphi Technique

In **Step 5**, use the **Delphi Technique**, for which the steps are described below:

5.1 The Brainstorming exercise would have generated a list of the underlying concepts and philosophy of Panchayati Raj Governance and each idea/concept would have been recorded on a card (only one idea per card).
5.2 The cards are then grouped according to the concept areas such as "units of self governance", "power to the people" and so on. One, some or all the participants can do this exercise. Exact duplicates are removed.
5.3 Each concept cluster denotes a particular theme area which is then discussed with the participants.

6. Do Matrix Scoring to examine the functioning of the Village Panchayat

In **Step 6, Listing, Scoring** and **Matrix Scoring** are done by the participants on the responsibilities of the Village Panchayat. This exercise helps the participants to:

- Facilitate so that the participants catalogue their responsibilities as members of the Village Panchayat.
- Facilitate so that the participants reflect on the concept of self government

The steps to be followed in this exercise are given below:

6.1 Explain clearly the purpose of the exercise to the participants, namely, that it will help to bring out their responsibilities as Village Panchayat functionaries.
6.2 Initiate a discussion about the responsibilities of the Village Panchayat. Let the participants list down the various responsibilities that are discussed, one on each flash cards. Place the flash cards as one column.

6.3 Ask the participants to score or rank their responsibilities scoring can be done by either the free, fixed or vector scoring method.

6.4 Now ask the participants the criteria against which they have ranked/scored their responsibilities. Place these as the first row.

6.5 Now facilitate so that the participants score each responsibility against the criteria.

6.6 Ensure that the criteria are all positive and precise. Use of positive and negative criteria in the same exercise can be confusing.

6.7 Help the participants to draw up a matrix with the responsibilities top to bottom and criteria left to right. The participants can do it the other way round also. However, keep in mind that the comparisons are made by the participants criterion-wise and not responsibility-wise. It means that the participants take up a criterion and then do scoring for all the responsibilities. Once one criterion is over, they move to the next, do the scoring for all the responsibilities and record them until all criteria are covered for each of the items.

6.8 Now ask the participants to score/rank each responsibility against "*accountability*" and "*transparency*".

6.9 (*Note*: There will be two Matrices scored, one with the criteria against responsibility suggested by the participants, and the other with the criteria of "*accountability*" and "*transparency*" against the responsibilities).

6.10 Now initiate discussion. See if they perceive that the more important responsibilities (according to the first Matrix mentioned above) are also the responsibilities that they carry out with transparency and accountability. If not, explore these questions:
- What are the reasons?
- What needs to be done?
- What are the inhibiting and facilitating factors? etc.

6.11 *Figure 3* gives an example of using the **Matrix Scoring Method** for the institutions that the Village Panchayat has to network with. The same method can be used for analysing the functioning of the Village Panchayat as described above.

7. Visual Method for synthesising what we have learnt from this Session

In Step 7, the Trainer fills in any knowledge gaps that may remain and then concludes the session by synthesising the learning points. The Trainer should point out that she is now trying to fill in Box 3 of Johari's Window. This may be done by using a set of overhead transparencies stating the points in very simple language. The flip charts or the cards prepared by the participants can be used. Alternatively, one of the participants can be requested to do the synthesis.

Figure 3: Example of Matrix Scoring for Institutional Analysis[8]

Criteria / *Institutions*	*Sensitivity to the Problems of the Village Panchayat*	*Willingness to work in Villages*	*Enforcement/ compliance with rules*	*Honesty*	*Local problem solving ability*	*Overall rank*
Police Station	●●	●●●●● ●●●●● ●●●●	●●●●● ●●●●	●	●●●●● ●●●●● ●●●●	3
Health Centre	●●●●● ●●●●●	●●●●●● ●●●●●●	●●●●● ●●●●● ●●●●	●●●●●	●●●●● ●●●●●	2
School	●●●●● ●●●●●	●●●●●● ●●●●●●	●●●●● ●●●●●	●●●●● ●●●●● ●●●●	●●●●● ●●●●● ●●●●	1
Patwari's Office	●●●●● ●●	●●●●●● ●●●	●●●●	●	●●●●● ●●●●● ●●●●	5
Block Office	●●	●●●●●● ●●●●	●●●●● ●●●	●	●●●●● ●●	8
Collector's Office	●●	●●●●●●	●●●●● ●●●●● ●●●●	●●●●	●●●●●	6
DRDA	●●●●●	●●●●●	●●●●● ●●●●● ●●●●	●●●●	●●●● ●●●●● ●	4
Election Commission	●	●●	●●●●● ●●●●●	●●●●● ●●●●● ●●●●	●●●	7
State Government	●●	●●	●●●●● ●●●●●	●●●●●	●●	9

Note:

1. **Free Scoring** has been used. The ranking has been done vertically for each criterion. The next step is to analyse the **Matrix Scoring** by highlighting the emerging issues and drawing relevant action points. For instance, from the above **Matrix Scoring** exercise, the following points emerge:

---

8. *Source*: Training of Trainers Workshop at HIPA, Gurgaon; Participants: Rajeshwari, Ramakanthan, Rita Singh, Pokhriyal and others; Facilitated by Amitava Mukherjee and Mitali Sen Gavai.

2. Very few of the institutions is sensitive to the problems of the Village Panchayat.
3. All the institutions are very keen to implement and enforce rules and are bureaucratic.
4. A majority of the institutions get low scores for the criterion of "*Honesty*".
5. The institutions outside the village do not score well for the criterion "Willingness to work in villages".
6. This exercise, therefore, conscientises the participants about these institutions. They can consider the following course of action for their Village Panchayats:
   - The participants, especially the elected Village Panchayat members can demand that these institutions became more sensitive to their needs and helped effectively in solving local level problems. They can demand better quality service from them.
   - After exploring as to why these institutions are not rated very high on "honesty", the participants can seek greater transparency, accountability and social audit.

Base Module *Session 3* — Section I General Orientation

Session Theme	GENDER AND SOCIAL JUSTICE
Duration	165 minutes
Venue	Classroom without fixed furnitures
Seating	Sit/stand on the ground forming a circle for the group work, move around the room for the games
Session Objective	*To conscientise the participants about the social concerns related to gender, social justice and social exclusion*

Expected Learning Outcomes

- The participants understand the issues related to gender and social exclusion that are prevalent in village-level society
- They become aware of the duty of the Village Panchayat for promoting social justice through both its governance and development related functions

Content Flow and Training Methodology

Sr. No.	*Content*	*Training Methodology*	*Training Aids*	*Duration (in minutes)*
1.	Energising Game	Step 1 Who are We?	None	15
2.	Concept of Gender, Differences between sexuality and gender	Step 2 Gender Analysis through Pictures	Flip Charts and marker pens	45[9]
3.	Neglect of gender and social justice	Step 3 Gendered Resource Mapping	Flip Charts and marker pens	45

9. It is suggested that the duration be factored thus: preparation time: 30 minutes, presentation and Discussion time: 15 minutes, total: 45 minutes. However, the trainer is free to vary these according to the needs of the trainees

Sr. No.	*Content*	*Training Methodology*	*Training Aids*	*Duration (in minutes)*
4.	Explore ways and means to rectify the situation	**Step 4** Access Social Mapping **Step 5** Solution Tree	Flip Charts and marker pens	45
5.	Synthesis of learning points by Trainer/ Participant (s)	**Step 6** Visual Method	Overhead slides/maps, pictures	15

THE METHODOLOGICAL STEPS FOR SESSION 3

1. Know each other better by playing Who are We?

In **Step 1**, an energising game, **Who are We?**[10] has been suggested, the steps for which are given below:

1.1 The objective of the game is to familiarise the participants with each other even further and promote group bonding.

1.2 Ask participants to raise their hands in response to some questions, like:
- Who is a sarpanch/upasarpanch?
- Who is a Village Panchayat member for the first time?
- Who is a Village Panchayat member for a second term?
- Who has been a Village Panchayat member more than twice?
- Whose Village Panchayat has a problem related to drinking water?
- Who has been trained before?

1.3 Use as many questions as possible. Briefly discuss after each such question. Most of the participants are interested in knowing more about the others. This exercise raises mutual awareness among them about each other.

2. Use pictures to understand the concept of gender

In Step 2, for the **Gender Analysis**, follow these steps:

10. Adapted from Pretty *et al.*, 1995.

2.1 Ask the participants to draw two pictures, one of a man and the other of a woman showing what each one does. The trainer analyses the pictures with them. Usually, in most cases, the participants draw the eyes, ears, etc. in both the pictures and add bindis and ornaments on the picture of the woman.

2.2 Initiate the gender related discussions based upon these pictures. The trainer should encourage the participants to talk about the differences. The trainer points out that many of the differences between a man and a woman are biological. This is **not** gender. They relate to the sexuality of man and woman. Gender is different. Gender relates to the social construction of the roles of man and woman and the power relationship between them. To help introduce the concept of gender, the trainer can facilitate the participants to analyse the pictures based upon questions, like:

- What are the tasks done by man and woman?
- Who decides what the woman will do?
- Who decides when the woman will do what?
- Who decides when the woman will work?
- Who decides why the woman will work the way she does?

---

3. Do Gendered Resource Mapping to understand deprivation due to gender discrimination

---

In **Step 3**, the **Gendered Resource Mapping** will help the participants to explore the gendered dimensions of social justice. An example of the Gendered Resource Mapping is given in *Figure 4* and *Figure 4A*. The steps for the Gendered Resource Mapping are described below:

3.1 The participants draw a map of the available resources in one of their villages. The map can be drawn on the floor of a building, on the ground or on paper.

3.2 Then ask the participants to choose symbols for showing the following:

- control over the natural resource, say 'C'
- providing labour and inputs for using the natural resource, say 'L'
- having end use of the products of the resource, say 'U'

3.3 Participants then choose symbols to show a man and woman, for example & can show a man and % depict a woman.

3.4 Next, ask the participants to combine the two of symbols for control, labour, inputs and man and woman and show who controls, who provides labour and inputs and who uses the

Figure 4: Resource Map from Ghusel, VDC, Lalitpur District, Nepal

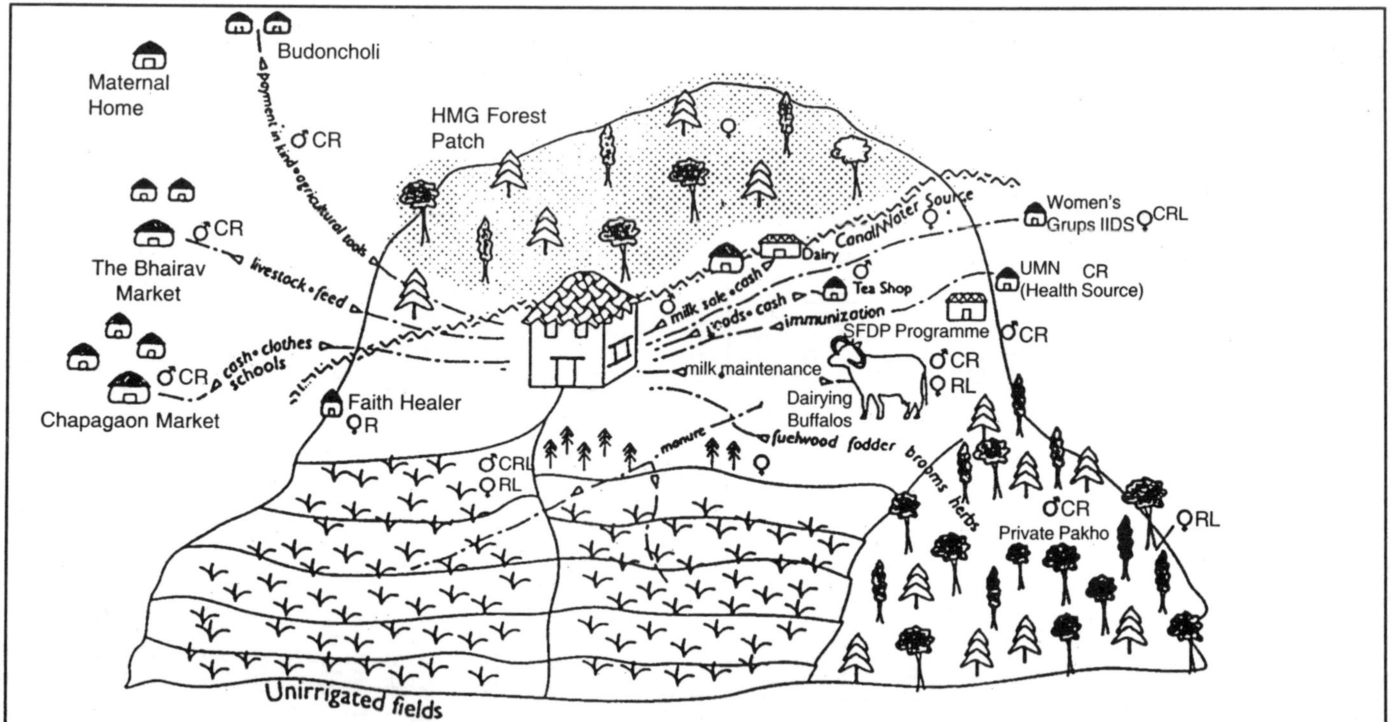

Pakho: Informal management system in which village households plant species suitable for fuelwood and fodder on government 'wasteland' (once forested, now barren), thereby converting that land to private property. Access to Pakho land varies widely by class, caste, and ethnicity.

UMN : United Mission to Nepal
SFDP : Small Farmer Development Programme
HMG : His Majesty's Government

C = Control of site/plants/products/relationship
R = Responsibility to provide products from the site
L = Labour input on site/actual use

Source: *Power, Process and Participation* (London: Intermediate Technology Press) 1996.

Figure 4A: Gendered household and community resources in Panano, Dominican Republic

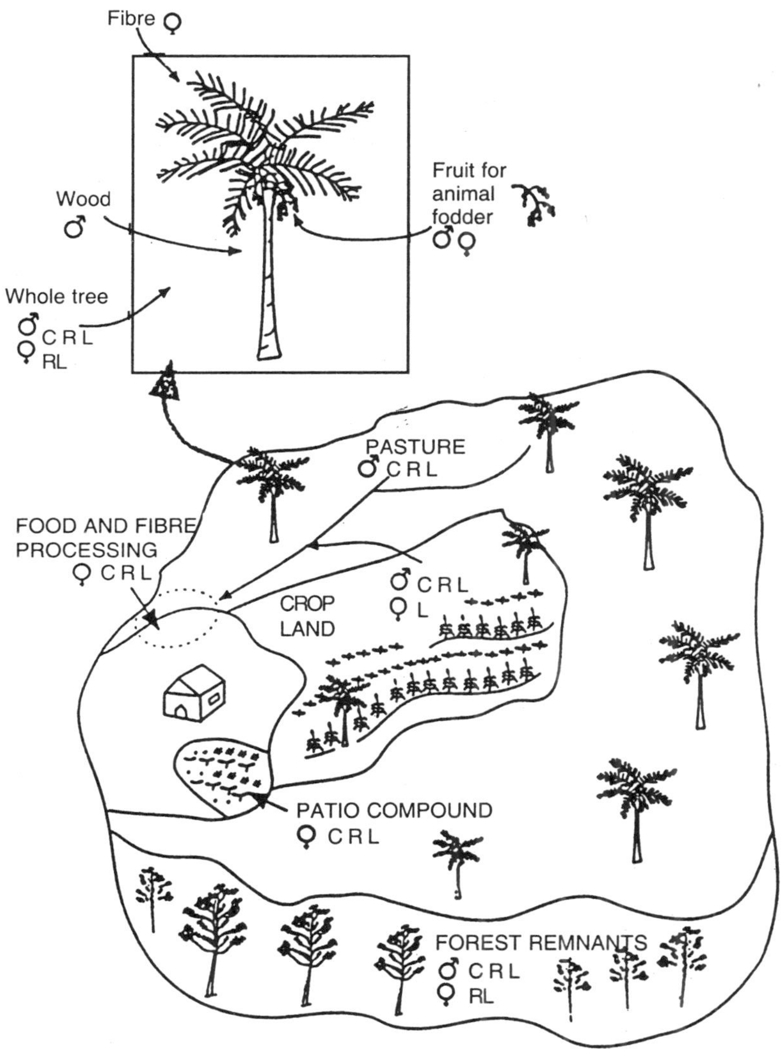

Multi-purpose use of land and trees in Pananao (La Sierra, Dominican Republic), Both men and women are present in this household, R = responsibility to provide a product thereof to the household, L = labour for the establishment, maintenance or harvest, and C = control of resource or process.

resources. Thus, for example and against coconut trees shows that the man controls them and also uses the income from the trees. Similarly, % shows that women put in labour to grow/ maintain the tree and also use the income from it. And so on.

3.5 This exercise should be done for every resource shown on the map.

3.6 From this exercise, the participants would understand the following issues, namely:
- How much labour do both men and women contribute in generating resources different used in pursuing rural livelihoods?
- Who controls the resources required for the livelihoods?
- Who puts in the labour? And in which resource?
- Who controls the production of the resources?

3.7 Then discuss with the participants:
- Is there equity in providing labour?
- Is there equity in the use of the benefits of the resources?
- Is the control fair? Is the control of the resources commensurate with the labour and inputs provided by women and men?
- Ask other questions which you may consider appropriate.

3.8 Once the participants have drawn the **Gendered Resource Map**, it is displayed on the wall. In order to bring out the gender justice dimension with respect to the control over resources, the participants are again asked to identify the following resources:
- For which resource they provide labour, but have no control over the produce.
- For which resource they provide labour and share control over the produce with the men.
- For which resource they provide labour and have full control over the produce.
- Is the control over produce equitable?
- What can be done to remedy the situation?

---

4. *Do Access Social Mapping to understand deprivation from access to social development services/public utilities due to gender discrimination*

In **Step 4**, the **Access Social Mapping** will help the participants understand the phenomenon of social exclusion whereby certain groups like gender, Scheduled Castes, Scheduled Tribes and others, have limited or no access to public utilities, development resources and services. This will help the participants to identify injustices and explore ways of rectifying them. *Figure 5* is an example of Access Social Mapping. The steps for the **Access**

Figure 5: Access Social Maping

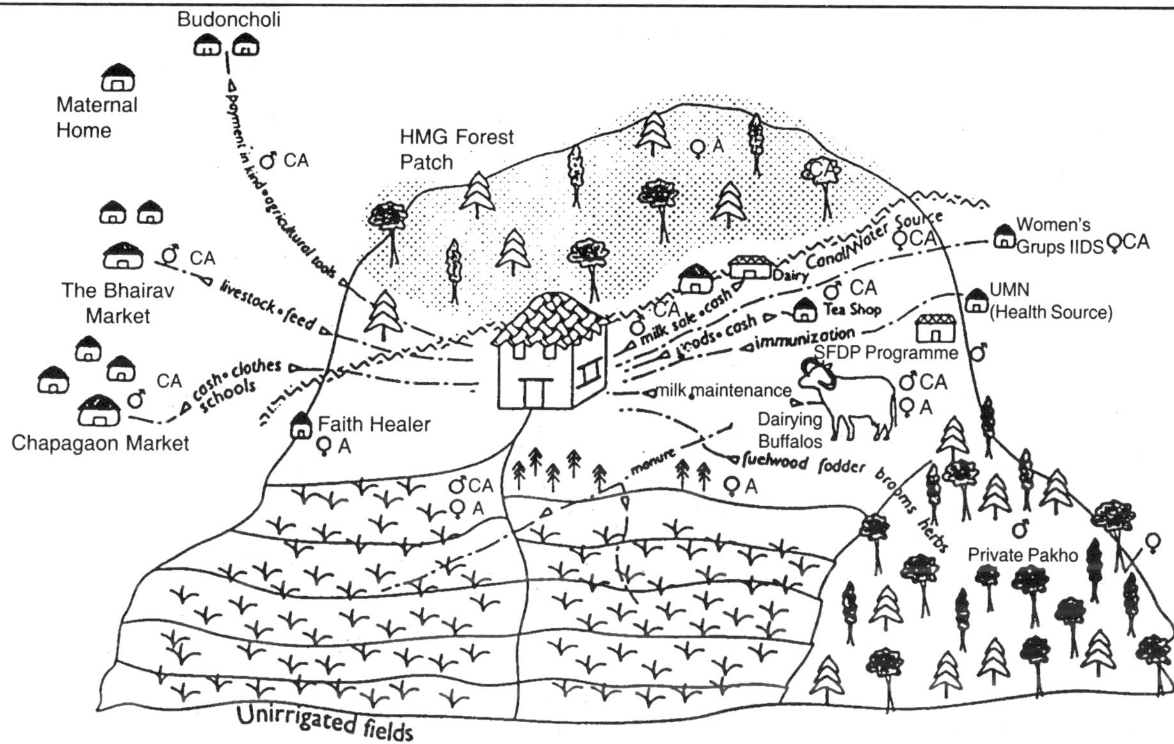

Pakho: Informal management system in which village households plant species suitable for fuelwood and fodder on government 'wasteland' (once forested, now barren), thereby converting that land to private property. Access to Pakho land varies widely by class, caste, and ethnicity.

UMN : United Mission to Nepal
SFDP : Small Farmer Development Programme
HMG : His Majesty's Government
C : Control
A : Access

Source: Modification from *Power, Process and Participation* (London: Intermediate Technology Press) 1996.

Social Mapping are given below:

4.1 The participants draw a Social Map of a village showing the social infrastructure like anganwadis[11], primary schools, community health centres, etc. The process of **Social Mapping** is described below:

4.2 Explain the purpose of the exercise to the participants. Request them to start with drawing the prominent physical features of their village. One way to start is to request the participants to mark the roads in the village or the Temple or the village pond etc.. Leave it to them to use whatever materials they choose — local as well as other materials as creatively as possible.

4.3 Keep a track of which participants are actively involved and which sections of the society they belong to and who are left out. Take proactive steps to involve those participants who are not involved in the mapping process.

4.4 *The trainer's role is that of mere facilitator*. Intervene when strictly necessary especially when the participants are in a rough patch.

4.5 If the trainer has something to add or clarify, she would wait for the right moment and not disrupt the process.

4.6 After the mapping is over, ask the participants to devise separate symbols to show full, partial and nil access, e.g. a shaded circle can show full access; a partially shaded circle shows partial access and a blank circle shows no access.

4.7 The participants then choose symbols to show a man and woman, as done earlier in case of Gendered Resource Mapping

4.8 Then mark each social institution drawn on the map by combining the two sets of symbols for access and man and woman to show what kind of access is available. For example if only men have access to the temple, mark ♀ beside the temple; if women have no access to the temple, mark ♂ beside the temple; and if both have access then mark ♀ ♂.

4.9 A similar exercise may be done for the Scheduled Castes, Scheduled Tribes and other socially excluded groups, as may be necessary.

4.10 Once the **Access Social Maps** are prepared, the participants are required to paste them on the wall and make a brief presentation.

4.11 Ask the participants whether the **Access Social Map** shows that women have less access than the men to the social infrastructure, development services, etc. existing in the village or not. In this

11. Village child-care centre providing services under the Integrated Child Development Services Programme.

context, the Trainer should now draw the attention of the participants to the concerns related to gender in equality and social justice for the socially excluded groups like women, Scheduled Castes, Scheduled Tribes, etc. and lead a discussion.

4.12 Draw the attention of the participants to the social injustices/ inequities, which may emerge from the mapping exercise. Discuss the obligations of the Village Panchayat for promoting social justice through their local governance and village development related functions. These discussions should increase the participants' sensitivity to the phenomenon of social exclusion whereby certain groups because of reasons of gender, caste, ethnicity, age group, lack of control over resources, etc. are excluded from participating in the activities and benefits of the social infrastructure and development services.

4.13 Seek solutions from the participants. Request the participants to write down on separate cards the problems that may emerge from the mapping exercises and the discussions that follow.

5. Solution Tree Format for visualizing problems and their solutions

In **Step 5**, ask the participants to write down the solutions to the problems discussed in the previous step, in a **Solution Tree Format**. In this exercise, the problems are thought of as the roots of a tree and the corresponding solutions as the branches of the tree. An example of a **Solution Tree** is given in *Figure 6*.

6. Visual Method for synthesising what we have learnt from this Session

Step 6: The session ends with the trainer synthesising the learnings that have flowed. The trainer may like to invite one or more of the participants to help in the synthesis.

Figure 6: Solution Tree: equitable and sustainable development

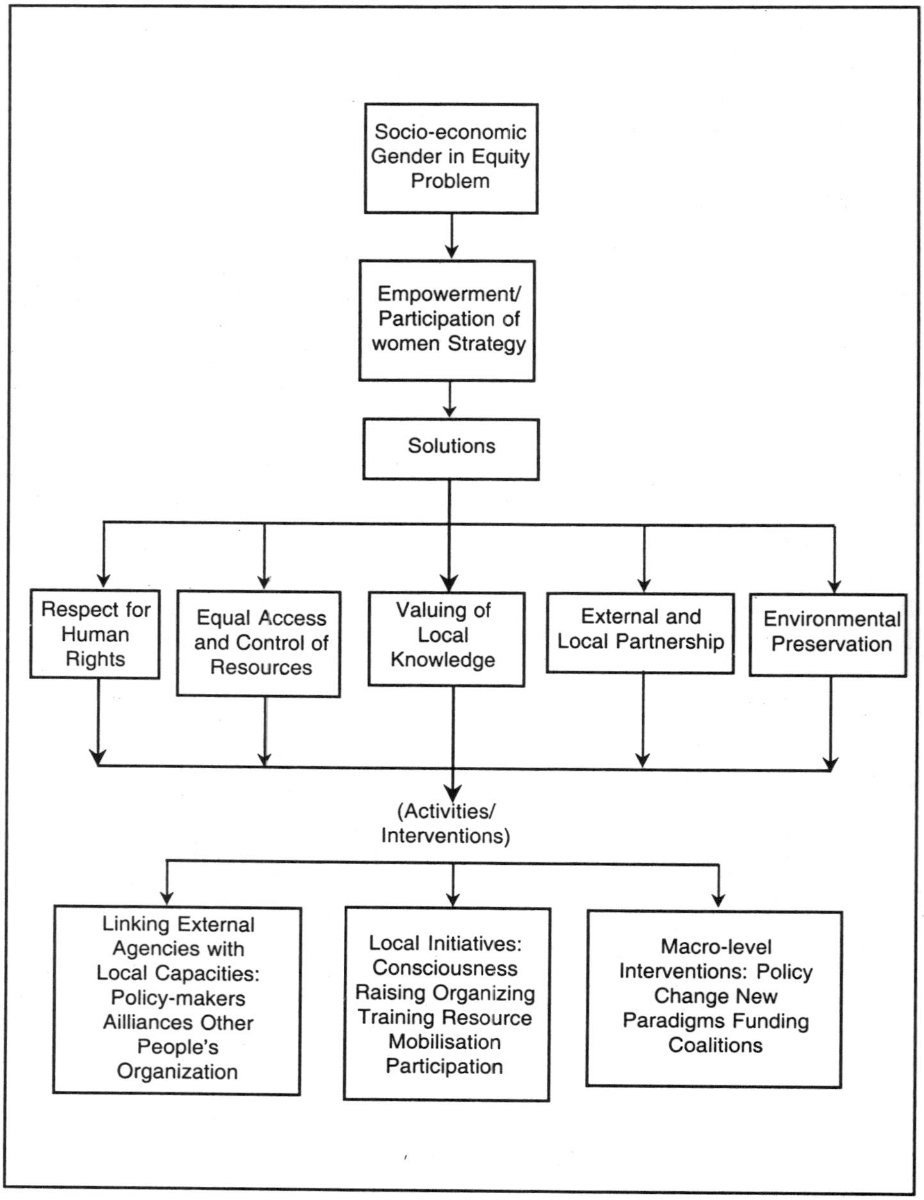

Base Module Section I
Session 4 General Orientation

Session Theme	PEOPLE-CENTRED COMMUNITY DEVELOPMENT
Duration	240 minutes
Venue	Classroom without fixed furnitures
Seating	Sit or stand on the floor forming a circle for group work; move around the room for the game and picture/poster sessions
Session Objective	*To impart to the participant a conceptual understanding of people-centred community development*

Expected Learning Outcomes

- The participants get acquainted with the different approaches and programmes for village development.
- They are able to appreciate the centrality of people-centred community development.

Content Flow and Training Methodology

Sr. No.	*Content*	*Training Methodology*	*Training Aids*	*Duration (in minutes)*
1.	(a) Changes in the development paradigm (b) The consistency of the status of decentralisation in India with the changing development paradigm	**Step 1** Historical Transect **Step 2** Lecture Method	Flip charts, marker pens, overhead slides, cards	60[12]
2.	Different approaches to development and the approach most appropriate for village level development	**Step 3** Matching Game	Cards, marker pens, seeds or pebbles	45

12. Preparation time: 25, Presentation and Discussion time: 20 minutes, Lecture: 15 minutes. However, the trainer can vary these time limits.

Sr. No.	*Content*	*Training Methodology*	*Training Aids*	*Duration (in minutes)*
3.	(a) Status of village development in India in the context of the different development approaches (b) Status of gender equity and social justice in this context	**Step 4** Pictures	Slides, drawings of cartoons	30
4.	Ways and means to improve the status of village development in India	**Step 5** Ranking and Scoring	Cards, marker pens, seeds or pebbles	45
5.	Development Programmes and ways and means to improve their efficiency	**Step 6** Pie Charts **Step 7** Ranking and Scoring	Flip Charts, marker pens, cards, coins of different denominations adding to a rupee, seeds or pebbles	45
6.	Synthesis of learning points by Trainer/ Participant (s)	**Step 8** Visual Method	Overhead slides/ Flip Charts prepared by the participants	15

THE METHODOLOGICAL STEPS FOR SESSION 4

1. Draw a Historical Transect to trace the shifts in the development paradigm

In **Step 1**, a **Historical Transect** is drawn to trace the important stages in the changes/shifts in the development paradigm. The trainer may need some outside help. It may be likely that the trainer will have to start from Box 3 of the Johari's Window, viz. *We Know and They do not Know* and then move to Box 2, that is *They Know and We do not Know*. An example of a Historical Transect is given in *Figure 7.*

2. Give a brief lecture about the status of decentralisation in India

In **Step 2**, by means of a brief lecture, discuss the consistency of the status of decentralisation in India compared to the changing development paradigm. For this purpose, the trainer is urged to use transparencies worded in simple language. The seating arrangement suggested for this purpose is that the trainer should be seated on the floor with the participants behind her, all of them facing the slide projector that is kept at a higher level.

3. Play the Matching Game to explore the different development approaches

In **Step 3**, for the **Matching Game**, follow this sequence:

3.1 **Brainstorm** the different development approaches with the participants. The trainer is requested to refer to *Figure 7* for details about development approaches.
3.2 Encourage the participants to write down each approach on a single card.
3.3 Facilitate so that the participants arrange the cards in one column.
3.4 Initiate discussions amongst the participants about the merits and demerits of each approach.
3.5 Let the participants write a merit/demerit of an approach on a single card.
3.6 Place these cards alongside the card for the concerned approach.
3.7 Use **Free Scoring** to explore the participants' views about which approach is the most appropriate for village-level development.
3.8 Discuss with the participants. Try and arrive at a conclusion about the approach that is best suited to the modern times.

4. Use cartoons to discuss the state of village development in India

In **Step 4**, **Pictures** used can be in the form of cartoons. Have a cartoon show with slides, transparencies or drawings. The cartoons of RK Laxman[13] have been published in several volumes. They have excellent material to make this show. Many of his cartoons deal with development problems and approaches. Ask the participants whether they can relate their situation to the pictures and lead a discussion. Separate the pictures with which

13. Laxman, 2000

Figure 7: Historical Transect of the Development Paradigm

Decade	*Development Paradigm*	*Programmes Initiated*	*Reasons for Success/Failure*
1950-60	• First phase of Panchayati Raj • Socialistic pattern of society • Plan emphasis on Industry	• Establishment of Community Development Blocks • Role of the public sector emphasised	• Public sector expanded • Agriculture neglected
1960-70	• Panchayati Raj established in many States like Maharashtra and Gujarat • Emphasis on agriculture and planned development • Trickle Down Theory	• Green Revolution (use of HYV seeds, fertilisers, irrigation) introduced.	• States did not want to devolve power to PRIs • Trickle Down theory did not deliver according to expectations
1970-80	• Food sufficiency achieved • Programmes for agricultural development given priority • Slogan of "Garibi Hatao"[14] • Launching of the Integrated Rural Development Programme and Integrated Child Development Services Programme with involvement of Panchayats in several States • First ever survey of Below Poverty Line Families	• Poverty alleviation programmes like IRDP and TRYSEM were initiated • Gender needs in development were being recognized • Maternal and child health received attention	• Emphasis on decreasing income poverty with no linkages for enhancing human capabilities • Social sector programmes were sectoral with little or no integration • Top-down development approach

(Contd.)

14. Slogan which literally means "Remove Poverty"

Figure 7 (*Contd.*)

1980-90	• Institutional reforms to reorganise the PRIs was done in Andhra Pradesh and Karnataka • IRDP continued but new programmes like Jawahar Rozgar Yojana, Jeevandhara Wells Programme, Indira Awas Yojana for ensuring wage employment on public works, land development and housing for the BPL were begun • Greater emphasis on the creation of social infrastructure	• Panchayats were given development funds under the new schemes • Involvement of poor stakeholders in development initiatives was emphasized • Village development plans prepared. ICDS Programme started	• Two-fold emphasis, viz. creation of self and wage employment and creation of rural social infrastructure • Village Panchayats were actively involved in development programmes
1990-2000	• Major shift in the development paradigm, viz. empowerment of PRIs through the 73rd and 74th Constitutional Amendment Acts • Micro-credit model initiated through Save and Thrift groups and later Self Help Groups • Social mobilization of poor stakeholders emphasised	• 73rd Constitution Amendment enacted • Many States passed new Panchayati Raj Acts or modified existing legislation • Capacity building of PRI functionaries commenced. • Revamping of IRDP • Micro-credit model based poverty alleviation programme launched. Revamped PDs started	• Social mobilisation seen as the vehicle for promoting social change • Poverty recognized as multidimensional and not limited to income poverty

Figure 7A: Historical Transects of Ardanarypura Village

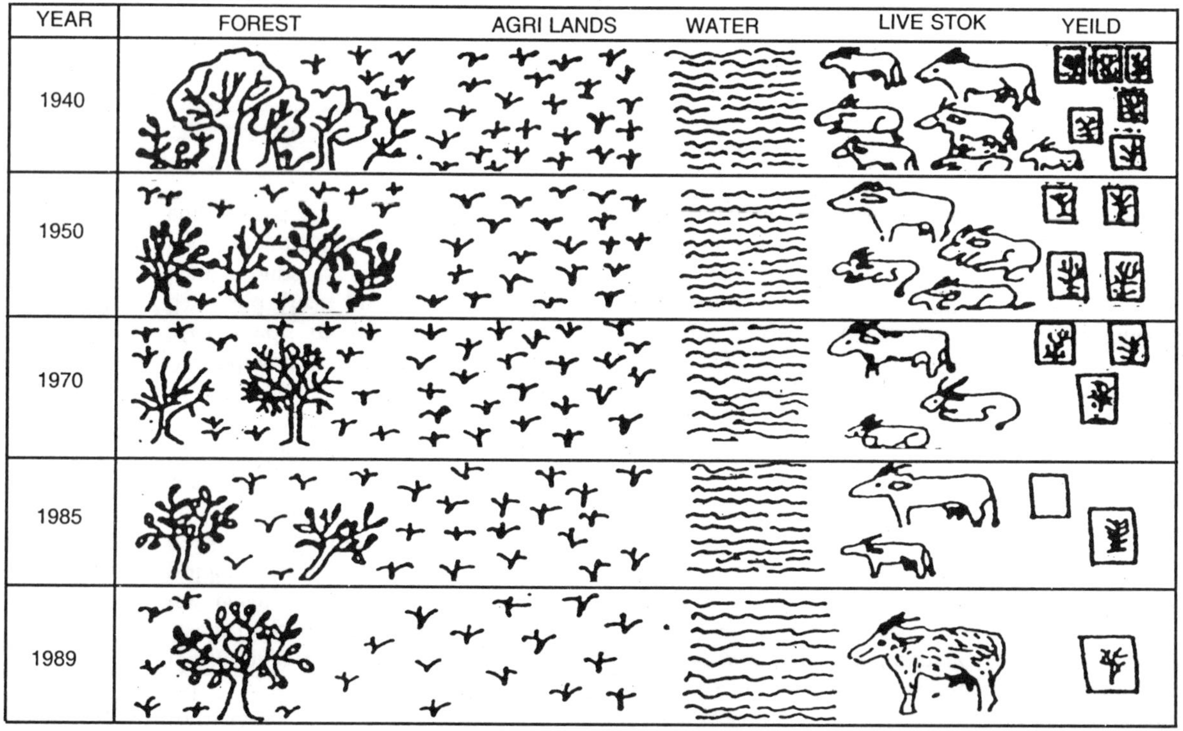

MYRADA STAFF
1. CHAKRA PAKI 2. KIRAN 3. VINSENT 4. SHELEA

PARTICIPANTS
1. SHUNDA DAMMA 2. MADAMMA 3. MARE 4. SODE MADAMMA 5. SHIDDAMMA

Source: Forest, Trees and People News letter no. 15/16

they can relate and discuss further. Use the learnings from the previous session to discuss the status of gender equity and social justice in this context. A set of cartoon showing the different kinds of development problems is at *Figures 8 to 12*.

---

5. *Rank and Score to determine ways to improve the status of village development in India*

In **Step 5**, for the **Ranking** and **Scoring** exercise, use the learnings from the cartoon show and ask the participants to write down the ways and means for improving the status of village development given the state of development they have depicted by the cartoons. The participants are encouraged to write each suggestion on a separate card. Sort the cards and arrange them in a column. Ask the participants to rank them.

Now after the **Scoring/Ranking,** use the ***Seven Helpers*** to interview the **Ranking** done by the participants:

- Who can improve the status of village development in India?
- Why is the status so?
- When can it be done?
- How can it be done?
- Where can it be done?
- Whom will it be done?
- For Whom will it be done?

---

6. *Draw Pie Charts for determining the relative importance of development programmes*

In **Step 6**, ask the participants to draw **Pie Charts** to depict the relative relevance/importance of development programme for the well-being of village communities. Follow these steps:

6.1 First ask the participants to list the development programmes which are being implemented at the village level.

6.2 Give the participants coins of different denominations adding upto a Rupee.

6.3 Then ask them to decide on the relative importance of the programmes by giving weights to each in terms of the coins provided. The weights are expressed in terms of a certain proportion of the Rupee, say 50 paisa, 5 paisa and so on, noting that the total cannot exceed Re. 1.

Figure 8: The Government's View of the Poor and the Poor's View of Themselves, Concerning Money

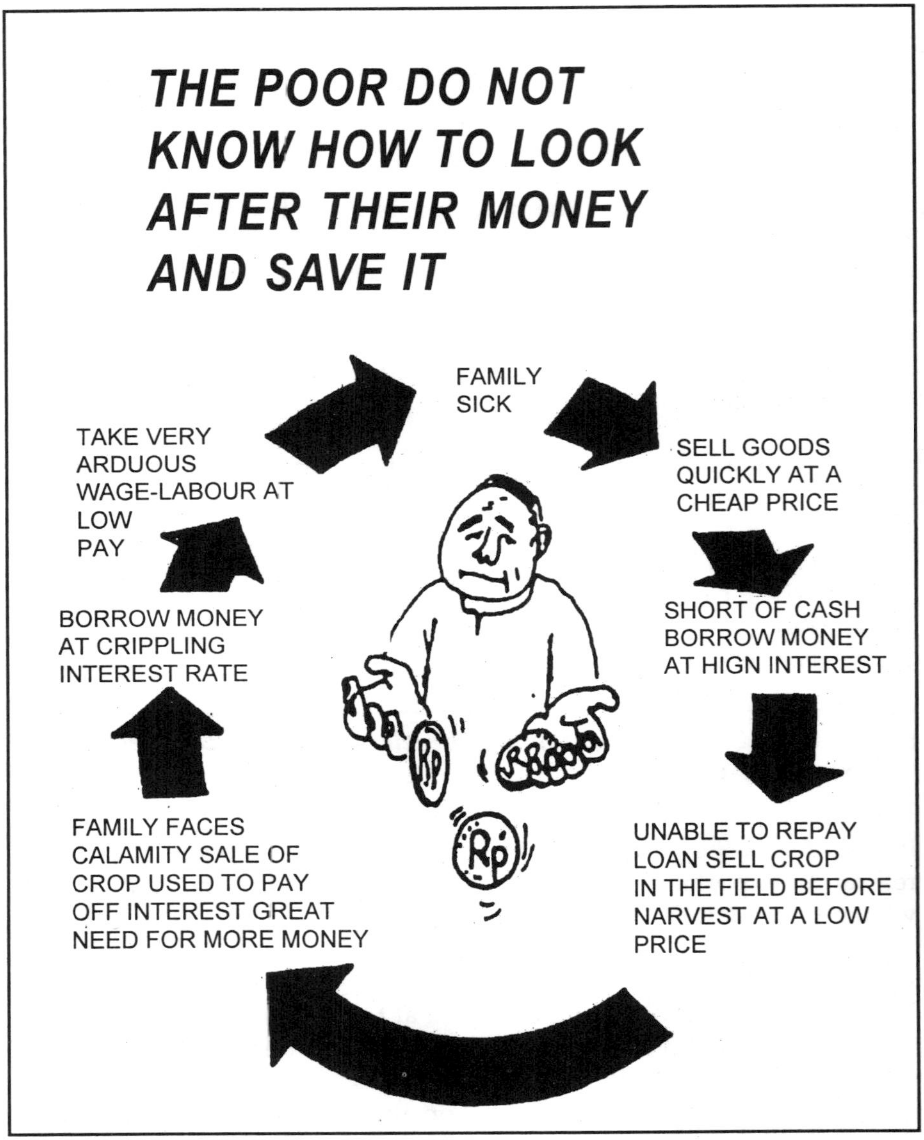

Source: Richard Holloway and David Watson (eds), *Changing Focus-Involving the Rural Poor in Development Planning* (Oxford and IBH Publishing: New Delhi, 1989).

Figure 9: Blockages in the System

Source: *Bulletin Nelayan*, a publication of the All Indonesia Fishermen's Association, out of print (1980).

Figure 10: "Leakages" and the Resultant Weakening of Government Policies

"You might just as well stay there—there's just not enough water to go round".

Source: Cartoon by Richard Wilson, reproduced by kind permission of *Development Forum*, a magazine published by the UN Division for Economic and Social Information, and the United Nations University: New York.

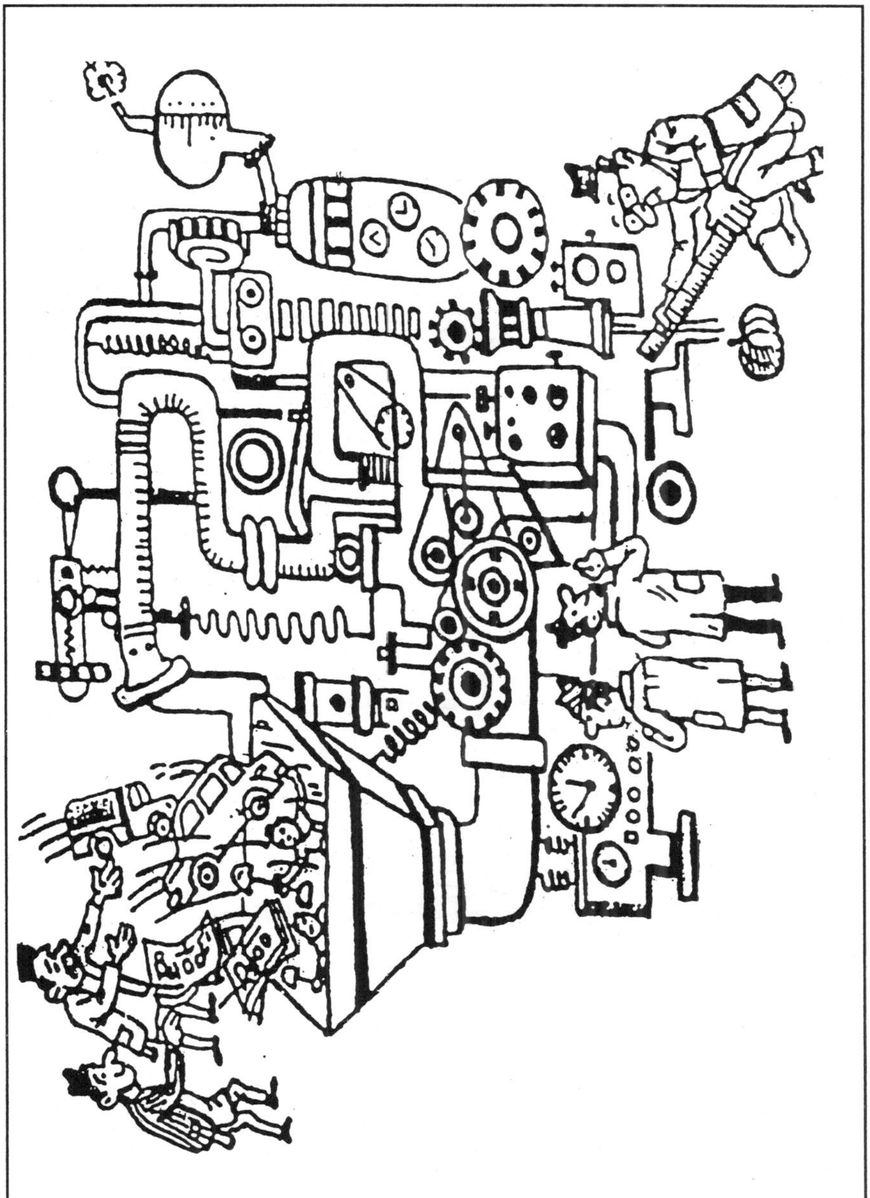

Figure 11: Disharmony Between Inputs, Complicate Process Output and Monitoring Quantitative Target

Figure 12: Target adjustment all the time and missing all the time

6.4 Then represent this analysis visually by asking the participants to draw a pie diagram where the entire circle is equivalent to a Rupee and different portions or quadrants to the proportionate weights assigned to them. Example of a **Pie Chart** is given at *Figure 13.*

6.5 Discuss about the different weights assigned to various development programmes.

Figure 13: Example of a Pie Chart[15]

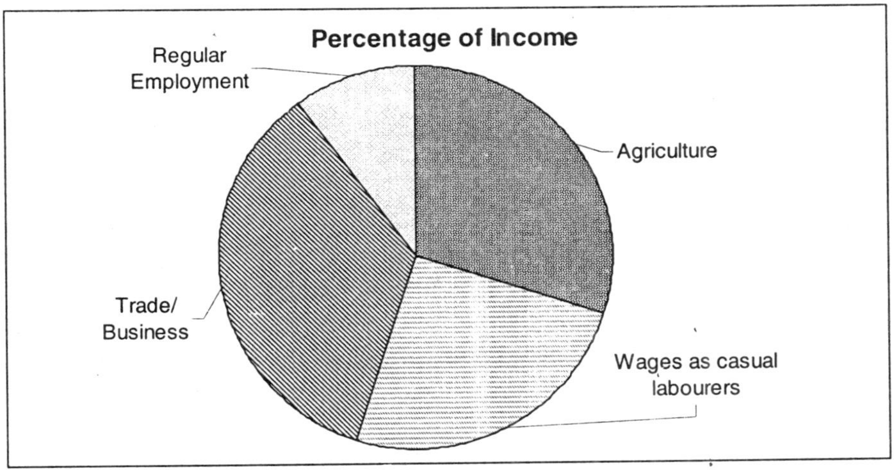

The Figure has been reconstructed from a Pie-Chart prepared by the villagers of Chandpur, Varanasi, Uttar Pradesh. The data set used by the villagers for the Chart is as follows:

Sources of Income	*Percentage of Income*
Agriculture	30
Wages as casual labourers	25
Trade/Business	35
Regular Employment	10
Total	*100*

15. *Source*: Amitava Mukherjee: *Hunger, Theory, Perspectives and Reality—Analysis Through Participatory Methods* (Aldershot: Ashgati Publishing Ltd. and New Delhi: Concept Publishing Company) 2002 pp.147.

7. *Rank and Score to determine ways to improve the status of development programmes*

In **Step 7**, for the second **Ranking** and **Scoring** exercise, ask the participants to repeat the process as in **Step 5** above. Participants will first list the ways and means for improving each development programme and proceed to analyse this information using the *Seven Helpers* that were discussed in Step 5 above.

8. *Visual Method for synthesising what we have learnt from this Session*

Step 8: The session ends with the trainer synthesising the learnings that have flowed. It is suggested that the trainer invites one or more of the participants to help in the synthesis.

Base Module: Section II
POLITICO-LEGAL ORIENTATION

CONTENT FLOW IN POLITICO-LEGAL ORIENTATION BASE MODULE: AT A GLANCE

Day 1		*Day 2*	
Time in minutes	*Session No. and Name*	*Time in minutes*	*Session No. and Name*
FORENOON			
90	5: Panchayati Raj Governance	60	8: Role of the Village Panchayat
20	*Break for Tea*	20	*Break for Tea*
90	6: Role of Panchayati Raj Institutions	120	8: Role of the Village Panchayat (continued)
60	*Break for Lunch*	60	*Break for Lunch*
AFTERNOON			
75	6: Role of Panchayati Raj Institutions (continued)		
20	*Break for Tea*		
140	7: Structure of Panchayati Raj Institutions		
380	*Total Duration of Training*	180	*Total Duration of Training*

DETAILED CONTENT FLOW IN SECTION II
POLITICO-LEGAL ORIENTATION

Day 1 (Time in minutes)	Day 2 (Time in minutes)
FORENOON **Session 5: Panchayati Raj Governance** **Duration: 90 minutes** **1. Content:** *Stepping Stones*—A Game for Experience sharing among the Participants about Village Panchayat Governance: **Duration:** 30 minutes **2. Content:** Self-government and the Panchayat Raj Institutions: Concept and Status **Training Methods:** Poster and Picture based discussions and Lecture **Duration:** 45 minutes **3. Content:** Synthesis by Trainer/ Participants **Training Method:** Visual **Duration:** 15 minutes *Break for Tea (20 minutes)* **Session 6: Role of Panchayati Raj Institutions (Duration: 150 minutes)** **1. Content:** Self–governance and PRIs: Implications and frame of action for economic development, gender equity and social justice **Training Method:** Visual using a cartoon show and picture based discussions **Duration:** 45 minutes **2. Content:** What were the original intentions of the legislations and protagonists of the movement? **Training Method:** Lecture **Duration:** 45 minutes *Break for Lunch (60 minutes)*	*FORENOON* **Session 8: Role of Village Panchayat** **Duration: 180 minutes** **1. Content:** *De jure* functions of the Village Panchayat **Training Method:** Brainstorming, Delphi Technique **Duration:** 60 minutes *Break for Tea (20 minutes)* **2. Content:** *De facto* functions of the Village Panchayat **Training Methods:** Brainstorming, Delphi Technique and Empowerment Circle **Duration:** 60 minutes **3. Content:** How empowered is the Village Panchayat? **Training Methods:** Empowerment Circle **Duration:** 45 minutes **4. Content:** Synthesis by Trainer/ Participants **Training Method:** Visual **Duration:** 15 minutes *Break for Lunch (60 minutes)*

Day 1 (Time in minutes)	Day 2 (Time in minutes)
AFTERNOON **Session 6: Role of Panchayati Raj Institutions** 3. **Content:** What happened to the original ideas and justifications for the PRIs? **Training Method**: Force Field Analysis, Brainstorming **Duration**: 60 minutes 4. **Content:** Synthesis by Trainer/Participants **Training Method:** Visual **Duration**: 15 minutes *Break for Tea (20 minutes)* **Session 7: Structure of Panchayati Raj Institutions** **Duration**: 140 minutes 1. **Content:** ***Saboteur***- A Game for Enhancing Group Dynamics **Duration**: 20 minutes 2. **Content:** The Seventy Third Constitutional Amendment Act and the State Conformity Act: Mandate and Salient Features **Training Method:** Lecture **Duration**: 60 minutes 3. **Content:** Structure of Panchayati Raj Institutions—Gram Sabha, Village Panchayat, Panchayat Samiti and Zilla Parishad **Training Methods:** Role Play/Drama and Lecture **Duration**: 45 minutes 4. **Content:** Synthesis by Trainer/Participants **Training Method:** Visual **Duration**: 15 minutes	
Total duration of Training: 380 minutes (6 Hours and 20 minutes)	Total duration of Training: 180 minutes (about 3 Hours)

NOTE TO TRAINERS FOR USING SECTION II POLITICO-LEGAL ORIENTATION

1. INTRODUCTION

Section II of the Module is designed for both the political and legal orientation of the participants. The previous Section had outlined the evolution of the PRIs and their role in the spheres of both village development and governance. The people-centred development paradigm that gives the overall context for the functioning of the PRIs, different development approaches and programmes were also discussed. The participants were broadly familiarised with the concepts of "democratic decentralisation" and "self government".

Section II coming as its sequel deepens the participants' understanding of both these concepts and serves for furthering the cause of raising the political consciousness participants. The participants get acquainted with the mandate and features of the Seventy-Third Constitutional Amendment Act and the State Conformity Acts which form the legal premise of the Panchayati Raj Institutions, which in turn is expected to induce in the participants an urge to demand their right to govern at the local level.

2. TRAINING OBJECTIVES

The Section has the following training objectives:

- To enhance the practical understanding of the participants about the concept of self government, its institutions, their structures and social mandate.
- To expand the knowledge of the participants about the legal premise of the Panchayati Raj Institutions.
- To conscientise the participants about their rights and duties as members of the Village Panchayat and generate an urge in them to seek their rights.

3. SESSIONS, THEIR TRAINING OBJECTIVES AND EXPECTED LEARNING OUTCOMES

There are four sessions in this Section. Out of these, the first two are geared to fulfil the first training objective, the third session is directed at both the first and the second objectives and the fourth session satisfies the third objective.

The session-wise *Training Objectives* and the *Expected Learning Outcomes* are given in the following table:

Session No.	*Session Description*	*Training Objective*	*Expected Learning Outcomes*
5.	Panchayati Raj Governance	To expand the practical under-standing of the participants about the concept of self government and its institutions	The participants have an increased understanding of the principles underlying the concept of self government, the role and functions of the PRIs as institutions for self government at the grassroots level
6.	Role of Panchayati Raj Institutions	To expand the practical under-standing of the participants about the social mandate of the Panchayati Raj Institutions	The participants have an enlarged comprehension about: • The social mandate of the PRIs for meeting the ends of gender equity and social justice • The extent of the fulfilment of the social mandate
7.	Structure of Panchayati Raj Institutions	To expand the knowledge of the participants about the legal premise and structure of Panchayati Raj Institutions	The participants are increasingly acquainted with the mandate and features of the Seventy Third Constitutional Amendment Act, the State Conformity Act for PRIs and structure of PRIs
8.	Role of the Village Panchayat	To conscientise the participants about their rights and duties as members of the Village Panchayat and generate an urge in them to seek their rights	The participants have increased awareness about: • their own rights and duties • the rightful place of the Village Panchayat in grassroots governance • its role, responsibilities and functions • what is necessary for having those rights, responsibilities and functions

4. THE RIGHTS OF PANCHAYATI RAJ FUNCTIONARIES

One very important feature of this Section is that its contents have been designed for directly functionalising the rights conferred upon the PRI functionaries by the Constitution of India. This is done by conscientising the participants about the right to self-government and political and development participation. The fourth session focuses on the role of the Village Panchayat, the institution which is at the very cutting edge of the development process. The Village Panchayat affords a wide range of poor stakeholders with the opportunity of direct political and development participation. In this session, the *de facto* and *de jure* functions of the Village Panchayat are discussed. This makes the participants aware of the powers and functions that are stated in Article 243 G Eleventh Schedule of the Constitution of India. These powers have to be endowed upon the PRIs for enabling them to function as institutions of self-government. The Schedule read with the under reference lists a total of 29 functions that have to be devolved upon the PRIs. Little progress has been made in this regard in most of the States. It is hoped that the training process will make the participants aware of the rightful powers of the Village Panchayat and their own rights and duties as members of this institution. This awareness should find expression subsequently, in suitable forums and platforms in raising a demand for a greater devolution of authority (in terms of functions, finances and functionaries) to the PRIs, in keeping with the letter and spirit of the Constitution.

5. SESSION 5 *(Note: Sessions 1, 2, 3 and 4 are in Section I of the Base Module)*

The first session of this section raises the curtain by exploring the practical experiences of the participants about Village Panchayat governance through a game called *Stepping Stones*. In the remainder of the session, the concept and status of PRIs is illustrated using a training methodology that is mostly picture/poster based.

6. SESSION 6

Based upon the concept of "self government", the second session of this section discusses the consequent implications and the desired agenda of proactive actions for the PRIs. The original mandate of the PRIs during their inception in some States in the sixties and seventies is then discussed. Force Field Analysis is used to identify how the positive and negative forces acts upon the functioning of the PRIs and the desired direction of future policy interventions.

7. SESSION 7

The Session begins with a game called the *Saboteur*, which is expected to enhance the negotiation skills of the participants thereby helping them to resolve conflicts in analogous Village Panchayat/ Gram Sabha scenarios. This Session coming at this juncture, deals with how the Seventy-Third Constitution Amendment Act and the State Conformity Acts were mandated to give the desired policy direction to the evolution of self-government in the country. The structures of the three-tiered PRIs and the Gram Sabha are also discussed in this session.

8. SESSION 8

The session as mentioned earlier, draws the attention of the participants to the 29 statutory development functions of the Village Panchayat. The extent of devolution of functions and funds and, therefore, the *degree of empowerment* of the Village Panchayat is analysed in this context through participatory exercises. As stated earlier, the underlying training approach relies heavily upon the Rights conferred on the PRIs by the Constitution. By conscientising the participants about the rights of the PRIs that are guaranteed to them by statute, it is expected that this may eventually lead to a demand for such rights. Such a demand may lead to policy changes or interventions for devolving functions, functionaries and finances to the PRIs.

9. TRAINING METHODOLOGY

The trainer is encouraged to use with ingenuity the training methodology suggested in this Section. It is an intermix of Participatory Learning and Action Methods, the lecture method, other visual method using posters and pictures and role play/drama. It has to be remembered that the contents of this Section are on the *heavier* side and, therefore, *learner motivation* has to be sustained by a greater degree of innovation on the part of the trainer. The trainer will be extensively dealing with *'hidden knowledge'* or *'What we know and they do not know'*, namely, Box 3 of the Johari's Window discussed in the previous section. For this purpose, the trainer is encouraged to use her judgement and introduce short duration energising games that alleviate *learner fatigue*. The trainer is referred to several such games that are described in the other sections of the Handbook.

10. DURATION OF TRAINING

The Section requires about one and a half training days. The total duration of training in estimated to be 560 minutes which is 9 hours 20 minutes.

Base Module Section II
Session 5 Politico-Legal Orientation

Session Theme	PANCHAYATI RAJ GOVERNANCE
Duration	90 minutes
Venue	Classroom without fixed furnitures
Seating	Sit and/or stand on the floor forming a circle; move around the room for the game and picture/poster sessions. The participants are free to sit on the chairs should they wish to.
Session Objective	*To expand the practical understanding of the participants about the concept of self government and its institutions*

Expected Learning Outcomes

- Increased understanding of the principles underlying the concept of self government, the role and functions of PRIs as institutions for self government at the grassroots level

Content Flow and Training Methodology

Sr. No.	*Content*	*Training Methodology*	*Training Aids*	*Duration (in minutes)*
1.	Game for Experience sharing among the Participants about Village Panchayat Governance	**Step 1** Stepping Stones	None	30
2.	Self-government and the Panchayat Raj Institutions : Concept and Status	**Step 2** Poster and Picture based discussions and Lecture Method	Posters/Pictures and any other aids as desired by the trainer	45
3.	Synthesis of Learning Points by Trainer/ Participants	**Step 3** Visual Method	Overhead slides, Flip Charts	15

THE METHODOLOGICAL STEPS FOR SESSION 5

1. *Play the game of Stepping Stones for experience sharing about Village Panchayat governance*

In **Step 1**, the *Stepping Stones* **Game**[16] is played by the participants. See the following steps:

1.1 The objective of this game is to share the experiences of the participants about Village Panchayat governance and discuss about what they think is important to them in this context. This helps the participants to comprehend the subsequent training sessions in the light of their own experiences.

1.2 First discuss and decide with the participants some key important events (or what are called *'Stepping Stones'*) in their experience of Village Panchayat governance that have significantly influenced them. Some suggested questions for eliciting the *Stepping Stones* are:

- How have the actions/inactions of the local Village Panchayat affected them in the past?
- What are the key events that made them elected members of the Village Panchayat?
- What are their main experiences since they became members in terms of realisations, meetings, training experience, social attitudes, barriers to political/development participation, interaction with extension staff, self esteem, satisfaction, frustrations, access to development information, etc.? (*Note*: Each item described in this point may be treated as a separate *Stepping Stone*).

1.3 The trainer can start the game by giving an example of one of her own *Stepping Stones*.

1.4 Ask the participants to work in pairs, interviewing each other. Each pair may interview about 3-4 *Stepping Stones* from the list.

1.5 The participants then present the findings of the interviews very briefly to the group. This can be done either by presenting directly to the group by paired introductions or visually by displaying the *Stepping Stone* for group viewing. The last method is recommended since this session relies heavily on the *Visual Method* as a training methodology for discussing the other training contents.

16. Adapted from Pretty *et al.*, 1995.

1.6 This game may take some time, especially in large groups of 20 or more. The trainer will have to remind the participants to keep to only 3-4 *Stepping Stones* and be brief.

1.7 The game is an experience sharing exercise and helps in placing the subsequent discussions in the session in the context of the participants' experiences about Village Panchayat governance. It also unlocks any reserve that the participants may still have about participating in the discussions.

---

2. Hold Poster and Picture based discussions about self-government and PRIs

---

Step 2 extensively uses the **Visual Method** involving discussions based upon posters and pictures, followed by a **Lecture**. Paste the posters on the walls all over the classroom before the participants arrive. A sample of posters/pictures is provided with this Handbook. The posters should relate to the Parliament, the State Legislature and the Panchayat Raj Institutions as also their functions. Lead the discussions from the posters and pictures in the following way:

2.1 On one table have cards on which the key concept areas and status of PRIs are written down, one on each card. For instance, *"The PRIs were created by the 73rd Constitutional Amendment Act"* is written on one card. *"One-third of the PRI members have to be women"* is written on another card. A third card can have *"The PRIs are the institutions of local self-government."* And so on. Now ask the participants to paste the cards at the foot of the corresponding pictures with which they are connected. For example, the first card with the comment *"The PRIs were created by the 73rd Constitutional Amendment Act"* could be pasted below the picture of the Parliament. The card with *"One-third of the PRI members have to be women"* could be pasted below the picture of the women's group. The third card with *"The PRIs are the institutions of local self-government"* could be pasted below the picture of the PRIs.

2.2 Check with the participants if all the "caption" cards and posters/pictures have been correctly paired. If not ask the participants to make amends. In case they are unable to do so, the trainer should help the participants to make the corrections.

2.3 Now provide the participants with Bindis or Post-It Stickers or any removable sticker. Ask them to place the stickers on these pictures about which they do not know or want to get more information about.

2.4 The trainer then provides the information sought by the participants through a brief lecture, pictures, drawings, video screening or whatever, followed by discussions among the participants.

3. Visual Method for synthesising what we have learnt from this Session

In Step 3, the trainer synthesises the session learnings as done in the earlier sessions. She can invite one or more of the participants to help in doing this.

Base Module
Session 6

Section II
Politico-Legal Orientation

Session Theme	ROLE OF PANCHAYATI RAJ INSTITUTIONS
Duration	150 minutes
Venue	Classroom without fixed furnitures
Seating	Sit/stand on the ground forming a circle; move around the room for the Force Field Analysis and picture-based discussions
Session Objective	*To expand the practical understanding of the participants about the mandate of the Panchayati Raj Institutions*

Expected Learning Outcomes

Enlarged comprehension of the participants about:

- The mandate of the PRIs for meeting the ends of gender equity and social justice.
- The extent of the fulfilment of the mandate.

Content Flow and Training Methodology

Sr. No.	*Content*	*Training Methodology*	*Training Aids*	*Duration (in minutes)*
1.	Self-government and PRIs: Implications and frame of action for economic development, gender equity and social justice	**Step 1** Visual Method using a Cartoon show and picture based discussions	Cartoons and pictures	45[17] minutes
2.	What were the original intentions of legislation and protagonists for the movement for self-government?	**Step 2** Lecture Method	Flash cards/ slides/ trans-parencies	30 minutes

17. It is suggested that the duration indicated for the sessions may be factored thus: Cartoon Show and Display of Pictured: 30; Discussion Time: 15; Total: 45

Sr. No.	*Content*	*Training Methodology*	*Training Aids*	*Duration (in minutes)*
3.	What happened to the original ideas and justifications for the PRIs?	**Step 3** Force Field Analysis **Step 4** Brainstorming	Different coloured cards, flip charts, Marker pens	60 minutes
4.	Synthesis of learning points	**Step 5** Visual Method	As desired by trainer	15

THE METHODOLOGICAL STEPS FOR SESSION 6

1. Use cartoons and pictures to illustrate the frame of action for PRIs

Step 1 uses the ***Visual Method*** with a Cartoon show and or picture based discussions to illustrate the frame of action for economic development, gender equity and social justice that the PRIs as institutions of self-government are expected to adopt.

2. ***Use a brief lecture to discuss the original intentions of legislation and protagonists for the self-government movement***

In **Step** 2 the trainer uses the **Lecture Method**, since this knowledge area is mostly situated in Box 3 of the **Johari's Window**. The trainer is required to use flash cards/transparencies/slides giving the original intentions of legislation and the protagonists. Discuss with the participants in order to identify which of them have been fulfilled. Write down the gaps on flip charts and paste them on the walls of the classroom. The context of this discussion is threefold:

- How is it possible to bring about village level economic development?
- What are the remedies for gender injustices as discussed in Session 3?
- How to remove/lessen social exclusion in the development process?

3. *Do the Force Field Analysis to determine the positive and negative forces that influence the gap between the original intentions and actual functioning of the PRIs*

Step 3: For analysing the forces that have caused the gap between the original ideas and justifications for the PRIs and what is happening in practice, a **Force Field Analysis** is done. The steps for doing the **FFA** are described below:

3.1 Explain the objectives of the exercise to the participants.
3.2 Please clarify that force is an energy that can cause or tend to cause a change. This is different from a problem or an advantage. Also, distinguish between positive and negative forces.
3.3 Keep a sheet of paper with the problem written or depicted on it, in front of the participants and ask them to concentrate on the problem. Ask them to visualize the problem situation in a state of temporary equilibrium by two sets of opposing forces, one favouring changes (positive forces) towards closing the gap and the other thwarting them (negative forces), that is, preventing the gap from being closed. Ask them to list one set of forces first followed by the other.
3.4 Ask the participants to write down or depict the forces identified on flash cards in bold letters. Write one force on one card. Clarify that if a force seems to be made of multiple elements, each component should be listed separately as a force. Different colour cards can be used for positive and negative forces.
3.5 Keep the sheet of paper with the problem written on it in the centre and draw a line across it. This line represents the present state of the PRIs. Ask the participants to spread the cards with negative forces below the line and those with positive forces above the line.
3.6 Ask them to take a look at the cards and see if they would like to make any changes.
3.7 Next ask the participants to assign weights to each of the forces by requesting them to keep each card force with the name of the force written on it, at varying distance from the present status line in such a way that the distance denotes the strength of the force. Greater the distance, the stronger is the perceived effect of the force on the problem. Arrows pointing downwards may be used to indicate negative forces. Arrows pointing upwards may be used to indicate positive forces.
3.8 Check with the participants whether they are satisfied with the diagram and relative strength of the forces as depicted or would they like to make any modifications.
3.9 Once they are satisfied with the diagram, ask them to discuss on how they can bring changes in the situation. Which of the positive forces can be reinforced and which negative forces can be diminished?
3.10 An example of a Force Field Analysis is at *Figure 14.*

Figure 14: Example of a Force Field Analysis[18]

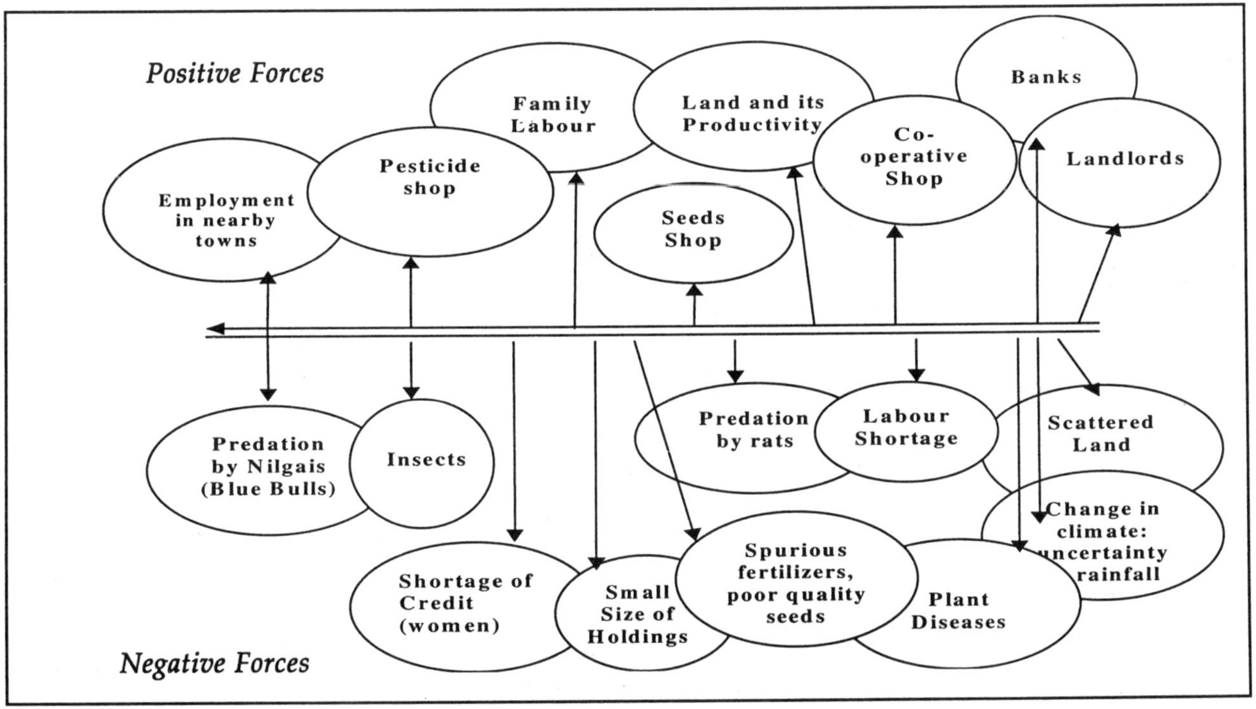

Note: (1) The central line denotes the present status of hunger.
(2) The villagers of Tikri, Varanasi participated in the FFA.

18. *Source*: Mukherjee, Amitava: *'Hunger: Theory, Perspectives and Reality—Analysis Through Participatory Methods'* Aldershot: Ashgate; Publishing Ltd. and Concept Publishing Company, New Delhi, 2002, pp. 292.

4. Brainstorm about how to strengthen positive forces and reduce negative ones

Use the **Brainstorming** technique for detailed analysis and in-depth probing by the participants. Smaller cards, preferably of different colours can be used to write down possible interventions for each of the positive or negative forces to increase or reduce its magnitude, respectively. Each of the possible interventions can be further weighed in the light of various factors, e.g., resources available, time, ideology of the organization etc. The idea is generally to capitalize on those that would bring the greatest change.

5. Visual Method for synthesising what we have learnt from this Session

In **Step** 5, the trainer synthesises the session learnings as done in the earlier sessions. She can invite one or more of the participants to help in doing this.

Base Module **Section II**
Session 7 **Politico-Legal Orientation**

Session Theme	STRUCTURE OF PANCHAYATI RAJ INSTITUTIONS
Duration	140 minutes
Venue	Classroom without fixed furniture
Seating	Sit/stand on the ground forming a circle
Session Objective	*To expand the knowledge of the participants about the legal premise and structure of Panchayati Raj Institutions*

Expected Learning Outcome

- Increased acquaintance with the mandate and features of the Seventy Third Constitutional Amendment Act, the State Conformity Act for PRIs and the structure of PRIs

Content Flow and Training Methodology

Sr. No.	*Content*	*Training Methodology*	*Training Aids*	*Duration (in minutes)*
1.	Game for Enhancing Group Dynamics	**Step 1** Saboteur	None	20
2.	The Seventy Third Constitutional Amendment Act and the State Conformity Act: Mandate and Salient Features	**Step 1** Lecture Method	As desired by the trainer	60
3.	Structure of Panchayati Raj Institutions — Gram Sabha, Village Panchayat, Panchayat Samiti and Zilla Parishad	**Step 2** Lecture Method **Step 3** Role Play/Drama of a Gram Sabha	As desired by the trainer	45
4.	Synthesis of learning points by Trainer/ Participant (s)	**Step 4** Visual Method	Overhead slides, Flip Charts	15

THE METHODOLOGICAL STEPS FOR SESSION 7

1. Play Saboteur for modelling different kinds of behaviours

Step 1: The trainer may begin this session with a game. The participants play a game ***Saboteur***[19] for which the details are given below.

1.1 The game has three objectives:
- It shows how communication and group work can be easily disrupted.
- It creates a group strategy for recognising and dealing with sabotage.
- It is also successful as an equaliser and as an energiser.

1.2 Divide the participants into sub-groups of consisting three members by any method, like making them pick up cards from a pack from which all 13 cards of either Clubs, Diamonds, Hearts or Spade have been discarded. Grouping together the participants who have picked up the same number i.e. one's, two's and so on then forms the threesomes.

1.3 The three participants within each subgroup have to fulfil three roles—the speaker, the listener and the saboteur. The speaker and the listener face each other to talk, while the saboteur can move about. The speaker is asked to describe what should be the development priorities of her Village Panchayat or any other related issue to the listener. The saboteur is asked to try to sabotage or disrupt this discussion in any non-violent manner.

1.4 Roaming saboteurs can move between groups. The trainer can also participate as a saboteur.

1.5 After two minutes ask the participants to change roles. Then again after two minutes do the same so that each participant has the opportunity to play all three roles. Everybody should know what it feels like to be a saboteur and also to be sabotaged.

1.6 After this exercise, discuss and ask the participants to reflect upon:
- What was it like to be a saboteur or to be sabotaged?
- Did you find it easy or difficult to disrupt the conservation?

1.7 Then ask every participant to speak about the different types of sabotage they have experienced in a Village Panchayat or a Gram Sabha meeting in the past. Record these on a flip chart in categories: dominance, gender-based, rigidity, interruptions, jokes, not being

19. *Source*: Pretty *et al.*, 1995.

taken seriously, rudeness, silence, walk-outs, physical distractions like drunkenness, violence, fidgeting, etc.

1.8 Ask the participants to reflect upon ways to deal with each kind of sabotage and record these strategies on the flip chart. Some examples of strategies are: ignore politely, stop talking, talk it out, acknowledge and postpone, divert attention, ask others for help, walk away, etc, as may be appropriate.

1.9 This game makes the participants aware of the kinds of sabotage they are likely to face while participating in the business of the Village Panchayat. They also identify the strategies for negotiating them and resolving conflicts. It also discourages the participants to become saboteurs in the training programme or later on in life, making them reflect on their own behaviour and that of others.

---

2. Give a lecture about the Seventy-Third Constitutional Amendment Act and State Conformity Act

---

In **Step 2**, the trainer can begin with the learning points of the previous session. The Force Field Analysis done by the participants earlier is an analysis of the extent to which the PRIs have fulfilled their destined roles. This exercise indicates the desired direction of policy intervention. In this context, it is suggested that the trainer uses the **Lecture Method** with suitable visual aids for presenting the mandate and features of the Constitution Amendment and Conformity Act.

---

3. Give a brief lecture about the structure of PRIs

In **Step 3**, the trainer uses the **Lecture Method** to fill in any knowledge gaps that still remain about the structure of PRIs. The role of the Gram Sabha is discussed in detail.

---

4. Use role play/drama to demonstrate the proceedings of a Gram Sabha

---

In **Step 4**, stage a role play or drama or use a video cassette. A reference has been given in this Handbook and a sample provided. In the role play for showing the proceedings of a Gram Sabha, assign different kinds of roles, viz. Sarpanch, Upa Sarpanch, Gram Sevak, SHG member, women Panchayat members, etc. to the performing participants. Some of the suggested themes are: selection of beneficiaries, development works, presentation of Village Panchayat budget, accounts, etc. The game of

Saboteur played earlier will help the performers act differently as a dominant person, saboteur or listener.

5. Visual Method for synthesising what we have learnt from this Session

In **Step 5**, the trainer synthesises the session learnings as done in the earlier sessions. She can invite one or more of the participants to help in doing this.

Base Module **Section II**
Session 8 **Politico-Legal Orientation**

Session Theme	ROLE OF THE VILLAGE PANCHAYAT
Duration	180 minutes
Venue	Classroom without any fixed furnitures
Seating	Sit/stand on the ground forming a circle
Session Objective	*To conscientise the participants about their rights and duties as members of the Village Panchayat and generate an urge in them to seek their rights*

Expected Learning Outcomes

Increased awareness about:

- Their own rights and duties.
- The rightful place of the Village Panchayat in grassroots governance.
- Its role, responsibilities and functions.
- What is necessary for having those rights, responsibilities and functions.

Content Flow and Training Methodology

Sr. No.	*Content*	*Training Methodology*	*Training Aids*	*Duration (in minutes)*
1.	*De jure* Functions of the Village Panchayat	**Step 1** Brainstorming **Step 2** Delphi Method	Flip charts, flash cards, marker pens	15 45
2.	*De facto* functions of the Village Panchayat	**Step 3** Brainstorming **Step 4** Delphi Method	Flip charts, flash cards, marker pens	15 45

Sr. No.	*Content*	*Training Methodology*	*Training Aids*	*Duration (in minutes)*
3.	How empowered is the Village Panchayat?	**Step 5** Empowerment Circle	Large sheets of paper, flip charts, several coloured marker pens, flash cards, seeds, Post-It stickers, bindis	45
4.	Synthesis of learning points by Trainer/ Participant (s)	**Step 6** Visual Method	Overhead slides, Flip Charts	15

THE METHODOLOGICAL STEPS FOR SESSION 8

1. Brainstorm the de jure functions of the Village Panchayat

In **Step 1**, use **Brainstorming** to determine the *de jure* functions of the Village Panchayat, i.e., those functions, which the Village Panchayat is required to perform according to the rules or statute. The attention of the participants should be drawn to the 29 development functions that are listed in the Eleventh Schedule to the Constitution. These may be discussed with particular reference to the following areas:

- The raising of resources in the Village Panchayat.
- The powers of taxation and borrowing of the Village Panchayat.
- Planning for social development at the Village Panchayat level.
- Affirmative action for gender and social justice.
- Management of programmes for social and economic development at the Village Panchayat level.
- Public Service delivery by the Village Panchayat based upon the principles of equity, responsiveness, transparency, accountability, etc.

2. Use the Delphi Method to make the concept clusters of the de jure functions

2.1 Request volunteers to write each function on a card/paper (only one function per card/paper).

2.2 The cards/papers are then placed upon the ground or pinned or pasted on the wall and grouped according to their concept areas. One, some or all the participants can do this exercise. Exact duplicates are removed.

2.3 The participants must agree on the criteria for grouping or clustering, since these provide the theme areas.

2.4 Now discuss each theme with the participants.

---

3. Next brainstorm the de facto functions of the Village Panchayat

---

In **Step 3**, again use brainstorming to generate the *de facto* functions, i.e., those functions, which the Village Panchayat performs, but is not required, repeat **not** required to perform according to the rules or statute.

---

4. Use the Delphi Method to make the concept clusters of the de facto functions

---

In **Step 4**, use the ***Delphi Method*** to form the concept clusters of the *de facto* functions of the Village Panchayat.

---

5. How empowered is the Village Panchayat? Draw the Empowerment Circle to explore to what extent it performs its de jure functions

---

In **Step 5**, first discuss and compare the *de jure* and *de facto* functions of the Village Panchayat. Discuss the variations, the gaps and what needs to be done to close the gap. That is, reduce the *de facto* functions which do not add value to the work of the Village Panchayat and increase the *de jure* functions which will make the Village Panchayats the true units of self-government.

5.1 Next use the **Empowerment Circle**[20] for focussing attention on the extent to which the Village Panchayat is empowered. Since the *de jure* functions are guaranteed by statute, and if functions, functionaries and finances have been transferred to the Village Panchayat, these could be used as a measure of its degree of empowerment. An example is given in *Figure 15*. The steps for drawing the Circle are as follows:

5.2 Ask the participants to define the concept of "*empowerment*" and identify its elements. List the elements thus if there are seven elements that constitute empowerment, there will be seven radii.

5.3 Ask the participants to draw a large circle on a sheet of paper or

---

20. Adapted from the field notes of Mukherjee, 2002.

Figure 15: Empowerment Circle

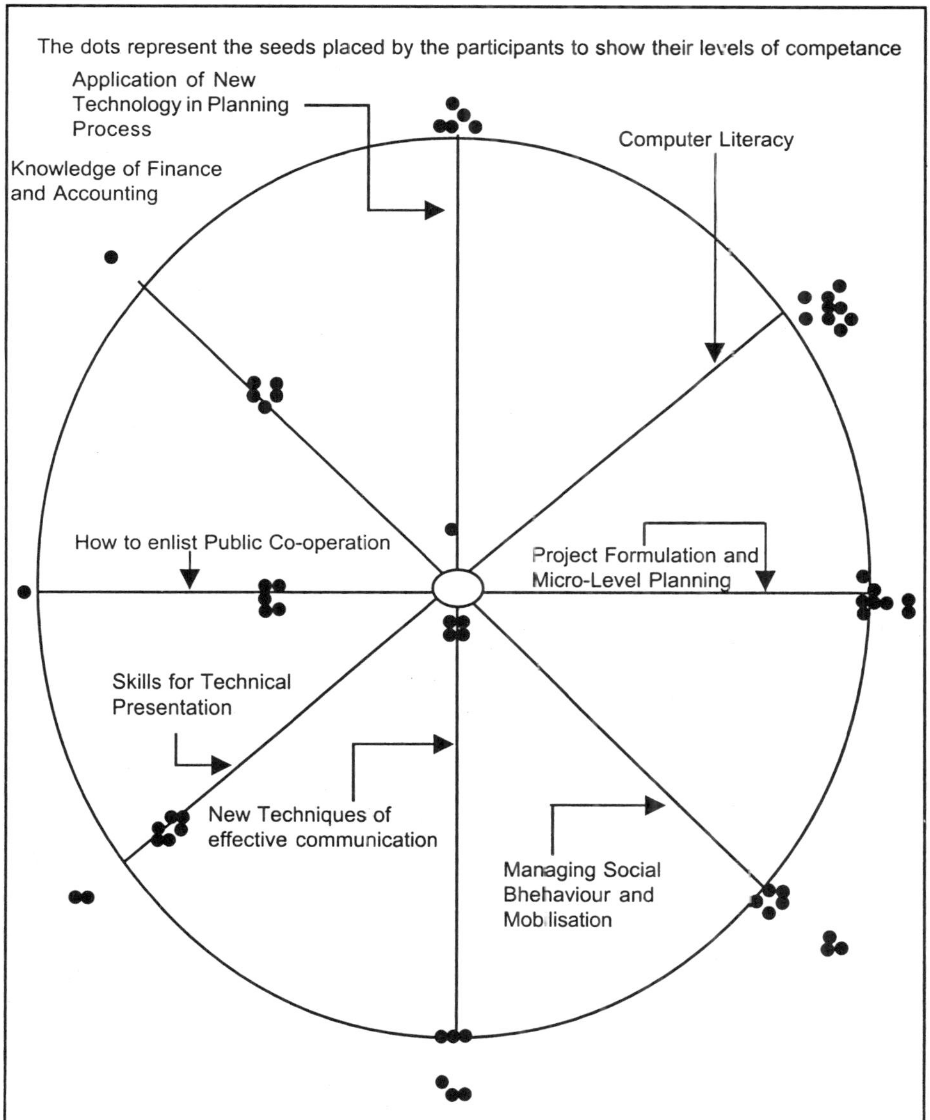

on the floor with as many radii originating from the centre of the circle as there are elements that make the Village Panchayat feel that it is empowered. Write one element along one radii.

5.4 Now explain that the centre of the circle from where the radii originate indicates the position that the Village Panchayat feels it is 100% empowered in respect of the respective element. Therefore, if the Village Panchayat is at the centre of the circle on any radius, then in respect of the element represented by that radius, the Panchayat is fully empowered.

5.5 The position halfway on any radius indicates that the Village Panchayat feels that on the element of empowerment represented by that radius, it is empowered to the extent of 50%. Thus the distance from the centre of the circle along any radius measures the extent to which the Village Panchayat feels it is empowered.

5.6 Any point on the circumference or outside the circle indicates the zero position, that is, the Panchayat in respect of the element shown by the radius is fully disempowered.

5.7 Now discuss each concept of the elements that constitute *empowerment* and facilitate the participants to decide to what extent the Village Panchayat is empowered with respect to that element. Facilitate so that the participants stick either *bindis* or Post-It Stickers along the radius for each cluster at an appropriate distance to indicate the extent to which the Village Panchayat is empowered.

5.8 If most of the stickers or *bindis* are at the centre of the circle, Panchayats are empowered. If most of the stickery or *bindis* are at the middle of the raddi, the Panchayats are moderately empowered. If most of the stickers or *bindis* are on the circumstances and beyond, the Panchayats are disempowered. If the stickers or *bindis* depict no pattern, then there is confusion about the empowerment of the Panchayats.

5.9 Discuss the Empowerment Circle with the participants and the ways and means of empowering the Village Panchayat. What are the factors that restrain the empowerment process? Who are the principal individuals/institutions responsible for the impediments? What are the policy measures suggested for improving this situation?

---

6. Visual Method for synthesising what we have learnt from this Session

---

In **Step 6**, the trainer synthesises the session learnings as done in the earlier sessions. She can invite one or more of the participants to help in doing this. In particular, focus during the synthesis on the **Empowerment Circle**.

Base Module: Section III
MANAGEMENT ORIENTATION

CONTENT FLOW IN MANAGMENT ORIENTATION BASE MODULE: AT A GLANCE

Day 1		*Day 2*		*Day 3*	
Time in min.	*Session No. and Name*	*Time in minutes*	*Session No. and Name*	*Time in min.*	*Session No. and Name*
			FORENOON		
90	9: Village Panchayat Administration	90	10: Management of Community Development (continued)	105	11: Financial Management of the Village Panchayat (continued)
20	*Break for Tea*	20	*Break for Tea*	20	*Break for Tea*
90	9: Village Panchayat Administration (continued)	90	10: Management of Community Development (continued)	60 90	11: Financial Management of the Village Panchayat (continued) 12: Good Governance by the Village Panchayat
60	*Break for Lunch*	60	*Break for Lunch*	60	*Break for Lunch*
			AFTERNOON		
120	10: Management of Community Development (Field Work)	105	10: Management of Community Development (continued)	75	12: Good Governance by the Village Panchayat (continued)
		20	*Break for Tea*	20	*Break for Tea*
		90	11: Financial Management of the Village Panchayat	75	12: Good Governance by the Village Panchayat (continued)
300	*Total Duration of Training*	375	*Total Duration of Training*	405	*Total Duration of Training*

DETAILED CONTENT FLOW IN SECTION III MANAGEMENT ORIENTATION

Day 1 *(Time in min.)*	*Day 2* *(Time in min.)*	*Day 3* *(Time in min.)*
FORENOON **Session 9: Village Panchayat Administration** **Duration: 180** **1. Content:** Functions of the Sarpanch and Upa Sarpanch of a Village Panchayat **Training Methods:** Brainstorming and Delphi **Duration:** 45 **2. Content:** Legal Provisions for the Disqualification of the Sarpanch and Upa Sarpanch of a Village Panchayat **Training Methods:** Case Study and Lecture **Duration:** 45 *Break for Tea (20)* **3. Content:** No Confidence Motion: Rules and Procedures **Training Methods:** Role Play and Lecture **Duration:** 30 **4. Content:** Village Panchayat Administration **Training Methods:** Case Study and Lecture **Duration:** 45 **5. Content:** Synthesis by Trainer/Participants **Training Method:** Visual **Duration:** 15 *Break for Lunch (60)*	*FORENOON* **Session 10: Management of Community Development** **3. Content:** Administrative Management of Community Development Programmes **Training Methods:** Case Study and Lecture **Duration:** 90 *Break for Tea (20)* **4. Content:** The Village Panchayat and the Community Development Network **Training Method:** Venn Diagramming **Duration:** 45 **5. Content:** Management and Delivery of Community Development Services **Training Method:** Communication Linkage Matrix **Duration:** 45 **Break for Lunch (60)**	*FORENOON.* **Session 11: Financial Management of the Village Panchayat** **3. Content:** Financial Management of the Village Panchayat **Training Methods:** Case Study and Lecture **Duration:** 45 **4. Content:** Village Panchayat Budgeting **Training Method:** Case Study **Duration:** 60 *Break for Tea (20)* **5. Content:** Financial Audit of the Village Panchayat **Training Method:** Lecture **Duration:** 45 **6. Content:** Synthesis by Trainer/Participants **Training Method:** Visual **Duration:** 15 **Session 12: Good Governance by the Village Panchayat** **Duration: 285** **1. Content:** Citizens' Charter for the Village Panchayat **Training Methods:** Case Study, Brainstorming, Delphi and Ranking **Duration:** 90 *Break for Lunch (60)*

Day 1 (Time in minutes)	*Day 2 (Time in minutes)*	*Day 3 (Time in minutes)*
AFTERNOON **Session 10: Management of Community Development** **Duration:** 405 *Field Work* 1. **Content:** Role of Village Panchayat in Community Development **Training Method:** Social Mapping **Duration:** 60 2. **Content:** Protection and Management of Common Property Resources **Training Method:** Resource Mapping **Duration:** 60	*AFTERNOON* **Session 10: Management of Community Development** 5. **Content:** Management and Delivery of Community Development Services (continued) **Training Methods:** Support System Diagramming, Role Play/Drama and Lecture **Duration:** 90 6. **Content:** Synthesis by Trainer/Participants **Training Method:** Visual **Duration:** 15 *Break for Tea (20)* **Session 11: Financial Management of the Village Panchayat** **Duration:** 255 1. **Content:** Financial Responsibilities of the Village Panchayat with reference to the Seventy-Third Constitutional Amendment Act **Training Methods:** Brainstorming and Lecture **Duration:** 30 2. **Content:** Income Maximisation by the Village Panchayat **Training Methods:** Brainstorming, Delphi and Lecture **Duration:** 45	*AFTERNOON* 2. **Content:** Role and Responsibilities of the Village Gram Sabha **Training Method:** Role Play/Drama **Duration:** 30 3. **Content:** Financial Transparency: Rationale and Practices **Training Methods:** Case Study and Lecture **Duration:** 45 *Break for Tea (20)* 4. **Content:** Social and Gender Audit of Community Development Initiatives **Training Methods:** Brainstorming, Delphi and Matrix Scoring **Duration:** 60 5. **Content:** Synthesis by Trainer/Participants **Training Method:** Visual **Duration:** 15
Total duration of Training: 300 (5 Hours)	Total duration of Training: 375 (6 Hours, 15 minutes)	Total duration of Training: 405 (6 Hours, 45 minutes)

NOTE TO TRAINERS FOR USING SECTION III: MANAGEMENT ORIENTATION

1. INTRODUCTION

Section III of the Module is designed for orienting the participants with the nitty-gritty of managing the Village Panchayat. An attempt has been made in this Section to consider all the managerial functions of the Village Panchayat, viz. the administrative, financial, community development and governance related. As mentioned in the introduction to the book, it is from this Section that the training process takes a definite turn from the conceptual to the practical, as its emphasis shifts from carrying out knowledge to effecting skill transfers to the participant-learners. This skill building process is continued in the next Section. Thus, the learnings flowing out of the third and fourth Sections are more strongly skill oriented than those in the preceding two Sections. It is expected that by now the participants have developed a understanding of the concept and philosophy of Panchayati Raj Governance and clarity about their roles as Village Panchayat members. They have thus reached a point where they can acquire and use the set of managerial skills associated with Village Panchayat governance with élan. The conceptual grounding achieved through the earlier Sections has also given individual participants an added confidence and an eagerness to learn how to face real life situations in their Village Panchayat scenarios.

2. TRAINING OBJECTIVES

The Section has the following training objectives:

- To equip the participants to perform their administrative functions.
- To empower the participants to function as agents of community development.
- To expand the practical understanding and skills of the participants for the financial management of the Village Panchayat.
- To orient the participants with the principles of good governance and the mechanisms for promoting them.

3. SESSIONS, THEIR TRAINING OBJECTIVES AND EXPECTED LEARNING OUTCOMES

There are four sessions in this Section and they serially satisfy the four training objectives. The *Training Objective* and the *Expected Learning Outcomes* that fulfil the Objective at the levels of both the individual participants and group are given in the following table:

Session No.	*Session Description*	*Training Objective*	*Expected Learning Outcomes*
9	Village Panchayat Administration	To equip the participants to perform their administrative functions	The participants understand: • The main functions of the Sarpanch and the Upa Sarpanch. • The formalities related to the disqualification of office bearers. • The passing of a No Confidence Motion. • The basics of Village Panchayat Administration.
10	Management of Community Development	To empower the participants to function as agents of community development	The participants know: • The fundamentals of managing community development. • The role of the Village Panchayat in this context. • The role of different development institutions and agencies and their linkages with the Village Panchayat.
11	Financial Management of a Village Panchayat	To expand the practical understanding and skills of the participants for the financial management of the Village Panchayat	• The participants understand the financial responsibilities of the Village Panchayat • They acquire skills for maximising its income, budgeting, observing financial propriety and keeping its financial records.

Session No.	*Session Description*	*Training Objective*	*Expected Learning Outcomes*
12	Good Governance by the Village Panchayat	To orient the participants with the principles of good governance and the mechanisms for promoting them	The participants understand: • The basic values related to good governance of transparency, responsiveness, participation and accountability. • The role of the Gram Sabha in this context. • They acquire skills for using the instruments of social and gender audit for promoting these values.

4. THE PARADIGM OF GOOD GOVERNANCE

The fourth session in this Section introduces the concept of good governance and discusses the diffusion of its underlying principles like, transparency, responsiveness, participation and accountability in Village Panchayat governance. The session also introduces the concept of the *Citizens' Charter* which is a self-declared charter of certain quality standards which the Village Panchayat is obligated to adhere to in the delivery of different public services to the village community. The Charter is in the nature of a written contract which the Village Panchayat voluntarily accepts as being duty-bound to follow. The Charter also gives information about the good governance practices which the Village Panchayat has adopted. The importance of the fourth session is underscored in the light of the fact that good governance is a pre-condition for any community development initiative to bear fruit.

5. SESSION 9

The content matter of the first session covers the nitty-gritty of Village Panchayat Administration including the functions of the Sarpanch and Upa Sarpanch, the conditions for their disqualification and the rules and procedures for passing No Confidence Motions. This session equips the participants to perform their administrative duties and conduct the business of the Village Panchayat. The training methodology suggested for use in this session is varied and sequenced with due regard to the content flow.

6. SESSION 10

The second session is one of the most important in the Module and great care has been taken while designing it. The essentials of the management of community development have been covered in this session. Very innovative participatory training methodologies have been suggested for use in this session in order to motivate the training audience consisting of adult learners. The session initiates the participants into the complex discipline of community development and imparts skills for them to adopt the role of development agents in their communities. The session contents are pitched at a very functional level to give the participants hands-on skills. It is recommended that the first part of the session be conducted in a village locale where the participants can engage in ***Social Mapping*** for appreciating the role of the Village Panchayat in community development. ***Resource Mapping*** is next done for learning about the mechanics of the protection and management of the Common Property Resources of the community. The participants also learn about the administrative side of managing development. The linkages between the Village Panchayat and the Extension Workers, NGOs, Banks, Self Help Groups, Users Cooperatives, Farmers Cooperatives and other institutions/ individuals operating at the Village Panchayat level are then explored by ***Venn Diagramming***. The administrative management of community level services, the concepts of the quality and convergence of the services delivered by these institutions/ individuals are then investigated through the ***Communication Linkage Matrix*** and ***Support System Diagramming***.

7. SESSION 11

This session expands the practical understanding and skills of the participants for the financial management of the Village Panchayat. Its contents extend over a broad spectrum. Beginning with the financial responsibilities of the Village Panchayat with reference to the Seventy-Third Constitutional Amendment Act, the session covers financial procedures, audit and related propriety issues, income maximisation by the Village Panchayat, the Village Panchayat Fund, maintenance of Accounts and Records and budgeting. The very nature of the contents makes the use of participatory training methods somewhat difficult, since the trainer is situated in Box 3 of the Johari's Window ('what we know and they do not know"). Despite this, some PLA based methods have been suggested whose use would definitely facilitate the learning process.

8. SESSION 12

The fourth session as mentioned earlier is significant since it breaks new ground by orienting the participants with the paradigm of *good* governance and its underpinning values. At the end of the session, it is expected that the participants acquire the skills necessary for functionalizing the paradigm through the use of instruments like Citizens' Charter, social and gender audit for promoting these values. The suggested training methodology for the session is in keeping with the value of *stakeholder participation* which the paradigm strongly upholds.

9. TRAINING METHODOLOGY

The trainer is encouraged to use with ingenuity the training methodology suggested in this Section. It is a mix of Participatory Learning and Action Methods, the lecture method, visual method using posters and pictures and role play/drama. It has to be remembered that the contents of this Section are on the *heavier* side and therefore, *learner motivation* has to be sustained by a greater degree of innovation on the part of the trainer. For this purpose, the trainer is encouraged to use her judgement and introduce short duration energising games that alleviate *learner fatigue*. The trainer is referred to several such games that are described elsewhere in the Manual.

10. DURATION OF TRAINING

The Section is of much longer duration than the previous two Sections which stretch for only two training days. This Section requires three training days and the total duration of training is estimated to be 1080 minutes which is 18 hours.

Base Module
Session 9

Section III
Management Orientation

Session Theme	VILLAGE PANCHAYAT ADMINISTRATION
Duration	180 minutes
Venue	Classroom without fixed furniture.
Seating	Sit/stand on the ground forming a circle; move around the room for the role play and group work
Session Objective	*To equip the participants to perform their administrative functions*

Expected Learning Outcomes

The participants understand:

- The main functions of the Sarpanch and the Upa Sarpanch.
- The formalities related to the disqualification of office bearers.
- The passing of a "No Confidence Motion".
- The basics of Village Panchayat Administration.

Content Flow and Training Methodology

Sr. No.	*Content*	*Training Methodology*	*Training Aids*	*Duration (in minutes)*
1.	Functions of the Sarpanch and Upa Sarpanch of a Village Panchayat	**Step 1** Brainstorming **Step 2** Delphi Method	Flip Charts, marker pens and cards	45
2.	Legal Provisions for the Disqualification of the Sarpanch and Upa Sarpanch of a Village Panchayat	**Step 3** Case Study Method **Step 4** Lecture Method	Documentation of Case Studies and other aids as desired by the trainer	45

Sr. No.	*Content*	*Training Methodology*	*Training Aids*	*Duration (in minutes)*
3.	No Confidence Motion: Rules and Procedures	**Step 5** Role Play **Step 6** Lecture Method	Proceedings Registers[21] of some Village Panchayats and others as desired by the trainer	30
4.	Village Panchayat Administration (a) Managing the Establishment (b) Conduct of Business (c) Passing of Resolutions (d) Supervision and Execution of Works Administrative Report	**Step 7** Case Study Method **Step 8** Lecture Method	Village Panchayat Records, like the Resolution Book[22], Proceedings Register, Administrative Report and other forms etc. as may be necessary.	45
5.	Synthesis of Learning Points by Trainer/ Participants	**Step 9** Visual Method	Overhead slides/Flip Charts	15

THE METHODOLOGICAL STEPS FOR SESSION 9

1. Brainstorming technique to catalogue functions of Sarpanch and Upa Sarpanch

In **Step 1**, use the **Brainstorming** technique to catalogue separate lists for the functions of both the Sarpanch and Upa Sarpanch of a Village Panchayat. This technique has been described in Session 8.

21. This is the record of the minutes of the meetings of the Village Panchayat. The trainer can use this record for those meetings where no-confidence motions have been tabled, passed or rejected.
22. This is the record of the resolutions passed by any Village Panchayat.

2. *Delphi Method for clustering the catalogued functions into concept areas*

Step 2: Use the **Delphi Method** separately for the functions of both the Sarpanch and Up Sarpanch, requesting the participants to write each of the functions on a card/paper (only one per card/paper).

2.1 The cards/papers are then placed upon the ground or pinned upon the wall and grouped according to their concept areas. One, some or all the participants can do this exercise. Exact duplicates are removed.

2.2 The participants must agree on the criteria for grouping or clustering, since this provides the concept areas like development functions, statutory functions, etc.

2.3 Now discuss each concept with the participants and fill in gaps wherever necessary. The Trainer will have to lead the discussions specifying the provisions in the State Panchayat Acts relevant to the functions of the Sarpanch and Upa Sarpanch.

3 & 4. *Case Study and Lecture Methods for discussing disqualification provisions*

In **Steps 3 and 4**, the trainer is encouraged to use any available documentation or her knowledge of case studies about cases of disqualifications of Sarpanch and Upa Sarpanch of Village Panchayats. Different circumstances and conditions for disqualifications can then be discussed along with a brief lecture about the legal provisions for them.

5 & 6. *Role Play and Lecture Methods for illustrating the Rules and Procedures for passing a No Confidence Motion*

In **Steps 5 and 6**, the trainer and some of the participants can stage a **Role Play** depicting the passing of a no-confidence motion, with a contentious debate on the underlying issues for passing such a motion. The trainer then can give a brief lecture discussing the legal provisions for such a motion. The outline for the Role Play should be jointly prepared by the participants and trainer and some script agreed upon. This exercise will not only be a learning process, but also provide a welcome energising break by generating a lot of interest and humour at the same time. Since there are many instances where no-confidence motions are being passed against women office bearers, this theme can be chosen as the focus of the Role Play. The ensuing discussions should also include the barriers to women's participation in the PRIs and the suggested policy implications in this context.

---

7 & 8. Case Study and Lecture Methods for discussing about the Village Panchayat Administration

---

In **Steps 7 and 8,** using the registers of some Village Panchayats as case studies, intersperse the discussions with brief lectures for discussing the administration of a typical Village Panchayat.

---

9. Visual Method for synthesising what we have learnt from the Session

---

In **Step 9**, while synthesising the learning points of the session, the trainer may ask different participants to list orally one important function of the Sarpanch/Upa Sarpanch. Similarly, the legal conditions for the disqualifications of the office bearers of the Village Panchayat may be reiterated.

Base Module
Session 10

Section III
Management Orientation

Session Theme	MANAGEMENT OF COMMUNITY DEVELOPMENT
Duration	405 minutes
Venue	Village Locale for the Social and Resource Mapping Classroom without fixed furnitures for the remaining session
Seating	Sit and/or stand on the ground or on the floor forming a circle; move around the room for the role play and group work
Session Objective	*To empower the participants to function as agents of community development*

Expected Learning Outcomes

The participants know about:

- The fundamentals of managing community development.
- The role of the Village Panchayat in this context.
- The role of different development institutions and agencies and their linkages with the Village Panchayat.

Content Flow and Training Methodology

Sr. No.	*Content*	*Training Methodology*	*Training Aids*	*Duration (in minutes)*
1.	Role of the Village Panchayat in Community Development	**Step 1** Social Mapping	Flip Charts, Marker pens	60
2.	Protection and Management of Common Property Resources	**Step 2** Resource Mapping	Flip Charts, Marker pens	60

Sr. No.	*Content*	*Training Methodology*	*Training Aids*	*Duration (in min.)*
Return to Classroom from Village Locale				
3.	Administrative Management of Community Development Programmes: Maintenance of Records and Accounts	**Step 3** Case Study Method **Step 4** Lecture Method	Village Panchayat Records for different development programmes and other aids as desired by the trainer	90
4.	The Village Panchayat and the Community Development Network	**Step 5** Venn Diagramming	Flip Charts, marker pens, white paper, cards, scissors, glue	45
5.	Management and Delivery of Community Development Services:		Flip Charts, marker pens, white paper, cards, scissors, glue, seeds and as desired by trainer and participants	45
	(a) Role of Extension Workers, NGOs, Banks, Self Help Groups, Users Cooperatives, Farmers Cooperatives, MLAs, MLCs and MPs and other institutions/ individuals operating at the Village Panchayat level	**Step 6** Communication Linkage Matrix		45
	(b) Quality of Service delivered by these institutions/ individuals			45
	(c) Convergence of Development Services			

Sr. No.	*Content*	*Training Methodology*	*Training Aids*	*Duration (in minutes)*
	(d) Administrative Management of Primary Schools, Anganwadi, Water supply schemes, etc. by the Village Panchayat	**Step 7** Support System Diagramming **Step 8** Role Play/ Drama **Step 9** Lecture Method		Variable Time
6.	Synthesis of Learning Points by Trainer/ Participants	**Step 10** Visual Method	Overhead slides/Flip Charts	15

THE METHODOLOGICAL STEPS FOR SESSION 10

1. *Social Mapping for focusing on what kinds of Community Development initiatives the Village Panchayat can undertake*

Step 1 involves a **Social Mapping** exercise which can be done in any village. A Social Map depicts the social aspects of a locality like households, their social categories, literate/illiterate households, schools, roads, hospitals, etc. The participants prepare the map, complete with all the household-wise details e.g., caste composition, school aged children etc. The households on the map are also numbered. The procedure for facilitating a mapping exercise has been discussed earlier. The trainer then leads a discussion about the features of the map by asking probing questions, like:

- What is the condition of the houses?
- What is the state of health of the villagers?
- How many people are literate?
- Is the social infrastructure in the village enough and in good shape?

For each aspect and household shown on the map, the problems and opportunities along with the role of the Village Panchayat in that context are discussed. Ask the participants to discuss the role of the Village Panchayat with regard to each item shown on the map. Some of these could be:

- Housing
- Literacy
- Primary education
- Health
- Maintenance of roads

Now compare these with the 29 items given in the Eleventh Schedule of the Constitution. Next discuss what development programmes exist for the improvement of the aspects shown in the Social Map. Then discuss in which of these areas the Village Panchayat actually executes programmes. If they do not, then discuss why this is so and what could be done.

Examples of social mapping are at *Figures 16, 17 and 18.* It may be noted, that social map by men and women could be different, and hence the trainer may like to stress and demonstrate the importance of this difference in perspective.

---

2. *Resource Mapping for focusing on how to protect and manage Common Property Resources in a village*

Step 2 is also a participatory exercise done in a village locale where a **Resource Map** is prepared by the participants. The method for facilitating resource mapping is similar to the process of facilitating social mapping. This map will show the resources of the village like fields, water bodies, trees, forests, plantations under social forestry, roads, public buildings, etc. The common property resources to which the villagers and the Village Panchayat have access are then identified and a discussion initiated about their protection and management. The role and responsibilities of the Village Panchayat in this context are listed. The trainer can use the **Delphi method** here, if desired, and record each concept area on a separate card for further discussions.

Examples of resource map are at *Figures 19 and 20.*

---

3. *Case Study and Lecture Methods for demonstrating how to administratively manage Community Development Programmes*

In **Step 3**, the trainer uses the **Case Study Method** for discussing the administrative responsibilities of the Village Panchayat for the management of different kinds of Community Development Programmes. The relevant records for different development programmes maintained by some Village Panchayats are used as illustrative case studies. All details

Figure 16: Social Map of A Village in Upper Egypt

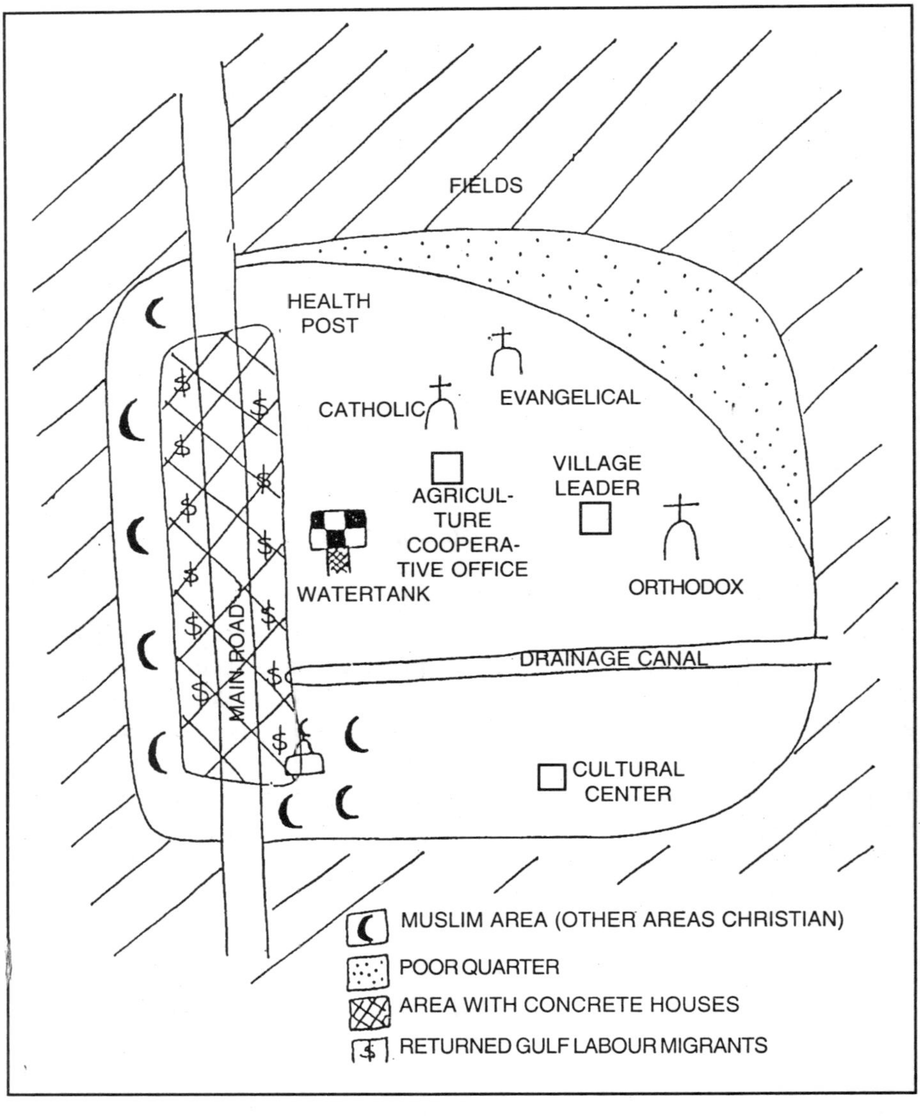

Source: Amitava Mukherjee, *Participatory Rural Appraisal: Methods and Applications in Rural Planning* (New Delhi: Vikas Publishing House Pvt. Ltd. and 2nd revised edition by New Delhi: Concept Publishing Company) 2003.

Figure 17: Social Mapping Ramenahally Village

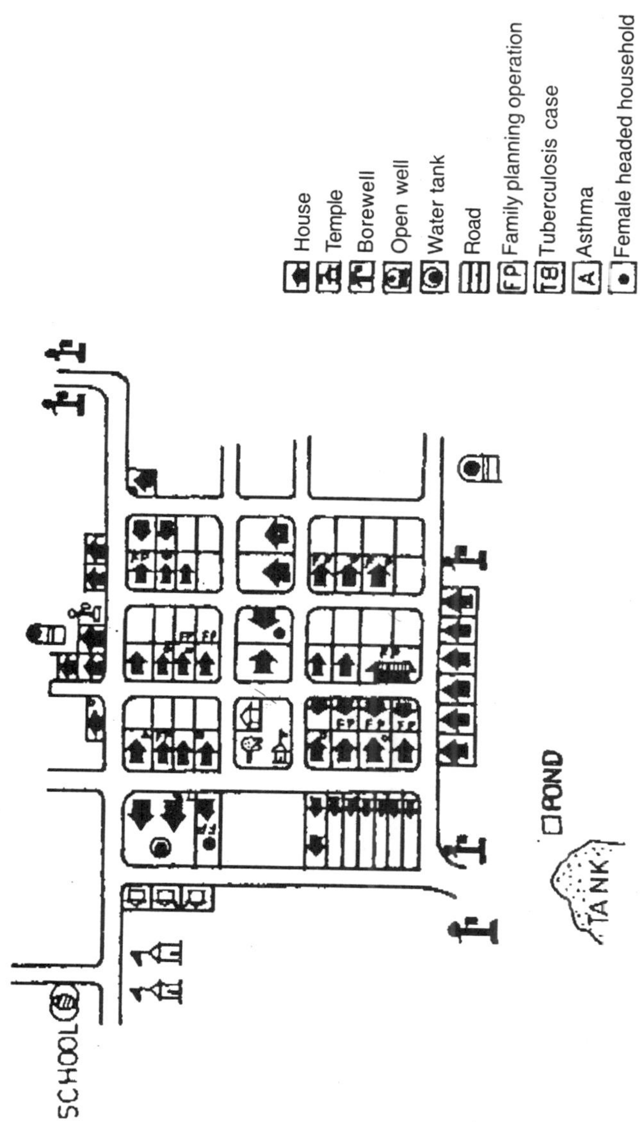

Social Mapping: This map was drawn by villagers of Ramenahally Village

Source : Forest, Trees and People News Letter no. 15/16

Figure 18: Social Map with Asset Details

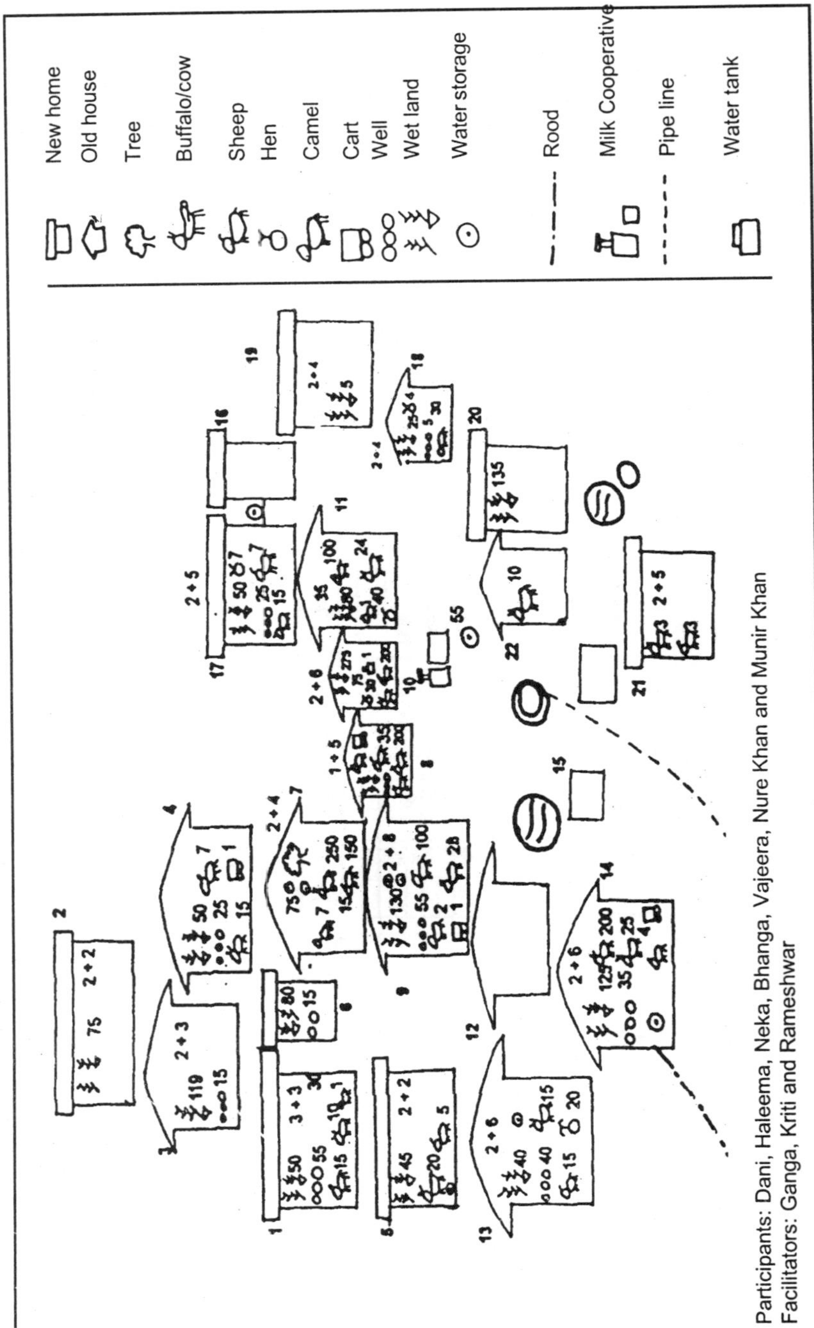

Participants: Dani, Haleema, Neka, Bhanga, Vajeera, Nure Khan and Munir Khan
Facilitators: Ganga, Kriti and Rameshwar

Source: Somesh Kumar: *Methods for Community Participation* (Sage, New Delhi) 2002.

Figure 19: A Resource and Social Map of A Village

Source: Neela Mukherjee: *Participatory Rural Appraisal: Methodology and Application*. (Concept, New Delhi) 1997

Figure 20: Participatory Sanctuary Map

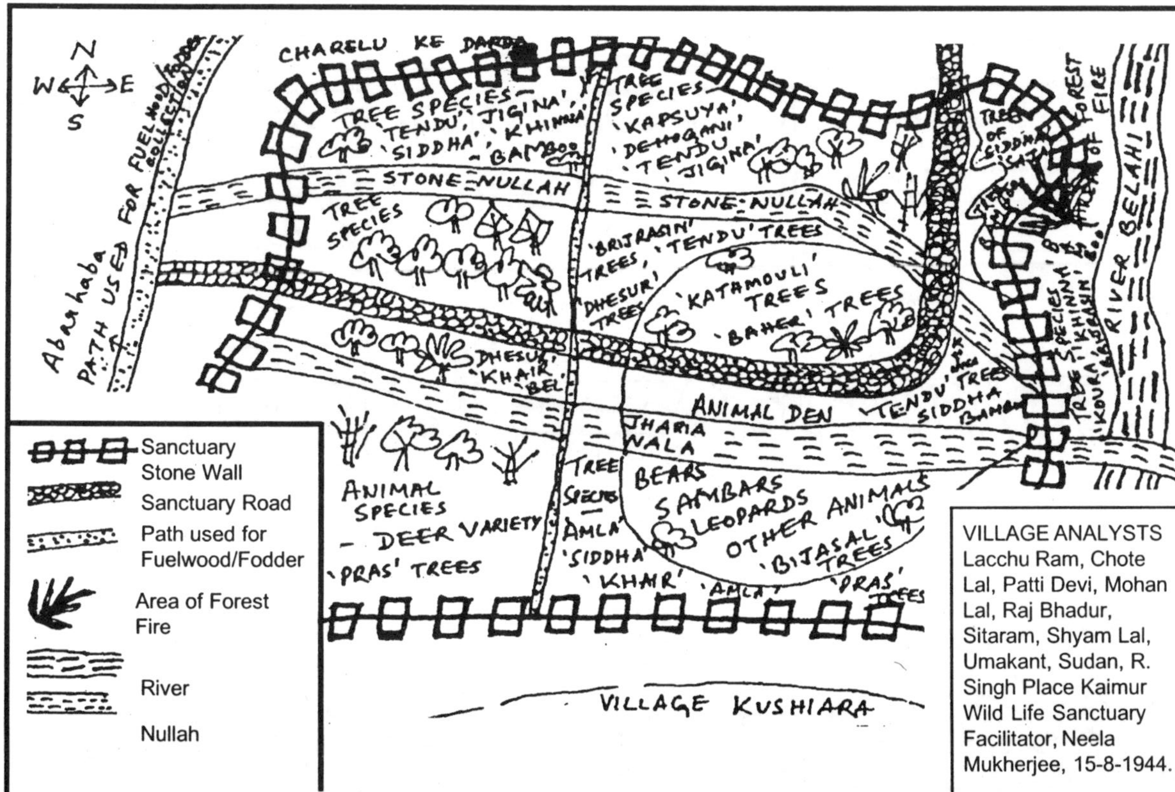

Though called a Participatory Sanctuary Map the Map depicts all the sources

Source: Neela Mukherjee: *Participatory Rural Appraisal: Methodology and Application*. (Concept, New Delhi) 1997

regarding flow of funds, record keeping, transparency of accounts, selection of stakeholders, implementation, monitoring and evaluation, etc. are discussed in detail in this session.

4. *Lecture Method of Reinforcement*

In **Step 4**, the **Lecture Method** is used by the trainer to reinforce the learning process flowing from the discussion of the case studies.

5. *Draw Venn Diagrams for depicting the different institutions/individuals with which/whom the Village Panchayat interacts*

In **Step 5**, the participants draw a **Venn Diagram** for studying the relationships of the Village Panchayat with the institutions/individuals with which it interacts for fulfilling its governance and development related functions. We especially refer to the newly created self-help groups and parallel bodies established by the government for the implementation of development programmes. Attention is also given to the emerging roles of MLAs, MLCs and MPs in the Panchayati Raj System and their linkages with the Village Panchayat as also development work. The suggested steps in the process of doing a Venn Diagram are as follows:

5.1 Explain the purpose of the exercise to the participants.

5.2 Ask them to list the various institutions or individuals with which the Village Panchayat interacts with.

5.3 Ask them to write and/or depict each institutions or individuals on small cards. Visual depiction becomes necessary if there are neo-literates or non-literate participants.

5.4 Ask the participants to place the cards in a descending order according to the perceived importance of the institutions from the point of view of the Village Panchayat. Make sure a common understanding is reached about what makes an institution important. Once the cards are arranged in an order, ask them whether they agree or would like to make modifications. Encourage them to make changes, if they think changes are required.

5.5 Ask them to assign stones, leaves, paper circles etc. of different sizes to the institutions or individuals in such a way that bigger the size of the stone, leaf or circle, the greater is the importance of that institution or individual for the Village Panchayat. Write or depict the institutions or individuals on the circles. Thus, the size of the stone, leaf, paper circle denotes the importance of the institutions or individuals to the Village Panchayat.

5.6 Ask the participants to make a small circle or any other symbol on the middle of a chart paper representing the Village Panchayat. Ask the participants to place the different stones, leaves or paper circles representry the institution, in such a way, around or symbol the circle depicting Village Panchayat, that those institutions or individuals which are more accessible to the Village Panchayat are kept close, while those which are loss accessible are kept further away from the circles representing the Village Panchayat. Thus, the distance of a stone, leaf or paper circle (representing an institution/individual) from the central circle (the Village Panchayat) denotes its degree of accessibility to the Village Panchayat.

5.7 Once all the circles are placed, discuss the placement and if they want to make any changes, encourage them to do so.

5.8 In case, certain institutions/individual are equally accessible to the Village Panchayat, they could be placed with an overlap or at equal distances.

5.9 Please note that the participants can use the distance of the circles representing the institutions from the central circle or symbol (the Village Panchayat) to denote the efficiency, usefulness, honesty, or whatever attributes they wish to or are necessary for the analysis.

5.10 Discuss why they have assigned different sizes to different institutions and why they have placed the cards at different distances from the Village Panchayat in such a manner.

5.11 An illustration of a Venn diagram is given in *Figure 21*. In this figure, judging from the size of the circles, the Gram Sevak, The SHG and the Extension Workers are the most important individuals/institutions from the point of view of the Village Panchayat. Judging from the distance of each circle from the central circle, the Gram Sevak, the local NGO and the Police Station are the most accessible.

5.12 Interview the Venn Diagram using the six helpers: why, what, whom, when, where and how.

---

6. *Draw a Communication Linkage Matrix for studying the quality of the relationships between the Village Panchayat and institutions/individuals*

Step 6 involves the preparation of a **Communication Linkage Matrix** by the participants. This Matrix is a tool for studying the quality of the relationship between the Village Panchayat and the different individuals/

Figure 21: Venn Diagram for the Village Panchayat and the Interacting Institution/Individuals

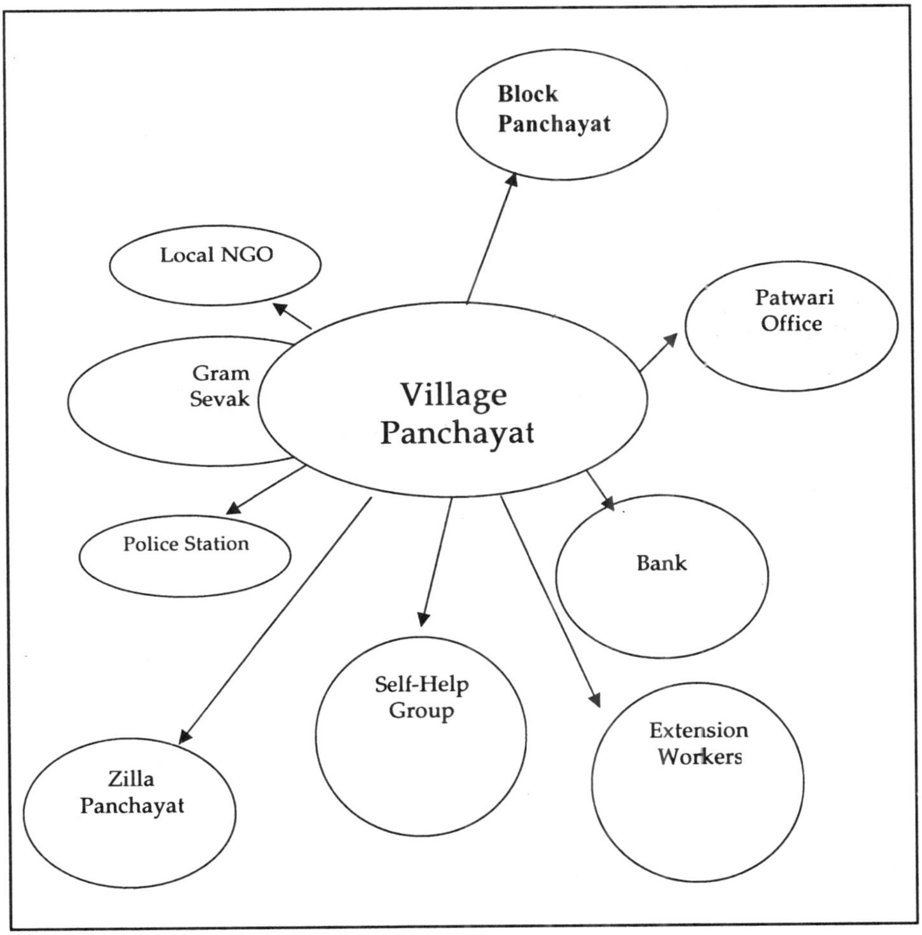

Notes: Sizes of the "Circles" show the importance of the Institutions. Distance of the "Circles" from the Village Panchayat shows the accessibility of the Institution to the Village Panchayat.

Facilitator: Amitava Mukherjee.

institutions listed in the previous step, assessed on the basis of multiple criteria. The Matrix provides a mechanism for the analysis of the Venn Diagram in terms of criteria like 'attitude', 'timeliness of service', 'availability of information', etc. under which they judge the accessibility, efficiency etc. of the institutions.

6.1 First the participants should **Brainstorm** the list of criteria with the participants for assessing the utility, accessibility, efficiency etc. of the institutions/individuals that interact with the Village Panchayat. The participants should start with the Venn Diagram, and complete it. Once the criteria are mutually agreed upon, and the Venn Diagram completed, the group can proceed with the assessment for each individual institution/individual.

6.2 Take the case of the Venn Diagram at *Figure 21* where the gram sewak is (nearest to the Village Panchayat) most accessible and the Zila Pancayat least accessible.

6.3 Write these institutions as the first column of a Matrix.

6.4 Take the criteria (and write them as the first row) on the basis of which the people have determined the relative position of the different institutions/ individuals, in order of accessibility.

6.5 Now starting with each criteria, rank the institution, as in Matrix. Do **Free Scoring,** fixed scoring or vector scoring against each criterion for all the institutions/individuals listed in Column 1. Move on to the next criterion after that and repeat the process till all the criteria are covered.

6.6 Now generate ideas from the participants, what could be done to bring the least accessible institution/individual (in the instant example, the Zila Parishad) to at least the level of the most accessible institution/individual (which in the instant example is the Gram Sevak).

6.7 Write the recommendations against each individual/institution.

6.8 Discuss the reasons for this state of affairs and how it can be improved.

Figure 22 is an example of a Communication Linkage Matrix following from the Venn Diagram of *Figure 21.*

---

*7. **Draw the Support System Diagram to understand what convergence of development services means?***

In **Step 7,** the participants do the **Support System Diagramming**[23] for

23. Adopted from Mukherjee, 2002.

Figure 22: An Example of the Communication Linkage Matrix for the Village Panchayat and some Village level Individuals/Institutions

Criteria / Institution/ Individual	*Attitude*	*Time-liness of Service*	*Infor-mation is made available*	*Quality of Infor-mation*	*Accessible*	*Suggestions for impro-ving the quality of accessibility/ utility*
Gram Sevak						
Block Panchayat						
Zilla Panchayat						
Local NGO						
Police Station						
MLAs/ MLCs/MPs						
Self-Help Group						
Bank						
Patwari Office						

Note: The other institutions/individuals can be Extension Workers like Anganwadi Worker, Auxiliary Nurse Midwife, Agricultural Assistants, etc.

illustrating the idea of the convergence of development services at a single delivery point. Consider the Self Help Group of a village as a single delivery point and the services required by it. The first step is to **brainstorm** the kinds of services the SHG requires from its inception to maturity and the different service providers. A suggested listing of the services which the SHG requires at different stages is given in the table below. The meetings of the SHGs, especially when they have women members should be the delivery points for nutrition and health related information and services. Thus, the idea of service convergence is to provide all the necessary development services from the single platform/ window of the SHG, i.e., to make the SHG the meeting point of different kinds of extension services. This is done by different extension agents participating in the meetings of the SHG and closely interacting with its members.

After obtaining a listing as suggested above, use the technique suggested for Venn Diagramming for drawing the **Support System Diagram** for the SHG. The central circle is the SHG and the other service providers make up the other circles, the sizes of which depend on their relative importance from the point of view of the SHG members. The distance of a circle from the SHG-circle is proportional to the degree of accessibility of that particular extension service to the SHG members, i.e., the extent to which it is available to them. The delivery of all these services when convergent at the level of the SHG provides for the holistic development of the SHG and its members. The focal point for illustrating the concept of convergence of services can also be chosen as the village anganwadi, farmers' cooperative, primary school, etc.

Sr. No.	*Nature of Service Required*	*Service Provider*
1.	Group formation and facilitation	Facilitator
2.	Bank Credit and Information about Banking Formalities	Bank Manager
3.	Development information about micro-enterprises and development programmes	Extension Worker
4.	Market related information about products	Extension Worker/Bank/ Consultant/NGO
5.	Preparation of Bankable Proposals for obtaining credit	"
6.	Training about accounting/book keeping	NGO
7.	Entrepreneurial Training	NGO
8.	Skill Training	NGO
9.	Nutrition and Health related Information and Services	Anganwadi worker, ANM, NGO

8 & 9. Use Role Play and Lecture Method to show what difficulties the Village Panchayat faces while managing programmes for social development

In **Step 8 and 9**, use **Role Plays/Dramas** with themes illustrative of the difficulties that the Village Panchayat faces in the course of the administrative management of any of the social development schemes like the village primary school, anganwadi, water supply schemes, etc. Different groups of participants can be given the task of staging separate Role Plays for different schemes. A discussion is then initiated and the trainer fills in gaps by brief lectures.

10. Visual Method for synthesising what we have learnt from the Session

In **Step 10**, while synthesising the learning points of the session, the trainer may ask different participants to list orally what they think is the most important learning from the session.

Base Module **Section III**
Session 11 **Management Orientation**

Session Theme	FINANCIAL MANAGEMENT OF THE VILLAGE PANCHAYAT
Duration	255 minutes
Venue	Classroom without fixed furniture
Seating	Sit and/or stand on the floor forming a circle; move around the room for the group work. Participants should be free to sit on chairs if they wish to.
Session Objective	*To expand the practical understanding and skills of the participants for the financial management of the Village Panchayat*

Expected Learning Outcomes

- The participants understand the financial responsibilities of the Village Panchayat Acquire.
- Acquire skills for maximising its income, budgeting, observing financial propriety and keeping its financial records.

Content Flow and Training Methodology

Sr. No.	*Content*	*Training Methodology*	*Training Aids*	*Duration (in minutes)*
1.	Financial Responsibilities of the Village Panchayat with reference to the Seventy-Third Constitutional Amendment Act	**Step 1** Brainstorming **Step 2** Lecture Method	Flip Charts, marker pens and others as desired by the trainer	30
2.	Income Maximisation by the Village Panchayat: (a) Imposition of Taxes and their efficient collection	**Step 3** Brainstorming **Step 4** Lecture Method	Flip Charts, marker pens, flash cards and others as desired by the trainer	60

Sr. No.	*Content*	*Training Methodology*	*Training Aids*	*Duration (in minutes)*
	(c) Levy of Fees for the Inspection of Records and obtaining their Certified Copies			
3.	Financial Management of the Village Panchayat: (a) The Village Panchayat Fund and How Fund Flow into it (b) Financial Procedures and Practices (c) Maintenance of Accounts and Record	**Step 5** Case Study Method **Step 6** Lecture Method	Records of some Village Panchayats and others as desired by the trainer	45
4.	Village Panchayat Budgeting	**Step 7** Case Study Method	Budgets of some Village Panchayats	60
5.	Financial Audit of the Village Panchayat	**Step 8** Lecture Method	Audit Reports of some Village Panchayats and other aids as desired by the trainer	45
6.	Synthesis of Learning Points by Trainer/ Participants	**Step 9** Visual Method	Overhead slides/Flip Charts	15

THE METHODOLOGICAL STEPS FOR SESSION 11

---

1. Brainstorm to catalogue the statutory financial responsibilities of the Village Panchayat

---

Step 1: First **Brainstorm** with the participants about the financial responsibilities of the Village Panchayat which have been provided in the

Seventy-Third Constitutional Amendment Act and/or the State Panchayati Raj Act and the Rules framed thereunder.

2. *Use a brief lecture to fill in any gaps*

The trainer then uses the **Lecture Method** to fill in any gaps in the information that flows out of the brainstorming exercise. The principle underlying **Johari's Window** as described in Session 2 is used in transiting from Box 1 ('What is known to both them and us') and Box 2 ('What they know and we do not know') towards Box 3 ('What we know and they do not know').

3. *Brainstorm again and Scoring/Rating the sources of revenue for the Village Panchayat*

In **Step 3**, use **Brainstorming** again to list the possible sources of revenue for a Village Panchayat. Give an example of a Village Panchayat where revenues have been generated in a substantial amount.

3.1 Facilitate a process where the different kinds/sources are recorded and Cards. One source/kind of revenue to be written on one card.
3.2 Lay the cards with kinds/sources of revenue written on them in one column.
3.3 How ask the participants to score the sources/kinds of revenue. Free scoring, fixed scoring or vector scoring may be used.
3.4 Rank the sources/kinds of revenues in descending order of score secured.
3.5 Interview the scoring using the six helpers: why, what, when, who, where and how.

4. *Use the Lecture Method to close any existing information gaps*

In **Step 4**, the trainer closes all information gaps by using the **Lecture Method** to discuss each possible source of revenue for the Village Panchayat.

5 & 6. Use Case Study and Lecture methods to show how to financially manage the Village Panchayat

In **Steps 5 and 6**, use the **Case Studies** of some Village Panchayats to illustrate the financial procedures, the working of the Panchayat Fund and the records that are required to be maintained. The trainer intersperses the discussions, wherever necessary with brief lectures. The trainer exhibits different forms, registers, record books, etc. in the class and requests the participants to identify them. In case of errors necessary corrections are suggested.

7. Use the Case Study method to illustratehow to prepare the annual budget of the Village Panchayat

Step 7 uses the Case Study method to illustrate how to prepare the annual budget of the Village Panchayat, using the budgets prepared by some Village Panchayats.

8. Give a lecture using case studies about financial audit practices

In **Step 8**, the trainer uses the **Lecture Method** for the discussions on financial audit by different statutory agencies, like the Auditor General, Local Fund Auditors, Internal Auditors of the Zilla Parishad, etc. The principles of financial good practices may be explained using the audit reports of some Village Panchayats as examples. Since this may be a technical session, the trainer may like to invite an external faculty (from financial departments of government/ local Chartered Accountant firms etc.) to take this session.

9. Visual Method for synthesising what we have learnt from the Session

In **Step 9**, synthesise the important learnings from the session by asking each participant to list at least one important lesson.

Base Module **Section III**
Session 12 **Management Orientation**

Session Theme	GOOD GOVERNANCE BY THE VILLAGE PANCHAYAT
Duration	285 minutes
Venue	Classroom without fixed furnitures
Seating	Sit and/or stand on the floor forming a circle; move around the room for the role play and group work. Participants should be also free to sit on chairs if they so desire.
Session Objective	*To orient the participants with the principles of good governance and the mechanisms for promoting them*

Expected Learning Outcomes

The participants understand the basic values related to good governance of transparency, responsiveness, participation and accountability; understand the role of the Gram Sabha in this context and acquire skills for using the instruments of social and gender audit for promoting these values.

Content Flow and Training Methodology

Sr. No.	*Content*	*Training Methodology*	*Training Aids*	*Duration (in minutes)*
1.	Citizens' Charter for the Village Panchayat	Step 1 Case Study Method Step 2 Brainstorming Step 3 Delphi Method Step 4 Ranking Method	Flip Charts, marker pens, cards and Citizens' Charter of some Village Panchayats as case studies	90
2.	Role and Responsibilities of the Village Gram Sabha	Step 5 Drama/Role Play	As desired by the trainer	30

Sr. No.	Content	Training Methodology	Training Aids	Duration (in minutes)
3.	Financial Transparency—Rationale and Practices: Gram Sabha, Publicity of Accounts and expenditure, monthly meetings, inspection of registers, financial audit	Step 6 Case Study Method Step 7 Lecture Method	As desired by the trainer	45
4.	Social and Gender Audit of Community Development Initiatives	Step 8 Brainstorming Step 9 Delphi Method Step 10 Matrix Scoring Method	Flip Charts, marker pens, cards, different varieties of seeds for the scoring	60
5.	Synthesis of Learning Points by Trainer/ Participants	Step 11 Visual Method	Overhead slides/Flip Charts	15

THE METHODOLOGICAL STEPS FOR SESSION 12

1. *What is a Citizens' Charter? Illustrate by means of a case study*

Step 1: The Citizens' Charter gives the quality standards for various public services delivered by the Village Panchayat to the village community, e.g. *say a time period of 5 days (from the date of receiving the application) to give a certified copy of any record like a death certificate.* The Charter is in the nature of a written contract which the Village Panchayat voluntarily accepts as being obligated to follow. The Charter also gives the practices which will promote the principles of transparency, responsiveness, participation and accountability in the affairs of the Village Panchayat, e.g., *presentation of detailed scheme-wise accounts before the Gram Sabha, display of boards at work sites giving details of estimates, expenditure, man-hours created, selection of programme stakeholders by the Gram Sabha, etc.* It is an obvious commitment on the part of the Village Panchayat to the cause of good governance. While framing its Charter, a Village Panchayat should begin by committing itself about a few work items and gradually expand its Charter depending upon its performance and public response. For explaining the importance and components of the Citizens' Charter to the participants, the trainer should use the **Case Study** of any Village Panchayat which already has a Charter.

---

2. *Brainstorm the kinds of public services provided by the Village Panchayat and some good practices to be included in the Charter*

Step 2: Next, engage the participants in an exercise for framing a Charter for a typical Village Panchayat. For this purpose, use the **Brainstorming** method to arrive at a list of public services delivered by the Village Panchayat which are to be included in the Charter. Let the participants also agree on the quality standards for each kind of service. The participants should also brainstorm about the practices that promote the principles of good governance and which should find inclusion in the Charter.

---

3. *Cluster the practices brainstormed using the Delphi Method*

At Step 3, use the ***Delphi Method*** to form separate clusters of the brainstormed ideas and record each idea on a separate flash card.

---

4. *Prioritise by ranking the concept clusters*

Step 4: Use the **Ranking Method** to compare and prioritise the concepts. Prepare a Charter which includes say the first 5-6 items and state their corresponding quality standards in terms of time limits, quantities, etc. Also, include some of the good practices in the Charter. Then compare with the existing Charters of some Village Panchayats. Discuss what steps should be taken to move towards the ideal Village Panchayat.

---

5. *Enact a Role Play showing what happens in a typical Gram Sabha*

In **Step 5,** request some of the participants to enact a **Role Play/Drama** depicting the proceedings of a Gram Sabha and follow this up with a discussion. The preparations for this should be done previously and a script prepared. The script should include the following subject areas:

- Issues related to gender development and other social causes.
- Some illustration of practices for promoting transparency e.g. declaration of the details of expenditure on public works by the Village Panchayat.

- Modelling of desired and undesired behaviours that are exhibited by community members in a typical Village Gram Sabha.
- The managing of conflicts which arise in a Gram Sabha.
- The caste, class and group dynamics that prevail in a Village Gram Sabha.

---

6 & 7. Use Case Studies and Lecture about why and how financial transparency is kept while managing the Village Panchayat

---

Steps 6 and 7: Use the **Case Study Method** with the **Lecture Method** to discuss the rationale and practices for maintaining Financial Transparency in the affairs of the Village Panchayat. Some of these practices may have already been discussed while framing the Citizens' Charter in Step 1.

---

8. Brainstorm a set of criteria for gender/social audit

In **Step 8**, first use the **Brainstorming Method** to evolve a check list of criteria to examine whether a community development programme reflects gender concerns. A similar checklist may be evolved for social concerns. Some criteria/evaluation questions to be used for examining for gender concerns are suggested below:

- What are the decision-making processes/mechanisms in place for preparing the village development plans, selection of sites, stakeholders, release of funds, review of programmes, financial audit which reflect the self governance nature of the Village Panchayats?
- Do women participate in these decision making processes and how?
- Whether women participation in the design, implementation and benefits of the programme?
- Whether the choice of the programme interventions are adapted to women's perspectives, practical convenience, expertise, land ownership patterns, control over resources required to participate in the programme, etc. (frame as separate criteria)?
- How favourable are the attitudes and behaviours of the programme extension staff towards women?

9. *Cluster the brainstormed criteria using the Delphi Method*

Step 9 uses the **Delphi Method** to form independent concept clusters of the checklists of criteria generated in the previous step, discarding duplicates.

10. *Do Matrix Scoring for different kinds of development programmes using the criteria clusters*

In **Step** 10 use the **Matrix Scoring Method** to help the participants audit development programmes using the set of criteria evolved in the previous steps. Help them to draw up a matrix with the programmes enumerated top to bottom as the first column and criteria left to right as the first row. Make the comparisons criterion-wise and not programme-wise. Take up a criterion and then do scoring for all the programmes. Once one criterion is over, move to the next, do the scoring for all the programmes. **Free Scoring Method** would suffice the purpose in the above exercise, but the trainer is free to use either free or fixed or vector scoring. Record the scores in the relevant cells using flexible material like seeds, pebbles etc. Request participants to re-examine the scoring if they wish, give them the choice to change the scoring.

10.1 Now lead a discussion about why a programme has been given a high or low score and what should be done for improving the quality of the low-scoring programmes. Use the six helpers to interview the scoring.

11. *Visual Method for synthesising what we have learnt from the Session*

In **Step** 11, ask each participant to describe one good governance practice which she thinks is the best and what she will do to ensure that her Village Panchayat emulates it. Reiterate the gender and social concerns that have flowed from the auditing exercise.

Base Module: Section IV
ROLE ORIENTATION

CONTENT FLOW IN ROLE ORIENTATION BASE MODULE AT A GLANCE

Day 1	
Time in minutes	*Session No. and Name*
FORENOON	
100	Session 13: People-Centred Behaviours and Attitudes
20	Break for Tea
105	Session 13: People-Centred Behaviours and Attitudes (continued)
60	Break for Lunch

DETAILED CONTENT FLOW IN SECTION V
ROLE ORIENTATION

DAY 1
(Time in Minutes)

FORENOON

Session 13: People-Centred Behaviours and Attitudes

1. Content: (a) How does a Village Panchayat member/development functionary usually behave?
(b) What are the appropriate behaviours for a member/functionary?
Training Methods: Game: "As a Village Panchayat member, I mainly..."[1] and Brainstorming
Duration: 75

2. Content: Non-Verbal Behaviour
Training Method: Energising Game: Non-Verbal Circles
Duration: 25
Break for Tea
Duration: 20

3. Content: Role of a Village Panchayat Member
Training Method: Role Play/Drama
Duration: 30

4. Content: Game for Enhancing Group Dynamics: Chairs
Duration: 30

5. Content: Modelling of People-Centred Attitudes
Training Methods: Johari's Window and Slide Show
Duration: 30

6. Content: Synthesis of Learning Points by Trainer/Participants
Training Method: Visual
Duration: 15
Total Duration of Session 13: 215

Break for Lunch
Duration: 1 Hour

Total duration of Training: 215 (3 Hours 35 minutes)

1. Adopted from Chambers, 2002.

NOTE TO TRAINERS FOR USING SECTION IV ROLE ORIENTATION

1. INTRODUCTION

Section IV of the Module consists of a single session, entitled "People-Centred Behaviours and Attitudes". This session, essentially makes the participants experience a process of sensitisation to the proactive behaviours and attitudes which are expected of them as members of the institution of the Village Panchayat. This sensitivity is imperative for enabling them to fulfil their roles with a high degree of commitment towards the poor stakeholders in the development process. The participants have to understand that their present day role as people's representatives is not one of being in control and exercising their powers arbitrarily. Their role is that of a facilitator. They have to remember that the development paradigm has shifted from a mechanistic top-down to an organic people-centred position. The patterns of normative behaviour and attitudes of the members have to be convergent with the principle of people-centricity which underpins the development paradigm.

2. TRAINING OBJECTIVES

The training objective of the Section has been articulated as:

- To enable the participants to comprehend the different kinds of people-centred behaviours and attitudes.
- To arrive at an understanding of what kind of behaviours are most appropriate for ushering people-centred development.

3. EXPECTED LEARNING OUTCOMES FROM THE SECTION

The *Expected Learning Outcomes* that fulfil the stated Training Objective at the levels of both the individual participants and group can be best described as:

- The participants are conscientised about the desired pro-people and pro-poor behaviours and attitudes that are expected of a Village Panchayat member and learn to emulate them.

Because of the nature of its training content, this Section calls for greater communication and facilitation skills on the part of the trainers. Unlike the other Sections, the learning outcomes from this Section are not measured in terms of the transfer of knowledge or work-related skills. Instead, the single session involves a portrayal of the normative value systems and behavioural patterns which the participants as members of the Village Panchayat are expected to emulate. Given the nature of the learning outcomes flowing out, it is expected that they will not be apparent immediately after the session, but will lie embedded in the psyche of the participants.

4. THE PARADIGM OF PEOPLE-CENTRED BEHAVIOUR

It is important that the participants realize that their role as members of the Village Panchayats consists of facilitating a process of social and economic development. The participants have to be sensitized against adopting a superior stance whereby they regard the poor as beneficiaries and themselves as benefactors. Instead, they have to understand that it is their responsibility to foster the agency of the self and community, so that rural stakeholders can engage in whole-hearted political and development participation.

5. SESSION 13

This single session in this Section models a variety of people-centred behaviours and portrays many corresponding attitudes. It is important to remember that most often a person's behavioural patterns are the manifestations of her attitudes.

6. TRAINING METHODOLOGY

The trainer is encouraged to use with ingenuity the training methodology suggested in this Section. It uses a mix of Participatory Learning and Action Methods, games and role play/drama. The use of slides, cartoons, pictures and video is strongly advocated. The nature of the training contents renders the task of the trainer doubly difficult. Behaviour modelling on the part of the trainer is crucial in these sessions and in the entire training Module. The trainer has to adopt a learner-centric approach in the classroom. The trainer has to convey herself as a role model who believes in learner participation, even that of the most deprived learners. Only then can the trainer sincerely uphold the analogous philosophy of people-centred development and the inclusion of poor stakeholders in the development process.

7. DURATION OF TRAINING

The Section has only one session and is of much shorter than the others. It requires about half a training day. The total duration of training is estimated to be 215 minutes which is 3 hours 35 minutes.

Base Module
Session 13

Section IV
Role Orientation

Session Theme	PEOPLE-CENTRED BEHAVIOURS AND ATTITUDES
Duration	215 minutes
Venue	Classroom without fixed furnitures
Seating	Sit and/or stand on the floor forming a circle; move around the room for the role play and group work. Participants may also sit on chairs if they like to.
Session Objective	*To enable the participants to comprehend the different kinds of people-centred behaviours and attitudes*

Expected Learning Outcomes

The participants are conscientised about the desired pro-people and pro-poor behaviours and attitudes that are expected of a Village Panchayat member and learn to emulate them

Content Flow and Training Methodology

Sr. No.	*Content*	*Training Methodology*	*Training Aids*	*Duration (in minutes)*
1.	(a) How does a Village Panchayat member/ development functionary usually behave? (b) What are the appropriate behaviours for a member/ functionary?	**Step 1** Game "As a Village Panchayat member, I mainly..."[2] **Step 2** Brainstorming	Flash cards, marker pens, flip charts, slides, transparencies	45 30
2.	Non-Verbal Behaviour	**Step 3** Game: Non-Verbal Circles	Chairs, sticks to improvise	25

2. Adapted from Chambers 2002.

Sr. No.	*Content*	*Training Methodology*	*Training Aids*	*Duration (in minutes)*
3.	Role of a Village Panchayat Member	**Step 4** Role Play/ Drama	As may be necessary	30
4.	Game for Enhancing Group Dynamics	**Step 5** Chairs	Chairs	30
5.	Modelling of People-Centred Attitudes	**Step 6** Johari's Window **Step 7** Slide Show	Slides, sketches	30
6.	Synthesis of Learning Points	**Step 8** Visual Method	Flip Charts, marker pens	15

1. Game: "As a Village Panchayat member, I mainly..."

In **Step 1**, play the game **As a Village Panchayat member, I mainly...** This is a game for reflecting on one's own behaviour and how we are seen by others. Follow these steps:

1.1 Facilitate a brainstorming exercise to complete the sentence 'As a Village Panchayat member, I mainly...' make a short list of behaviours like, listen, think, argue, lecture, dominate, lead, facilitate, and of roles, listener, thinker, debater, leader, facilitator, etc. Ask participants to record each idea or similar ideas on a flash card.

1.2 The next step is to join others who are similar. Post the words in different parts of the room and ask the participants to move **quickly** to the word each thinks represents her best. Encourage the participants to move fast at this stage of the game. If any participant cannot choose a word, they can form their own group.

1.3 The groups formed under each word then discuss their roles or behaviours and decide:

- What is helpful about it?
- What is unhelpful about it?
- How do others see me?
- Do I want to make any changes?

- How does it affect my role as a Village Panchayat member or development functionary?
- Does it meet the needs of people-centred development? If not why?
- Any other reflections.

1.4 The groups discuss their insights with the other groups. These discussions can help the participants recognize the value of all kinds of behaviours and roles and identify which of these are congruent with the philosophy of people-centred development.

---

2. Brainstorming for the appropriate behaviours of a member or functionary

---

In **Step 2**, based upon the previous discussions, **Brainstorm** with the participants about the appropriate behaviours for a member or functionary. Use slides and transparencies of pictures, wherever possible. Some behaviours are suggested below:

- *Avoid Dominance*. Dominant behaviour is characterized by the inability to listen to others and appreciate the fact "that they know"; the tendency to ignore/override the development interests of others, impose one's own views and beliefs upon others, etc.
- *Avoid Biases* there are eight kinds of biases to be avoided:

  (a) *Gender Bias*—ignoring men or women.
  (b) *People Bias*—talking to vocal people, clean people, people with clean clothes, etc.
  (c) *Road side Bias*—visiting places nearer the road.
  (d) *Project Bias*—look at pet projects where nothing has gone wrong.
  (e) *Professional Bias*—looking at development problems and solutions from the narrow respective of one profession.
  (f) *Seasonal Bias*—carrying out field work, important sessions etc. when it is most inconvenient for the people.
  (g) *Time Bias*—carrying out field work, important meetings (like a Gram Sabha) etc., when it is not convenient for the people.
  (h) *Diplomacy Bias*—not expressing opinions or view in order not to offend others *or* when people say what they think "outsiders" want to hear.

- *Eschew arrogance* like not listening to others' views; acting as "Mr/ Mrs Know — All;" being disrespectful towards the views of socially excluded sections; being very conscious of one's own status as a Village Panchayat member, etc.

- *Do not lecture* since this is against the principle of participation. They know their problems and solutions.
- *Do not seek 'blueprint'* since development interventions have to be specific to community/stakeholder needs and hence cannot conform to one fixed pattern.
- *Seek and respect diversity* since there are diverse perspectives and needs of development stakeholders and "their reality" counts.
- *Be self critical and be self aware. Do not be judgmental.* Encourage others to express themselves freely and listen to them. Be self introspective and realize your strengths and weaknesses.
- *Be culturally sensitive* by recognizing the tradition, usage, dress, culture, language and religion, customs etc. of the different sections of society and communities and respecting them.
- *Respect others and their points of view* by listening to others and encouraging debates.
- *'Deal with People', do not avoid them or cut them out if they are 'difficult' or if they do not agree with you.* Difficult people are dominant people, "Mr/Mrs. Know-All", the "trappers", the "arrogant people", the "destroyers", the "thick skinned" and bored people, the shy people, people with limited vocabulary and the procrastinators. Such people may include some government functionaries who do not wish to share information and power or community members who ask many questions in the Gram Sabha to disturb the proceedings only.

---

3. Game to sensitise the participants to non-verbal behaviour

---

In **Step 3, Non-Verbal Circles,** an energising game has been suggested with the objective of sensitising the participants to how non-verbal behaviour can indicate dominance, submissiveness and friendliness. Follow the steps given below:

3.1 Form two sub-groups of the participants. The two sub-groups sit in two circles, facing inwards.

3.2 One person in each sub-group is elected scorer, who also takes part in the game.

3.3 The first competition for each sub-group is to show and perform non-verbal actions that demonstrate dominance. One person does the action, and then all other members repeat it for it to count in the score.

3.4 Continue until one of the two groups runs out of ideas.
3.5 Quickly ask the scores, and invite each sub-group to choose its best non-verbal action.
3.6 Repeat for submissiveness.
3.7 Repeat for being 'nice to people'.
3.8 Repeat for different kinds of behaviours which have been identified in the previous steps.
3.9 Now discuss about the importance of non-verbal behaviour. Analyse how much we communicate with our words and how much through non-verbal behaviour, especially in exhibiting the behaviours which have been either recommended or discouraged in the previous step.
3.10 Discuss the importance of paralinguistics and facial expression. Indicate that current thinking on the subject maintains that we communicate only 7% of what we communicate by words, 38% by paralinguistics (tone, voice inflexion, etc.) and 55% by facial expression.

4. Role Play or Drama to illustrate the Role of a Village Panchayat Member

In **Step 4**, highlight the role of a Village Panchayat member using **Role Play/Drama** staged jointly by the participants and trainers. The script can narrate **Case Studies** if so desired. Several role models may be portrayed by the script, like:

- Facilitator of participatory development and governance at the grassroots.
- Promoter of gender and social justice at the grassroots with special reference to the management of conflict and conflict resolution.
- Facilitator of the process of social and economic change.
- Proactive agent of community development.
- Regulator of the units of self-government at the village level.
- Custodian of public property at the village level.

5. Game for Enhancing Group Dynamics

In **Step 5**, the participants play a game of **Chairs**[3] for enhancing their group dynamics, even further. The steps to be followed are given below.

3. Pretty *et al.* 1995.

5.1 Prepare three kinds of instructions on slips of paper, an example of which is given below:

- A: Put all the chairs in a circle within 15 minutes.
- B: Put all the chairs near the door within 15 minutes.
- C: Put all the chairs near the window within 15 minutes.

5.2 Explain to the participants the objectives of the game which are:

- To illustrate how to manage conflict by turning it into co-operation.
- To help them focus on the possible differences in the interpretation of instructions.
- To make the participants aware of the cultural and gender differences in handling conflicts.

5.3 Give each participant one kind of instruction (either A, B or C), distributing equal numbers of the three instructions. Ask them to keep the instruction given to them a secret.

5.4 Tell the participants to start the game following the instructions they have been given.

5.5 The focus of the exercise is on cooperation and conflict resolution by non-aggression. The three sub-groups cannot carry out their given tasks unless they cooperate. Several mutual solutions are possible, like:

- Putting all the chairs in a circle between the door and the window.
- Putting first all the chairs in a circle, then near the door and next near the window.
- Putting one-third chairs in a circle, one-third near the door and one-third near the window.

5.6 The groups will be seen to be using force and carrying their chairs desperately away or sitting on them near the door or window to avoid the chairs being displaced. Some participants will be seen trying to find a co-operative solution, while others will continue collecting and defending their chairs. The latter will frustrate the good intentions of the former who then join the argument.

5.7 Analyse the experience with the participants exploring how they felt about their chairs, the others who tried to take their chairs away and about the participants who were trying to co-operate. Ask them whether they would play the game differently a second time. Also explore how they related the game to real-life situations, say the dynamics they experienced in a Gram Sabha or a meeting of the Village Panchayat.

6. *Use Johari's Window to Model People-Centred Attitudes*

In **Step 6**, use the **Johari's Window** see *Figure* 23 to focus attention on the fact that it is important to believe that people know their problems and are capable of suggesting solutions. Also, that the realities of the poor people count. People's analysis, people's criteria, people's monitoring, people's evaluation, people's views and people's knowledge count and not ours. Discuss how these principles have underpinned the entire training programme where the trainer has given more emphasis to the realities and knowledge of the participants than her own. The whole training process itself has been one of both behaviour and attitude modelling by the trainer. The trainer should discuss how the participants could use the training methods in their communities to elicit popular participation.

7. *Use Slides to Model People-Centred Attitudes*

In **Step 7**, use **Slides** with pictures/sketches to model a spectrum of people-centred attitudes with a particular reference to the following attitudes:

- *"They Know"*. It is important for a Village Panchayat member to appreciate the knowledge of the people since this is the first step towards facilitating their development through participation and understand that their knowledge, their technology, their priorities, their preferences, their planning, their monitoring and their evaluation count.
- *Embrace Error* since this ability denotes humility and non-dominant behaviour and leads to efficient development choices and decisions. This helps to inculcate the attitude of learning from mistakes and moving ahead.
- *"Fail Forward"*, i.e., learn through your mistakes and move forward but do not either repeat mistakes or get demoralised by failure.
- *Positive Person: "Yes, I have an Idea."* It indicates that the leader has enthusiasm. This is the essential quality of a leader as someone who has a vision and motivates others. If the leader is not enthusiastic, how can the people be expected to be.
- *"I will not talk the talk, unless I walk the talk."* The Village Panchayat member has to be a role model for her community and must exhibit the behaviours which she expects others to emulate. Practice what you preach.
- *Improvise, Innovate and Adapt.* The quality of village development depends upon the creativity and flexibility of the Village Panchayat

Figure 23: Johari's Window

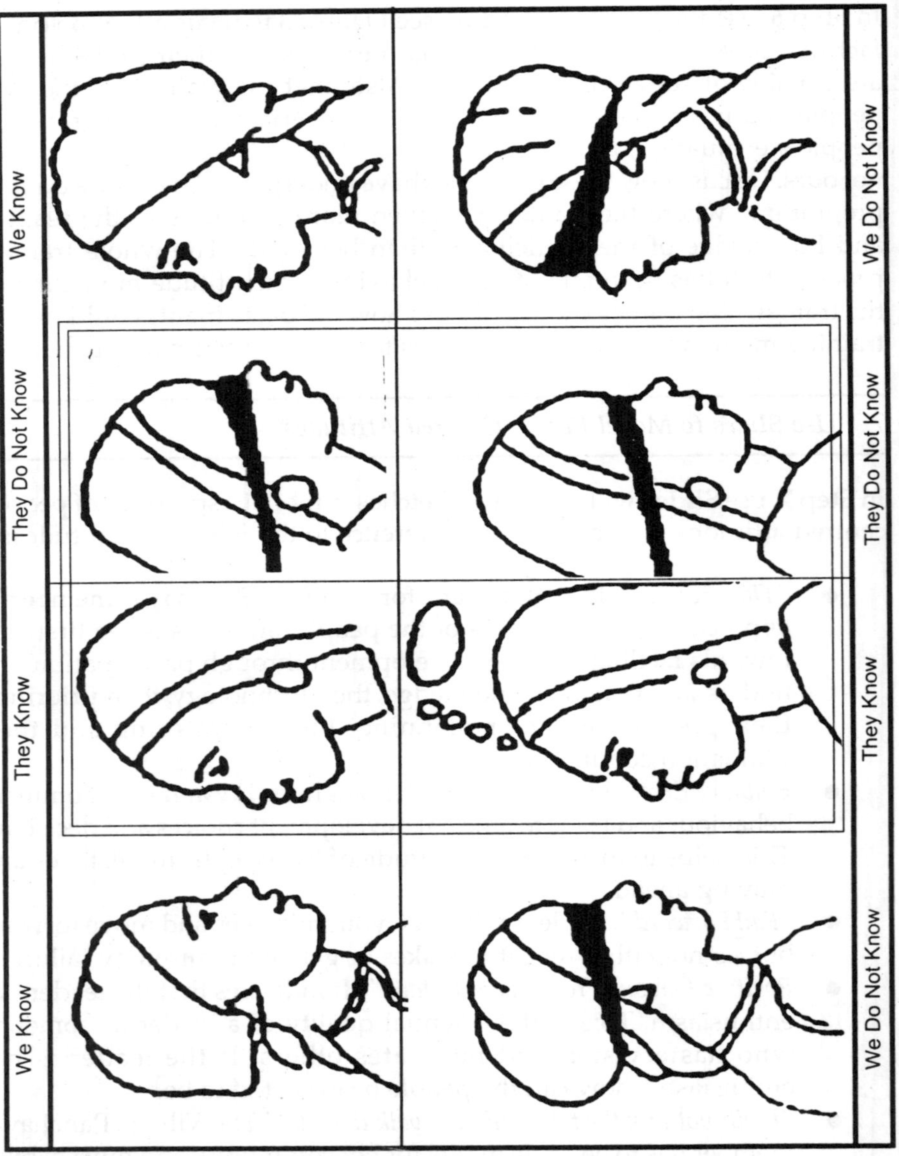

member. The Village Panchayat members must, therefore, constantly improvise, innovate and adopt existing ways of doing things.

- *Listening, Observing for Learning.* This attitude is significant because unless the Village Panchayat member is prepared to listen to people, she cannot learn and if she in not a state of continuous learning, she cannot innovate and adapt for the development needs of her community. Also, learning from the people is important for making informed development decisions which conforms to people's priorities, their needs, their preferences. To learn, it is imperative to listen, observe and learn.
- *Communicate Well,* so that others can understand and participate. Communication is critical to make the process of development interactive.
- *We are Facilitators: They do it.* People are the real actors; not us. We are there to facilitate the process so that people can analyze, plan, implement, act, monitor and evaluate. This attitude underlies non-dominant behaviour and is important for initiating stakeholder participation in development.

8. Visual Method for synthesising what we have learnt from this Session

In **Step 8**, the synthesis of the learning points is done by the trainer with help from the participants. To introduce good humour, do the synthesis by asking the participants to act out some of the desired and undesired behaviours and attitudes for a Village Panchayat member.

Base Module: Section V

MICRO-LEVEL PLANNING ORIENTATION

(for Social Justice and Economic Development)

DETAILED CONTENT FLOW IN SECTION V MICRO-LEVEL PLANNING ORIENTATION

DAY 1 *(Time in Minutes)*			
Forenoon **Session 1:** **Step 1** **Training Method:** **Duration:** 45 **Step 2** **Training Method:** **Duration:** 45 Break for Tea **Duration:** 20 **Step 3** Energising Game: Breakthrough **Duration:** 15 **Step 4 & 5** **Training Methods:** Mapping, Delphi Method **Duration:** 45+45= 90 **Step 6** **Training Methods:** Ranking, Scoring, Pair-wise Ranking **Duration:** 45 Break for Lunch **Duration:** 1 Hour			
Afternoon			
Total duration of Training: 420 minutes (7 hrs.)	Total duration of Training: 545 minutes (About 9 hrs.)	Total duration of Training: 565 minutes (About 9 ½ hrs.)	Total duration of Training:

NOTE TO TRAINERS FOR USING SECTION V MICRO-LEVEL PLANNING ORIENTATION

1. INTRODUCTION

Section V of the Base Module deals with the application of *Mirco-Level Planning* in development interventions.[1] This Section imparts a set of functional skills to the participants to facilitate micro-level planning that is necessary for initiating community development through *praxis.* The Section is a natural sequel to the previous ones which are designed to sensitise the participants to the philosophy of people-centred development and stakeholder participation in the development process. The seeds of the future involvement of stakeholders are sown at the planning stage. The Section thus completes the *Capability Spectrum* in terms of knowledge, skills and attitudes that the elected members of the Panchayati Raj Institutions must necessarily possess for facilitating the process of people-centred development in their communities.

2. TRAINING OBJECTIVES

The training objectives of this Section are stated as follows:

- *To enable the participants to comprehend the process of people's participation in planning for village development.*
- *To equip the participants with the functional skills required for engaging in planning for economic development and social justice at the micro-level.*

3. SESSIONS, THEIR TRAINING OBJECTIVES AND EXPECTED LEARNING OUTCOMES

The Section has five sessions on Micro-Level Planning. The first five sessions are geared to satisfy the two stated objectives. For each session, the *Expected Learning Outcomes* at the end of the session that demonstrate the fulfilment of the two training objectives, at the levels of both the individual participants and group have been identified.

---

1 Extracted from Amitava Mukherjee: *Participatory Rural Appraisal and Rural Development Planning*, Vikas Publishing Co. : New Delhi, 1994 (revised second edition 2003 by Concept Publishing Co., New Delhi).

The session-wise *Training Objectives* and the *Expected Learning Outcomes* are given in the following table:

Session No.	*Session Description*	*Training Objectives*	*Expected Learning Outcomes*
14.	The Dream Village	(a) To enable the participants to comprehend the process of stakeholder participation in planning for village development (b) To equip the participants with the functional skills required for engaging in micro-level planning	(a) The participants visualise their dream village and articulate their vision for village development. (b) They acquire functional skills for using PLA methods in developing a perspective for village development.
15.	Context Analysis for Action Planning	Same as above	(a) The participants are able to contextualise their dream map to the realities existing at the village level. (b) They acquire functional skills for using PLA methods in analysing the existing condition in the village.
16.	Problem Identification and Prioritization	Same as above	(a) The participants acquire functional skills for using PLA methods in identifying the problems contorting for village development. (b) They can adopt a problem-solving approach for prioritising development problems.

Session No.	*Session Description*	*Training Objectives*	*Expected Learning Outcomes*
17.	Solution Identification and Prioritization	Same as above	(a) The participants acquire functional skills for using PLA methods in finding solutions to problems identified in the previous session. (b) They can adopt a problem-solving approach for prioritising solutions for development problems.
18.	Action Planning	Same as above	(a) The participants acquire functional skills for using PLA methods in planning for village development. (b) They have a hands-on understanding of how to develop an Action Plan from a Tactical Plan.

4. SESSION NO. 14

In this initial session, the participants are encouraged to prepare a map of their dream village as a first step towards Micro-Level Planning. This session seeks to explore and expand the *development vision* of the participants and help them articulate their perspective of development. It is imperative for Village Panchayat members to possess the essential ability to envision village development in its entirety. They have first to understand what village development is all about. This session, therefore, attempts to develop the participants' vision based upon their own development perspectives.

5. SESSION NO. 15

In the second session, participatory methods are used to conduct the context analysis for preparing the village development plan. This analysis is done based upon village level realities and with reference to four areas:

- Analysis of space, which includes analysis of resources available, infrastructure social condition, etc.
- Analysis of time which includes evolution of the village, seasonality of income, food availability, employment, opportunities, credit needs etc.
- Analysis of relationships which includes an analysis of the importance of different institutions and their utility etc., to the community and the inter-relationships between the institutions, with which the community has interface.
- Analysis of preferences and priorities, which includes preferences for crops, trees, food, livelihood, seasons, institutions etc.

6. SESSION NO. 16

This session involves the participants in acquiring the skills required to facilitate the community in identification and prioritisation of village-level development problems and needs which have to be addressed by the plan. The problem identification is done by involving different groups in the process, especially women and other socially excluded groups. It may also be emphasised that there may be a need to carry out the exercise of problem identification with different group: men, women, aged and old, children, people with disabilities etc.

7. SESSION NO. 17

In this session, the skills to help communities identify or range of solutions or suitable development activities and match them with the needs voiced by the people in the previous session. A method/technique for prioritisation of the solution is then effected for arriving at an optimal set of development interventions. Perspectives related to gender and social justice are also explored and included in the set of activities that are listed.

8. SESSION NO. 18

In this last session, the *Micro-Level Plan* prepared by the process adopted in the last four sessions is transformed into a *Tactical Plan* by:

- Fitting it within a definite time frame by specifying the time horizons for the proposed development activities.
- Specifying the financial allocations available from different funding sources for each of these activities.

- Ascertaining the appropriateness of the Plan for marginalised groups.

9. PLANNING FOR THE RURAL PRODUCTION SECTOR

The sequence of steps and the planning process outlined in the Sessions Nos. 14 to 18 can be followed for the rural production sector whereby the participants prepare a participatory village plan for the development and strengthening of on-farm and/or off-farm livelihoods. The facilitator must ensure that the focus is on rural production sector. An indicative list of the possible activities is given below for guidance:

Rural On-Farm Productive Activities

1. Agriculture
2. Agricultural Extension
3. Land improvement
4. Implementation of agrarian reforms
5. Soil Conservation
6. Management of water resources
7. Watershed development
8. Regulation of manure pits in public places

Rural Off-Farm Productive Activities

9. Animal husbandry
10. Dairying
11. Poultry
12. Fisheries
13. Collection of minor forest produce
14. Khadi, village and cottage industries
15. Traditional Rural Artisanship

10. PLANNING FOR RURAL SOCIAL INFRASTRUCTURE

Similarly, the sequence of steps outlined in the five sessions (14 to 18 alone) may be used for planning for rural social infrastructure. The focus of micro-level planning here will be on social infrastructure. The trainer should impress upon the participants that one of the basic tenets of the people-centred development paradigm is that the agency of the individual/group/community has to be fostered by increasing the level of human well-being in terms of the social development indicators like literacy, health, sanitation, etc. This is particularly important for gender and other vulnerable groups. Poverty is a multidimensional phenomenon and not simply restricted to income poverty. It is equally important to address the social, economic and political dimensions of deprivation. It is only then that the development process leads to social change, which is the ultimate development goal. Therefore, special attention has to be given during planning for the creation of social infrastructure which enhances the quality of human capital in village communities. A suggested list for assisting the trainer in facilitating the planning process is given below:

Productive Activities for creating/strengthening the Village-level human capital

1. Education with special reference to the education of the girl child, including primary and secondary schools.
2. Adult and non-formal education.
3. Markets and fairs.
4. Family welfare, health, sanitation, primary health centres and dispensaries.
5. Women and child development.
6. Social Development of Scheduled Castes, Scheduled Tribes and physically and mentally challenged persons.
7. Public distribution system.
8. Relief and rehabilitation of disaster and project affected persons.
9. Maintenance of the record of village-level social development indicators.

Productive Activities for Social Infrastructure/ Physical Capital

1. Social forestry and farm forestry.
2. Management of common property resources.
3. Rural housing.
4. Drinking water.
5. Fuel and Fodder.
6. Roads, culverts, bridges, ferries and other means of transportation.
7. Non-conventional energy sources.
8. Maintenance of community assets.
9. Construction and maintenance of Dharmashalas and similar institutions.
10. Construction and maintenance of Cattle Sheds, Ponds and Cart Stands.
11. Construction and maintenance of Slaughter Houses.
12. Maintenance of public parks, playgrounds, etc.
13. Removal of encroachments on public properties.
14. Organising voluntary labour and contribution for community works.

11. TRAINING METHODOLOGY

The role played by the Participatory Learning and Action Methods in this Section is two-fold. First, as a training methodology used in this Section is also predominantly PLA-based. Second, the participants are prepared for field work where they can draw up a village level development plan.

Base Module Section V
Session 14 Micro-Level Planning Orientation

Session Theme	MY DREAM VILLAGE
Duration	150 minutes
Venue	Classroom without any fixed furnitures
Seating	Sit and/or stand on the floor forming a circle; move about for the game and group work. Participants should be free to sit on chairs if they so desire.
Session Objectives	• *To enable the participants to comprehend the process of people's participation in planning for village development and develop a perspective for development of the village.* • *To impart the functional skills required for engaging in micro-level planning to the participants*

Expected Learning Outcomes

- The participants visualise their dream village and articulate their vision for village development. This provides a perspective for mirco-level plan.
- They acquire functional skills for using PLA methods in micro-level planning for village development.

Content Flow and Training Methodology

Sr. No.	*Content*	*Training Methodology*	*Training Aids*	*Duration (in minutes)*
1.	Energising and Group Forming Game	**Step 1** Card Game	Flip charts, marker pens, boards.	15
2.	Game for Improving Listening and Observation	**Step 2** Matches	3-6 match sticks or coins for each participant	15

Sr. No.	Content	Training Methodology	Training Aids	Duration (in minutes)
3.	Creating/ Articulating the Development Vision or building the community's perspective	**Step 3** Dream Mapping	Flash cards, flip charts, marker pens, transparencies, slides and other aids as desired by the participants	45[2]
4.	Setting the Perspective for Village Development Planning: The Dream Map provides the perspective.	**Step 4** Visual Method for the Presentation and Analysis of the Dream Map and Identification of Key Elements	Same as above	60
5.	Synthesis by Trainer/ Participants.	**Step 5** Visual Method	Slides, aforesaid materials	15

THE METHODOLOGICAL STEPS FOR SESSION 14

1. Play an energising and group forming game

In **Step 1**, the **Card Game** is played with the objective to energise the group and form sub-groups of the participants for the group exercises that are an integral part of this session. The steps for playing the game are:

1.1 Make the participants stand in a circle.
1.2 Take a pack of playing cards and keep cards of the four houses, viz. *Clubs*, *Diamonds*, *Hearts* and *Spades* with their faces down in the middle of the circle. The total number of cards should be equal to the number of participants. Equal number of cards of each house should be kept if it is desired to form sub-groups of equal size.

1.3 Ask the participants to run in a circle and pick up a card each while keeping on running. The participants are then divided into four sub-groups, depending on the card they have picked up, viz., clubs, hearts, diamonds and spades.

2. Play a game for improving listening and observation

In **Step 2, Matches,** a game for improving listening and observation has been suggested, as given below:

2.1 The objectives of the game are to make each participant aware of the value of their contribution and encourage a listening attitude in the subsequent group work.
2.2 Give each participant the same number of tokens like match sticks or coins depending upon the time available for playing the game. Say each participant has 5 coins or match sticks.
2.3 Ask them to sit in circles in the sub-groups formed, viz. clubs, hearts, diamonds and spades.
2.4 Every time a participant speaks in her sub-group, she has to put one of her tokens in the centre of the circle.
2.5 If a participant has no token left, she cannot speak.
2.6 A participant realises that every remark is valuable and, therefore, evaluates her remark before speaking. Knowing that every speaker has made the evaluation, the other participants also listen.
2.7 The participants who has/have token(s) left are the winners.

3. Dream Mapping for creating and articulating the development vision

Step 3: For the **Dream Mapping** the participants work in the four sub-groups. Each sub-group holds discussions about what their dream village would look like and how they visualise village development over a given period of time, say 5 or 10 years. The participants together can choose to present their dream village through pictures, drawings maps or text highlighting the features it would possess. The trainer should enlist the support of a co-facilitator and jointly facilitate the group work. Provide whatever stationery the sub-groups may desire such as coloured papers, coloured cards, pens, markers, scissors, guns and glues, tapes etc. and encourage them to be very creative. At the end of this exercise, it is expected that each sub-group would have either depicted its dream village pictorially and/or prepared a presentation about the same on chart paper, transparencies, etc.

4. *Presentation and Analysis of Dream Maps for setting the perspective for village development planning*

In **Step 4**, each of the four sub-groups uses the **Visual Method** for makin a presentation about its dream village, followed by the trainer facilitating an analysis of the key elements of each dream map. These elements are either noted down on flip charts pasted around the room or on flash cards. After all four groups have made their presentations, the key elements of the dream maps analysed. The dream map would show how the fields will look, how the houses will look, how the forest would change, how the state of health and literacy would vary or how much industrialisation will advance over the chosen time frame. These key elements are then discussed further and the overall perspective for micro-level planning for village development is outlined by the participants.

5. *Visual Method for synthesising what we have learnt from this Session*

In **Step 5**, the synthesis of the learning points is done by the trainer with the help of the participants. The trainer should focus on the fact that the key elements of the dream maps prepare by the participants will form the perspective of the whole planning exercise in the next sessions. The village development plan which will thus be eventually prepared, would, therefore, be *People's Micro-level Plan* in the true sense of the term.

Base Module
Session 15

Section V
Micro-Level Planning Orientation

Session Theme	CONTEXT ANALYSIS FOR MICRO-LEVEL PLANNING
Duration	550 minutes
Venue	Village locale
Seating	Sit and/or stand on the floor forming a circle; move about for the game and group work.
Session Objectives	*To enable the participants to acquire skills for analysing the present situation of the village, to inform micro-level planning for economic development and social justice.* *To impart the planning skills required for engaging in micro-level planning to the participants.*

Expected Learning Outcomes

- The participants are able to contextualise their dream map to the realities existing at the village level.
- They acquire skills in using PLA methods in analysing the present conditions of their village for micro-level planning for economic development and social justice in their village.

Content Flow and Training Methodology

Sr. No.	*Content*	*Training Methodology*	*Training Aids*	*Duration (in minutes)*
1.	Context Analysis of Village Development: Analysis of Space	**Step 1** Joint Walk or Geographical Transect **Step 2** Social Mapping or Modelling	White paper, marker pens, flash cards, chalks, stones	45 30 45 25 Total: 145
2.	Energising Game	**Step 3** Breakthrough	None	15

Sr. No.	*Content*	*Training Methodology*	*Training Aids*	*Duration (in minutes)*
3.	Context Analysis: Analysis of Time	**Step 4** Historical Transect **Step 5** Time Line **Step 6** Oral History **Step 7** Seasonality Analysis	White paper, marker pens, flash cards, chalks, stones	45 45 30 45 Total: 165
4.	Context Analysis: Analysis of Relationships and institutions	**Step 8** Venn Diagramming **Step 9** Relational Matrices **Step 10** Card Matching Game	White paper, marker pens, flash cards, scissors, glue, seeds of different varieties or pebbles	45 45 45 Total: 135
5.	Context Analysis: Analysis of Priorities	**Step 11** Scoring, Ranking and Matrix Ranking **Step 12** Force Field Analysis	White paper, marker pens, different coloured cards, scissocrs, glue	45 45 Total: 90
6.	Synthesis by Trainer/ Participants	**Step 13** Visual Method	Slides, trans-parencies, maps and charts prepared by the parti-cipants during the session	15

THE METHODOLOGICAL STEPS FOR SESSION 15

1. Analysis of Space: Take a joint walk or a Geographical Transect in the village

In Step 1, let the participants take a **Joint Walk** with the villagers and discuss the changing face of the village, the natural resources and other features of the village during the walk. The usual method for Geographical Transect is to go to the highest point in the village and walk along with villager, down to the lowest point. If the highest point happens to be at the centre of the village, then there could be two joint walks, one or either direction. During the walk record all "elements" (trees, houses, fields, bushes, crops etc.) seen on the surface, as you walk along. Discuss with the villagers details of soil types, uses, problem etc. Record these. An example of a Geographical Transect is at *Figure 24 and 24-A*.

2. Analysis of Space: Draw a Social Map of the village

In Step 2, involve the participants and some villagers in drawing a Social Map of the village as done earlier in Session 10. **A Social Map**[1] depicts the social aspects of a locality like households, their social categories, literate/illiterate households, schools, roads, hospitals, etc. In this exercise, the Map is drawn for describing the present state of the village. The participants prepare the map, complete with all the household-wise details, e.g., caste composition, school aged children etc. The households on the map are also numbered. The trainer then leads a discussion about the features of the map by asking probing questions, like:

- What is the condition of the houses?
- What is the state of health of the villagers?
- How many people are literate?
- Is the social infrastructure in the village enough and in good shape? and so on.

For each aspect of the map and household shown on the map, the problems, opportunities, development programmes and ways of improvement are discussed. Ask the participants to discuss the development opportunities with regard to each item shown on the map. Some of these could be:

1. Mukherjee, 2003.

Figure 24: Geographical Transects: This is a transect of a village in northern Pakistan

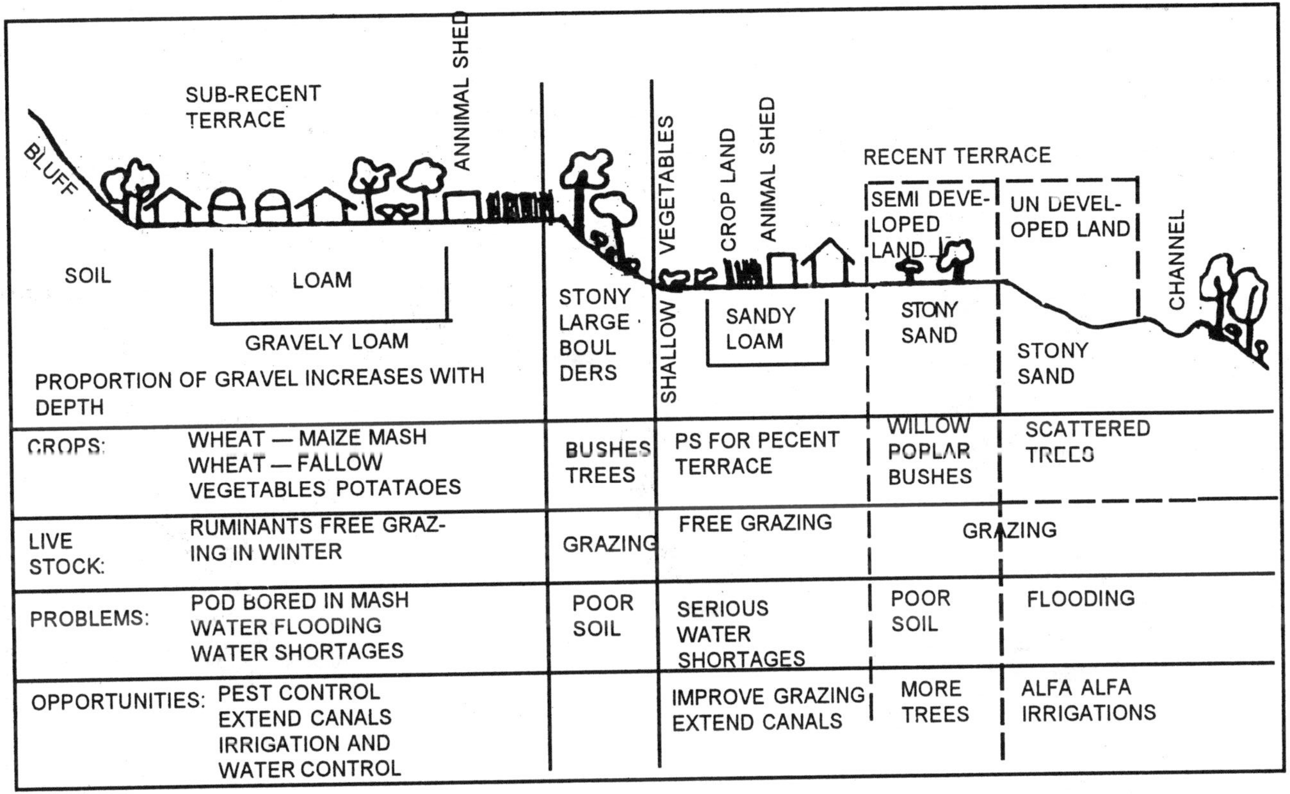

Source: Forest, Trees and People news Letter no. 15/16

Figure 24A: Transeet of Ghusel, Lalitpur District, Nepal

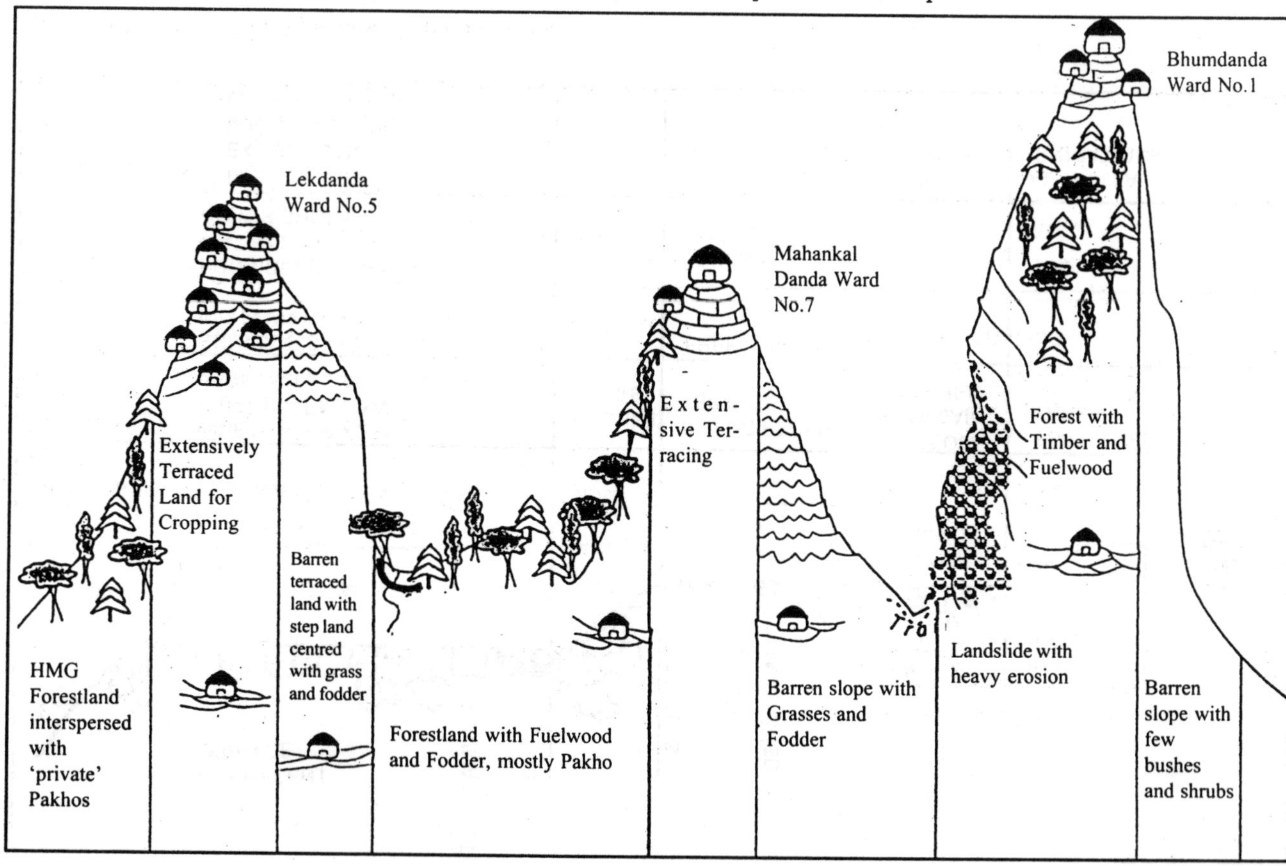

Source: *Power, Process and Participation* (London: Intermediate Technology Press) 1996.

- Housing
- Literacy
- Primary education
- Health
- Immunization
- Maintenance of roads
- Management of natural resources

The steps for developing a social map have been discussed earlier.

3. Analysis of Space: Modelling village development

In **Step 3**, in place of drawing a map, people can also build a model. In models, instead of drawing, objects are either placed or constructed to show different aspects of the village. For instance, in place of drawing trees in a map, branches or leaves are used to show location of trees in the village, on a model. Then for rivers or drainage, a small drain is actually dug out on the ground. For houses, stones or pieces of brick may be placed. *Figure 25* is an example of a model.

4. Play Breakthrough an energising game

In **Step 4**, play the **Breakthrough Game** with the participants as follows:

4.1 This game may be used to energise the participants and also illustrate the importance of co-ordination and communication.
4.2 Divide the participants into two groups (Groups A and B) of equal size and have them stand in two lines facing each other, about two metres apart.
4.3 Group A is asked to break through Group B. No one is allowed to talk.
4.4 When the breakthrough occurs, the one group is told they have five to ten minutes to plan a second breakthrough the other group is told that they have the same amount of time to organise a defence.
4.5 Repeat the attempt.
4.6 Ask the participants to reflect on the differences between the two breakthroughs. The first breakthrough usually occurs easily. The second is more difficult. Ask the participants to reflect upon the importance of coordination and communication, and what may be achieved as a group than as a set of individuals. Hint that

Figure 25: Model

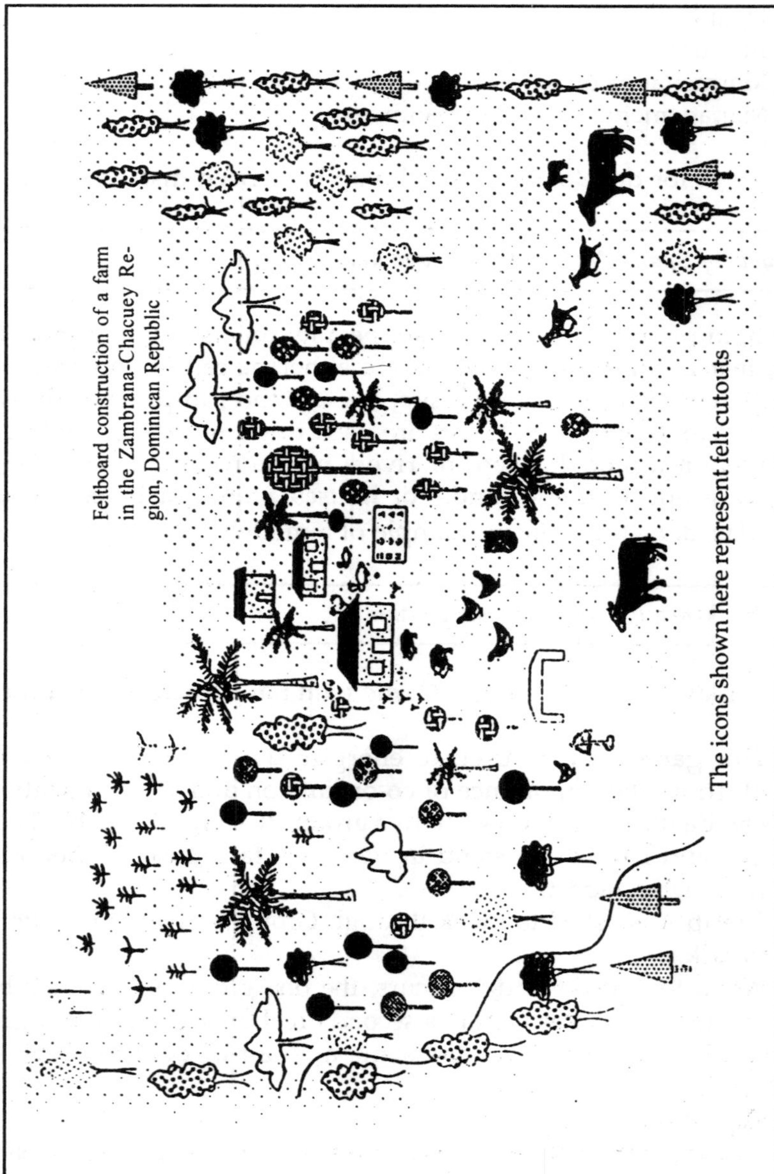

Source: *Power, Process and Participation* (London: Intermediate Technology Press) 1996.

for Group-B, defending their group was easier because they co-ordinated their efforts. Group-A similarly found organising the breakthrough easier, though they may not have succeeded.

---

5. *Analysis of Time: Draw a Timeline to trace the development of the Area being planned for*

In **Step 5**, involve the participants in drawing a **Timeline** as in Session 2 earlier. The steps in doing the **Timeline** are described below:

5.1 Identify an elderly person and request her to talk about the history of her village and initiate a discussion about the village. This can be done with a group of villagers also.

5.2 Some suggested key questions could be as under:

- When was the Village established?
- What are the important events in the history of the Village?
- What major changes took place?
- What are the reasons for these changes?
- How have these changes affected the community?

5.3 Ask one of the participants to note down the major events briefly on cards in bold letters as the group or the participants narrate the events occurrences. If the participants are unable to do so, one of the facilitators can help.

5.4 Once the participants feel the list of events is more or less complete, ask them to keep the cards in a chronological order — the earlier events on the top and the later events lower down. Request them to read out the events and ask them whether they are happy with the order or if they would like to modify it. Also ask the participants to add events etc. if they wished to.

5.5 Now request the participants to associate years/dates etc. with the events. If they can write them down.

5.6 Add years to the left side of the events. Failure of memory and not using their system of calendar may hinder the process of the participants getting the exact years. Use best judgement to arrive at the years. There is no need to have exact dates/years. Approximate years/dates are acceptable.

5.7 Now initiate a discussion on the Timeline to help the participants analyze and reflect on it. Interview the Timeline by asking open-ended questions to clarify doubts or to get an in-depth understanding about the evolution of the Village and any aspect of the village, including the evolution of the village Panchayat.

6. *Analysis of Time (continued): Listen to the Oral History of the village*

In **Step 6**, the participants listen to the "local people describe the trends in local conditions from a historical perspective. Such local trends are more of broad overviews of selected issues comparing two periods, an old period and the current period."[2] While the term seasonality or seasonal is used, the analysis could be in terms of seasons (winter, summer etc.) or months (Baisakh, Jeth etc.) or in terms of weeks. A reflection on oral history may help the participants to analyse the factors that helped or hindered the development of the village. And put the subsequent steps into perspective.

7. *Analysis of Time (continued): Do the Seasonality Analysis for the village*

In **Step 7**, the participants engage in drawing seasonal diagrams to show seasonal variations in availability of food, of employment, of diseases, of income, livelihood, and even problems. "Each season has its specific problems and the local people have different strategies for "sourcing" their livelihoods."[3] While the term seasonality or seasonal is used, the analysis could be in terms of seasons (winter, summer etc.) or months (Baisakh, Jeth etc.) or in terms of weeks. The suggested steps of seasonal diagrams are:

7.1 Explain the objective of the exercise to the participants.

7.2 Start discussions about the present season and the work they have been doing during the season with the villagers. Move to the present month and ask what other months are there. Facilitate so that participants/community write names of months on cards in bold letters. Write one month on one card.

7.3 Ask them to identify a unique thing about each month one by one, which would remind them of the month. It can be a symbol or drawing. Encourage them to do it themselves. Facilitate so that the participants write for redraw the unique thing on cards to represent season, months or weeks. This can be fun and adds to their involvement, even of the illiterates meaningfully. Mark cards bearing the unique things pertaining to different months or season or weeks, on the end with names of the respective month or season or week respectively written.

7.4 Facilitate so that participants can draw a grid with chalk on the floor or on the ground. Use of pens and several flip charts joined together can also be made. In the grid ensure that participants

2. Mukherjee, 2003.
3. Mukherjee, 2003.

have columns one column for each month or season or week and one additional column for the items to be studied and as many rows as the items you want to study. Keep the cards with names of the months or seasons or weeks and the corresponding visuals or symbols horizontally as the first row or the column heads.

7.5 Now on the first column, encourage participants to take the items whose seasonal variations they intend exploring. Ask the participants to show the condition, amount or state of the item, in months or season or weeks when the aspect or activity is on. Ask them to represent the magnitude of the activity using different numbers of leaves, seeds or sticks of different sizes or even lines. For instance one may be interested, say, in the availability of wage labour during various months. Seeds can be used to indicate the number of days employment in different months. Different kinds of seeds may be used to show availability of employment for men and women separately. Similarly, sticks of different sizes can be used to indicate the quantity of rainfall during each of the months. After completing one aspect or activity move to another, until all of them are similarly covered.

7.6 Give the participants an opportunity to think on whether they would like to take up any other aspect or activity or make any modifications to the diagram. If they wish to, facilitate changes.

7.7 Interview the diagram, i.e., ask them questions on aspects you are not clear. Use the six helpers — why, what, where, whom, when and how to interview the seasonality diagram.

7.8 Facilitate a discussion and analysis among the participants and others present. The points of discussion could include:

- Major findings and learning.
- Implications of the findings.
- Recommendations and action points.

7.9 Copy the diagram on a flip chart with legends and details of the participants, facilitators, locality and date, etc. if it is drawn on the ground or floor.

7.10 Triangulate the findings of the seasonality diagram with other key informants or groups or key performants.

Examples of seasonality Diagrams are at *Figures 26, 26A, 27 and 28.*

---

8. Analysis of Relationships: Do the Venn Diagramming for depicting the relationships with different institutions/individuals interfacing with the Village

---

In **Step 8**, the participants draw a **Venn Diagram** also called "Chapati

Figure: 26 Employment and Wages in Krishna Rakshit Chak (1998)

	Wages	*Days of Employment (W)*	*Days of Employment (M)*
Magh (Mid-January to Mid February	Rs. 30 plus a snack of puffed rice.	10-15 days in winnowing	5-10 days earth work.
Phalgun (Mid-February to Mid-March)	Rs. 30-40 per sq. feet of earth work	10-15 days carrying agricultural produce.	2-5 days work. Digging earth or stones.
Chaitra (Mid-March-to Mid-April)		Some work. Harvesting of Boro Paddy	Some work. Selling of Eucalyptus Leaves etc.
Baisakh (Mid-April to Mid May)			5-6 days
Jyastha (Mid-May to Mid June)			1-2 days in households of Landlord/large farmers.
Asardh (Mid-June to Mid July)	Rs. 30 plus a snack of puffed rice.	Some work in the fields	1-2 days preparing fields of other farmers
Srabon	Rs. 30 plus a snack of puffed rice.	15-16 days work in paddy transplantation	15-26 days cultivation work
Bhadra (mid-August to Mid-Sept.)			
Ashwin (Mid-Sept. to Mid-October)	Rs. 30	4-5 days work in deweeding.	
Kartick (Mid-October to Mid-Nov.)	Rs. 30 plus one Meal (M) Rs. 25 plus one Meal (W)	10d ays work in harvesting.	10 days work in carrying headloads, storing grains etc. for women. 15-20 days for men.
Ahgrayan (Mid-November top Mid-Dec.)	Rs. 30 plus one snack of puffed rice (W) Rs. 50 plus a snack of puffed rice (M)	15-20 days work	15-20 days
Poush (Mid-Dec. to Mid-January)	Rs. 30 plus a snack of puffed rice		15 days

Prepared by Women of Krishna Rakshit Chak, Midnapore, West Bengal.

Source: Amitava Mukherjee: *Hunger: Theory, Perspective and Reality—Analysis Through Participatory Methods* (Aldershot: Ashgate Publishing Ltd. and New Delhi: Concept, Publishing Company) 2002.

Figure 26A: Seasonality Matrix

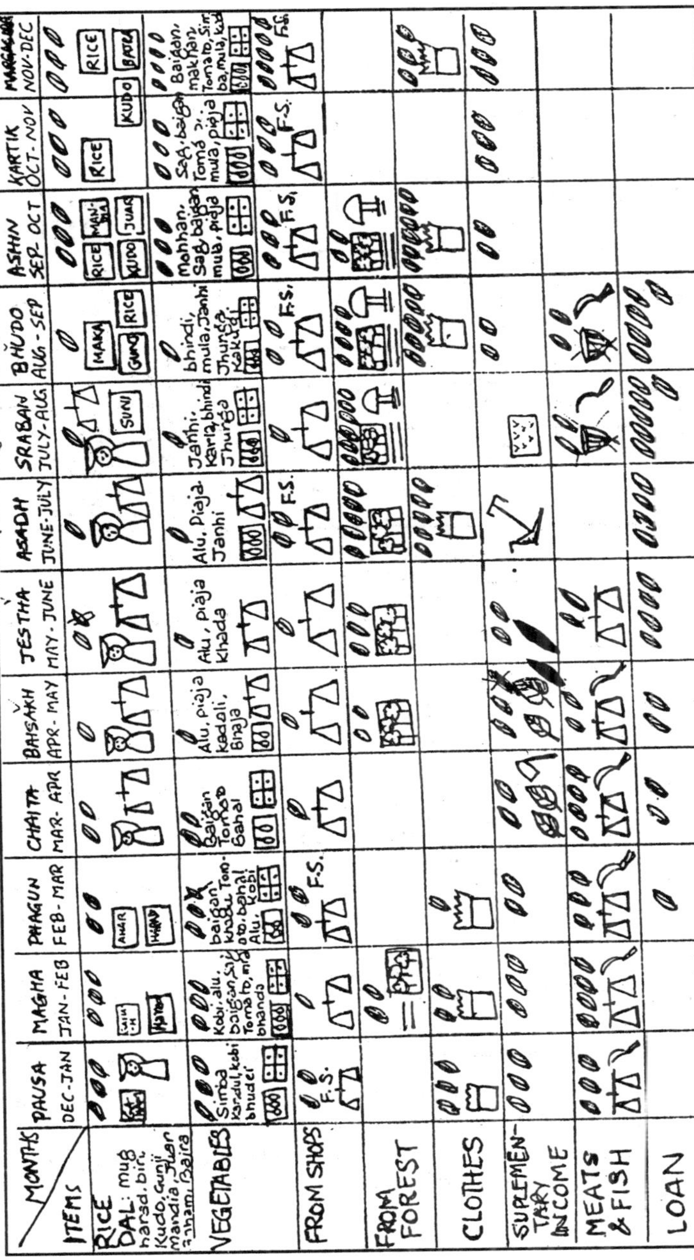

Vegetable Waste
Weekly Market
Gochar Forest
Resource Forest
Forest Cleaning
Agl Work
F.S. Festival Seasons
Open Animals
Cloth Merchant
Sal Leaf
Kendu Leaf
Crop Yield
Daily Wage
Shop
Own Forest

Participants : Indra Bho Pandit Bhol, Jojuroshan, Shyama Bhol Basudev.

Source: PRAXIS, 1998

Figure 27: Seasonality with Scoring

Months / Diseases	Jan	Feb	Mar	Apr	May	Jun	Jul	Aug	Sep	Oct	Nov	Dec
Fever				●●	●	●					● ●●●● ●●●● ●●●●	●● ●●
Cold and Whooping Cough	●● ●●										●●●● ●●●● ●●●●	●●●
Headache	●●●● ●●●●			●●●● ●●●●		●	●●●	●●●	●●● ●●	●●●● ●●●● ●●	●●●● ●●●●	●●● ●●●
Diarrhoea				●●●● ●●●● ●●●● ●●●●	●●●		●●		●	●●●● ●●●● ●●●● ●●●● ●●●● ●●●●	●●●● ●●●● ●●●● ●●●● ●●●● ●●●●	
Measles				●●●● ●●●●	●●● ●●● ●●●	●● ●● ●						
Jaundice	●●● ●●●	●●● ●●		●●● ●●● ●●								
Vomiting	●	●●●		●	●●● ●●● ●●●				●●●● ●●●●	●●●● ●●●●		
Scabies		●●	●●●	●●●● ●●●● ●●●● ●●●●	●●●● ●●●● ●●●●		●●	●●	●●●	●●●		
Tetanus									●	●●●● ●●●●	●●●● ●●	●●● ●●
Months	Jan	Feb	Mar	Apr	May	Jun	Jul	Aug	Sep	Oct	Nov	Dec

Note: Seasonal Health Calendar of Nine Diseases, Udayanampatti Village : Villagers Used Stickers to Depict Frequency of Disease.

Source: Devavaram Joh *et al.* (1991) PRA for Rural Resource Management *RRA Notes*. Number 13, August IIED. London.

Figure 28: Seasonal Diagrams

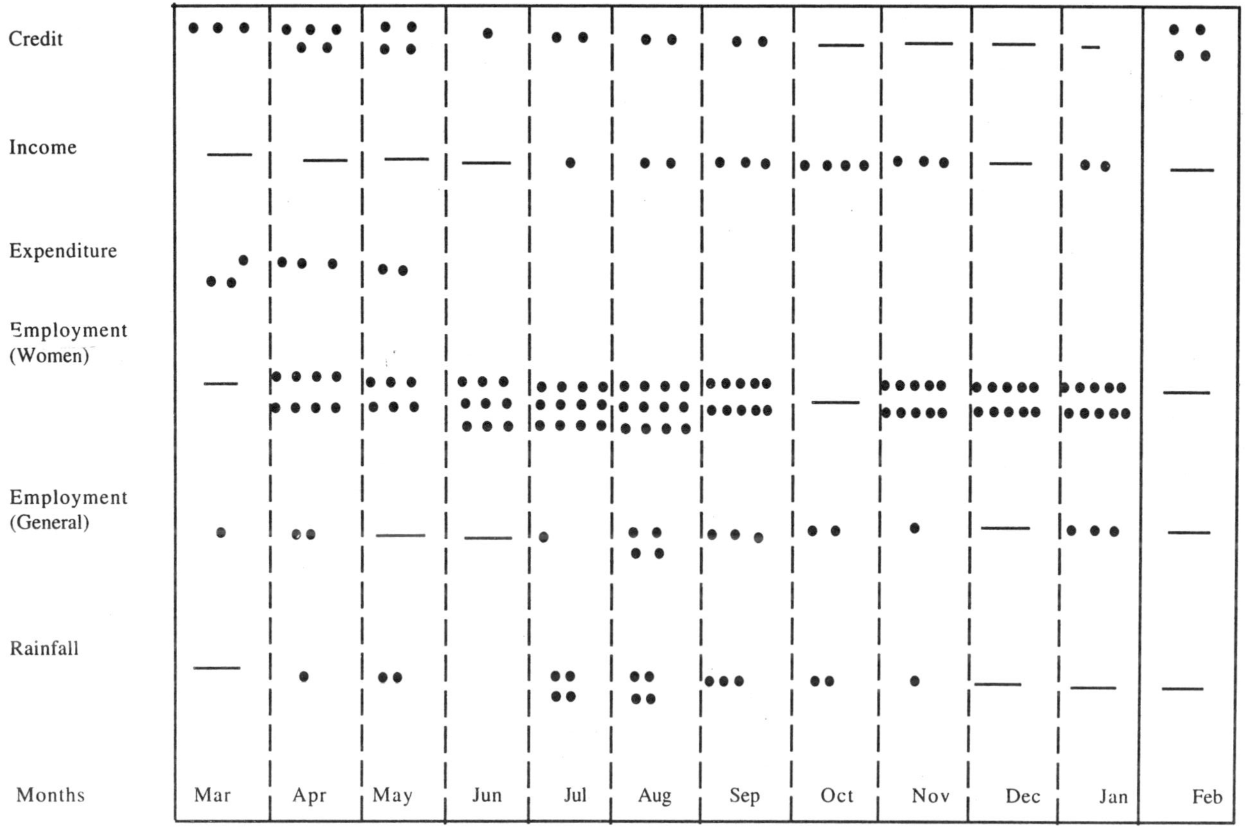

Participants : 1. Nagalingaiah B.D.O 2. Hanumantharaju 3 .Chandershekar B.D.O. 4. Vijay Kumar 5. Karumbaiah 6. Sheleikeri 7. M.K. Ali 8. Rame Gowda 9. Janiardhan 10. Chaluvachari 11. Ningachari

Source: Forest, Trees & People Newsletter 15/16.

Diagram" for studying the relationships of the Village with the institutions/individuals with which it interfaces. The diagramming process has earlier been described in Session 9. The only difference is that the central circle is now the Village. The suggested steps in the process of doing the diagram are as follows:

8.1 Explain the purpose of the carrying out Venn Diagramming to the participants. It is a diagram depicting two variables (relationships) between the village on the one part and the institutions or individuals on the other part.

8.2 Encourage participants to list the various institutions or individuals which the Village interacts with, such as the Police Station, Block Development officer etc.

8.3 Participants are facilitated to write and/or depict each institutions or individuals on small cards. Visual depiction with the help of symbols or pictures becomes necessary if there are non-literate participants.

8.4 Facilitate a process when the participants place the cards in a descending order according to the perceived importance of the institutions or individuals from the point of view of the Village. It is wise to help the participants arrive at a common understanding of what they mean by importance. Once the cards are arranged in an ascending or descending order of importance, ask the participants whether they agree or would like to make changes in order of importance. Encourage them to think and make changes, if they consider changes are required.

8.5 The participants may then assign stones, leaves or even paper circles of different sizes to the institutions or individuals in such a way that bigger the stone, leaf or paper circle, the greater is the importance of that institution or individual for the Village. Write or depict the institutions or individuals on the paper circles and in case of stones or leaves, name of the institution or individual is written on slips of paper and kept beneath the stone or leave which represents it. Make sure the name of the institution is visible. Thus, the size of the stone, leaf or paper circle denotes the importance of the institutions or individuals to the Village. Two institutions or individuals could be of same importance. In which case stones, leaves or paper circles of same size could represent them.

8.6 Ask the participants to make a small circle on the middle of a chart paper or on the ground, or on the floor representing the Village. The participants now place the stones or leaves or paper circles in such a way on the chart paper or on the ground or on the floor around the Village so that those institutions or individuals which are more accessible to the Village are kept close, while those which are less accessible are kept further away from the circles representing the Village. Thus, the distance of a paper circle or stone or leaf (representing an institution/individual) from the central circle (the Village) denotes its degree of accessibility to the Village. Greater the distance, lower is the accessibility. There is an inverse relationship shown between distance and accessibility.

The distance can also denote efficiency, honesty or efficacy of the institution/individual, instead of showing accessibility.

8.7 Once all the stones, leaves or paper circles of different sizes are placed around the small circle representing the village, discuss the placement and if the participants want to make any changes either of the size of the stone, leaves or paper circles or of the distance at which they are kept from the village, encourage them to do so.

8.8 Remind the participants that the distance in a Venn Diagram is not geographical, distance. It is the mental or social distance.

8.9 In case, certain institutions or individual are equally accessible to the Village or efficient or efficacious, they could be placed at an equal distance from the village.

8.10 It may be reiterated that the participants can use the distance of the stones, leaves or paper circles representing the institutions from the central circle (the Village) to denote the efficiency, usefulness, honesty, or whatever attributes they wish to or are necessary for the analysis.

8.11 Discuss why they have assigned different sizes to different institutions and why they have placed the cards at different distances from the circle denoting the Village in such a manner.

8.12 Interview the Venn Diagram using the six helper: why, what, where, whom, when and how. A Venn Diagram is at *Figure 29*. Also see *Figure 21*.

---

9. *Analysis of Relationships: Draw the Relational Matrices for the different institutions/individuals interfacing with the Village*

In **Step 9**, the participants draw the **Relational Matrices** for the different institutions/individuals interfacing with the Village. An example of a Relational Matrix is given in *Figure 30*. The steps for this exercise are:

9.1 The participants are encouraged to write the names of the different institutions/individuals interfacing with the Village

Figure 29: Gendered Institutional Diagrams from Choluteca, Honduras

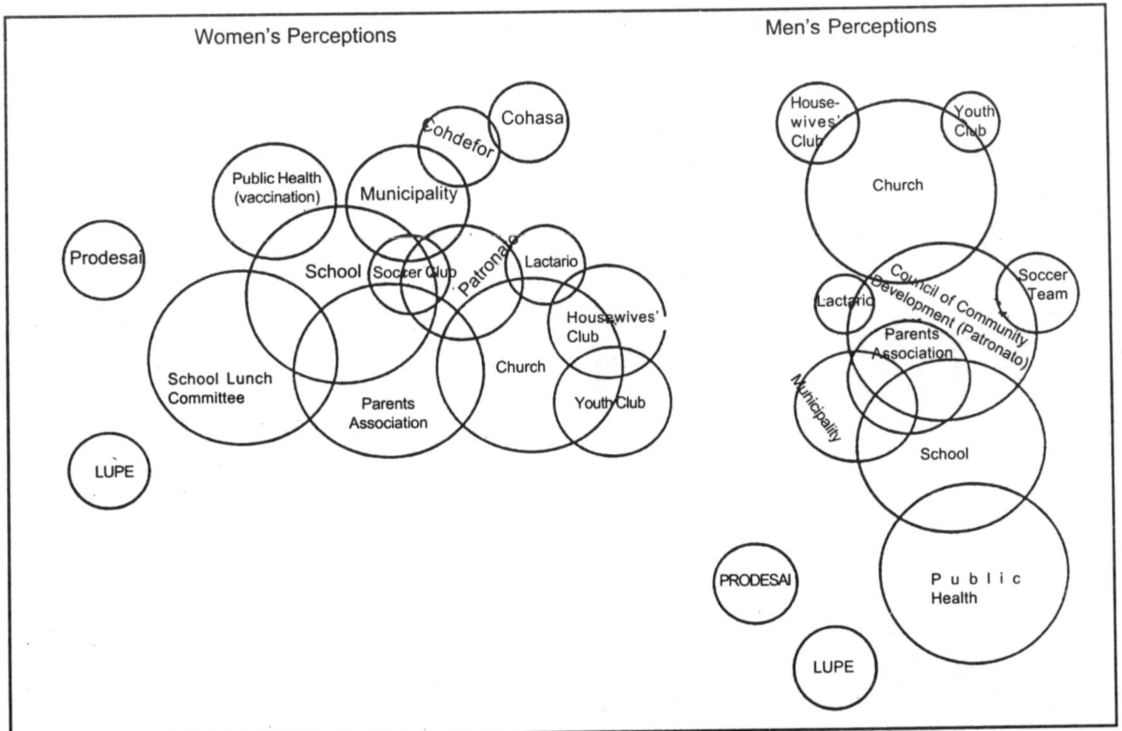

Source: ECOGEN Field Data, 1992 and Power, Process and Participation (London: Intermediate Technology Press) 1996

Focus groups of men and women, through a process of dialogue and consensus-building ranked each organization's importance (represented by the size of the circle). Using paper circles each group constructed diagrams indicating the relationships between and among different community institutions. Men and women ranked the significance of community groups for local welfare very differently. This exercise provided extensive information about men's and women's relationships with and attitudes about local and regional organisations.

Figure 30 : Relational Matrices

(a) Problem-Problem Matrix

PROBLEM \ PROBLEM	Low Income (1)	Low Productivity (2)	Lack of Water for Irrigation (3)	Non-Adoption of Improved Method of Cultivation (4)	Poor Health (5)	Mal-Nutrition (6)	Poor Sanitation (7)	Problem Problem Matrix
Low Income (1)	–	✓	✓	✓	✓	✓	✓	
Low Productivity (2)	✓	—	✓	✓	✓	✓	✗	
Lack of Water for Irrigation (3)	✓	✓	—	✓	✗	✗	✗	
Non-Adoption of Improved Method of Cultivation (4)	✓	✓	✓	–	✗	✓	✗	
Poor Health (5)	✓	✓	✗	✗	—	✓	✓	
Mal-Nutrition (6)	✓	✓	✗	✗	✓	—	✗	
Poor Sanitation (7)	✓	✗	✗	✗	✓	✗	—	
No. of Inter-Connections	6	5	3	3	4	4	2	

(b) Project-Project Matrix

PROJECT \ PROJECT	Off-Season Employment A	Supply of HYV Seeds & Feritiliser B	Agricultural Extension C	Lift Irrigation D	Vegetable Cultivation E	Toilet Construction F	Drinking Water G	Health Education H	Project Project Matrix
Off-Season Employment	–	✗	✗	✓	✗	✓	✗	✗	
Supply of HYV Seed & Fertilisers	✗	–	✓	✓	✓	✗	✗	✗	
Agriculture Extension	✗	✓	–	✓	✓	✗	✗	✗	
Lift Irrigation	✓	✓	✓	–	✗	✗	✗	✗	
Vegetable Cultivation	✗	✓	✓	✓	–	✗	✗	✗	
Toilet Construction	✓	✗	✗	✗	✗	–	✗	✗	
Drinking Water	✗	✗	✗	✗	✗	✗	–	✓	
Health Education	✗	✗	✗	✗	✓	✓	✓	–	

Figure. 30 *Contd*

(c) Project-Project Matrix

PROJECTS \ PROJECTS	Off-Season Employment A	Supply of HYV Seed and Ferilitisers B	Agriculture Extension C	Lift Irrigation D	Vegetable Cultivation E	Toilet Construction F	Drinking Water G	Health Education H	Project-Project Matrix
Off-Season Employment	—								0
Supply of HYV Seed and Ferilitisers	—	—							0
Agriculture Extension	I	D	—						3
Lift Irrigation	D	D	D	—					6
Vegetable Cultivation	—	D	D	D	—				6
Toilet Construction	I	—	—	—	—	—			1
Drinking Water	—	—	—	—	—	—	—		0
Health Education	—	—	—	—	—	D	D	—	4

(d) Project-Project Matrix

PROJECTS \ PROJECTS	NFE Centre	Health Centre	Hand Pump	IGP	Off Season Employment	Community Centre	HYV Seeds	Social Forestry	
NFE Centre		0	0	0	0	⊥	0	0	1
Health Centre	0		⊥	⊥	0	⊥	0	0	3
Hand Pump	0	⊥			⊥	0	⊥	0	3
IGP	0	⊥	⊥		⊥	0	⊥	⊥	5
Off Season Employment	0	⊥	0	⊥		0	0	⊥	3
Community Centre	⊥	⊥	0	0	⊥		0	⊥	4
HYV Seeds	0	0	⊥	⊥	0	0		0	2
Social Forestry	0	0	0	⊥	⊥	⊥	0		3

Figure 30A: Social Network Mapping

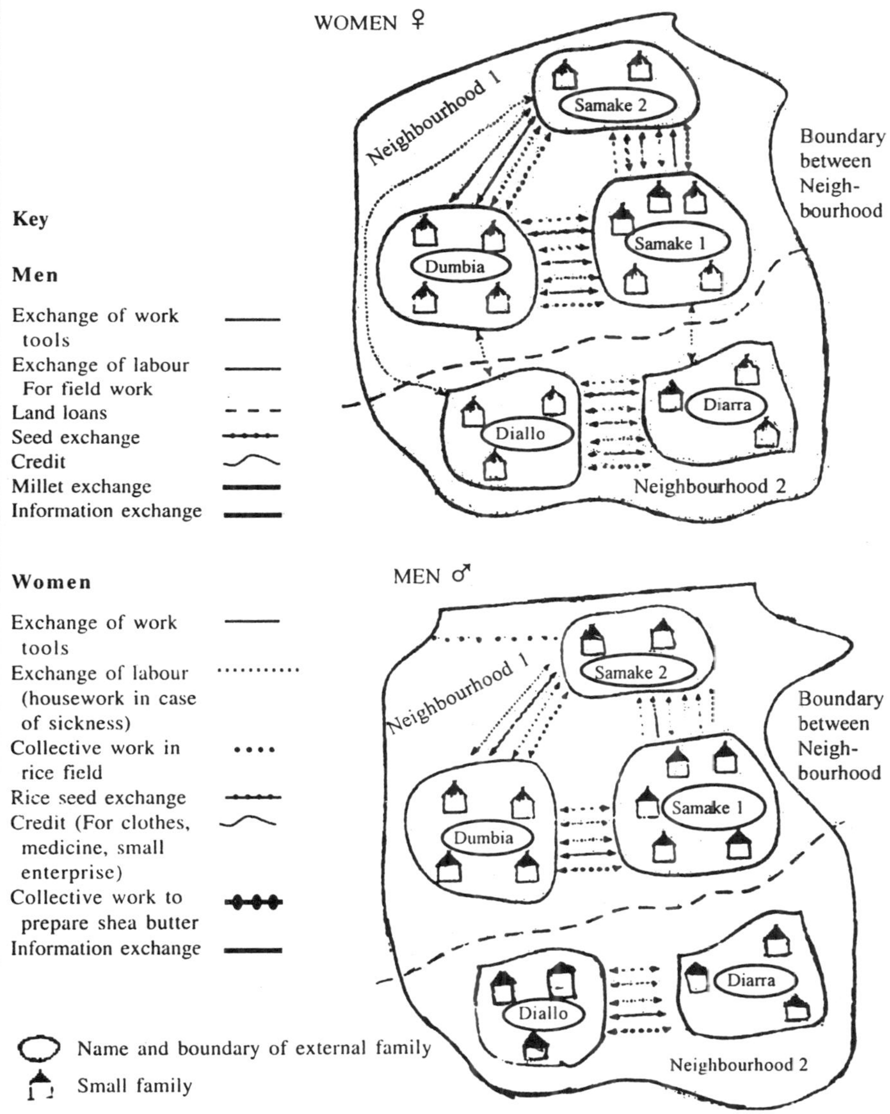

Multi-purpose use of land and trees in Pananao (La Sierra, Dominican Republic), Both men and women are present in this household. R = responsibility to provide a product thereof to the household, L = labour for the establishment, maintenance or harvest, and C = control of resource or process.

Source: *Power, Process and Participation* (London: Intermediate Technology Press) 1996.

on flash cards, ensuring that only one name is written or one flash card. Then these cards are arranged and as items in the first column of a Matrix.

9.2 Tell the participants that they are encouraged to write all the different kinds relationship that individuals/institutions can have with the with the villages. These relationships could be like technical support, finance, maintenance of peace etc. The cards bearing the names of relationships are placed as first row of the matrix.

9.3 Now encourage the participants to ask whether there is a direct or an indirect connection between the institution/individual at serial number 1 and its/her/his relationship with all the different relationships. It is possible that there exists no relationship.

9.4 If there is a direct connection between the two, write 'D' in the square common to them and if there is an indirect connection, write 'I' and if there is no connection, put a cross.

9.5 Repeat the process for all the institutions/individuals occurring in column 1 in relation to all the relationships occurring in row 1.

9.6 Repeat the process for all the institutions/individuals in relation to relationship 2.

9.7 Repeat the process till all the institutions/individuals have been pitted against all the relationships.

9.8 Remember always to ask the question whether a particular institutions/individuals has a direct or indirect or no relationship with the relationship. Never do it the other way around.

9.9 Now ask the participants to count the number of direct and indirect connections that each institution/individual has with the relationships.

9.10 Ask the participants to record each count at the end of each row.

9.11 One may give a score of two for each direct connection, a score of 1 for each indirect connection and 0 for no connection. Then work out a total score for each institution/individual.

9.12 The institutions/individuals are now ranked according to the number of direct/indirect connections or the scores obtained.

9.13 Interview the institutional diagram with the six helpers: why, what, where, whom, when and how.

---

10. Analysis of Institutions: Do the Venn Diagramming for depicting the different institutions/individuals interfacing with the Village

---

In **Step 10**, the participants draw a modified **Venn Diagram** as in Step 9 earlier, for studying the institutional linkages of different institutions/individuals with the village.

10.1 In studying relationship, like in Step 9, the participants assign stones or leaves, paper circles of different sizes to different institutions.

10.2 Those institutions which are closely related to each other are to be placed near each other.

10.3 Those institutions which have overlapping interest are represented by stones, leaves or paper circles, kept overlapping each other.

10.4 Encourage participants to make any change they want to make either about the size of circles or of their positions.

10.5 Interview the modified Venn Diagram using the six helpers: why, what, where, whom, when and how.

10.6 Discuss with the participants the implications of the relationship. For instance, if the institutions have considerable overlap, then there is congruity of interest, objectives, mission, vision and values of the institutions, which in turn shows cohesion.

An example of a Modified Venn Diagram is at *Figure 31*.

---

11. Analysis of Institutions (continued): Do the Force Field Analysis for Institution

---

In **Step 11**, the rationale for conducting the **Force Field Analysis (FFA)** is to determine which are the institutions which impart positive and negative forces on the development of the village.

The steps for doing the **FFA** have been described earlier in Session 6 and are reproduced below:

11.1 Explain the objectives of the exercise to the participants, viz., of finding institutions which impart positive and negative forces on the village or Gram Panchayat etc.

11.2 Please clarify that force is an energy which acting on a body is capable of or tends to change its position. Example of force could be the gravitational force, which pulls down objects to the earth. Also, distinguish between positive and negative forces.

11.3 Keep a large sheet of paper or a flip chart with the present state of the village written or depicted on it, in front of the participants and ask them to concentrate on the same. A horizontal live across the flip chart or floor could depict the present condition. The present condition of the village may also be depicted on the floor or ground with chalk/coloured powder etc. Ask the participants to visualize the village in a state of temporary equilibrium by two sets of institutions releasing

Figure 31: Modified Chappati (Venn) Diagram village Tien Phong, Quang Binh (Vietnam)

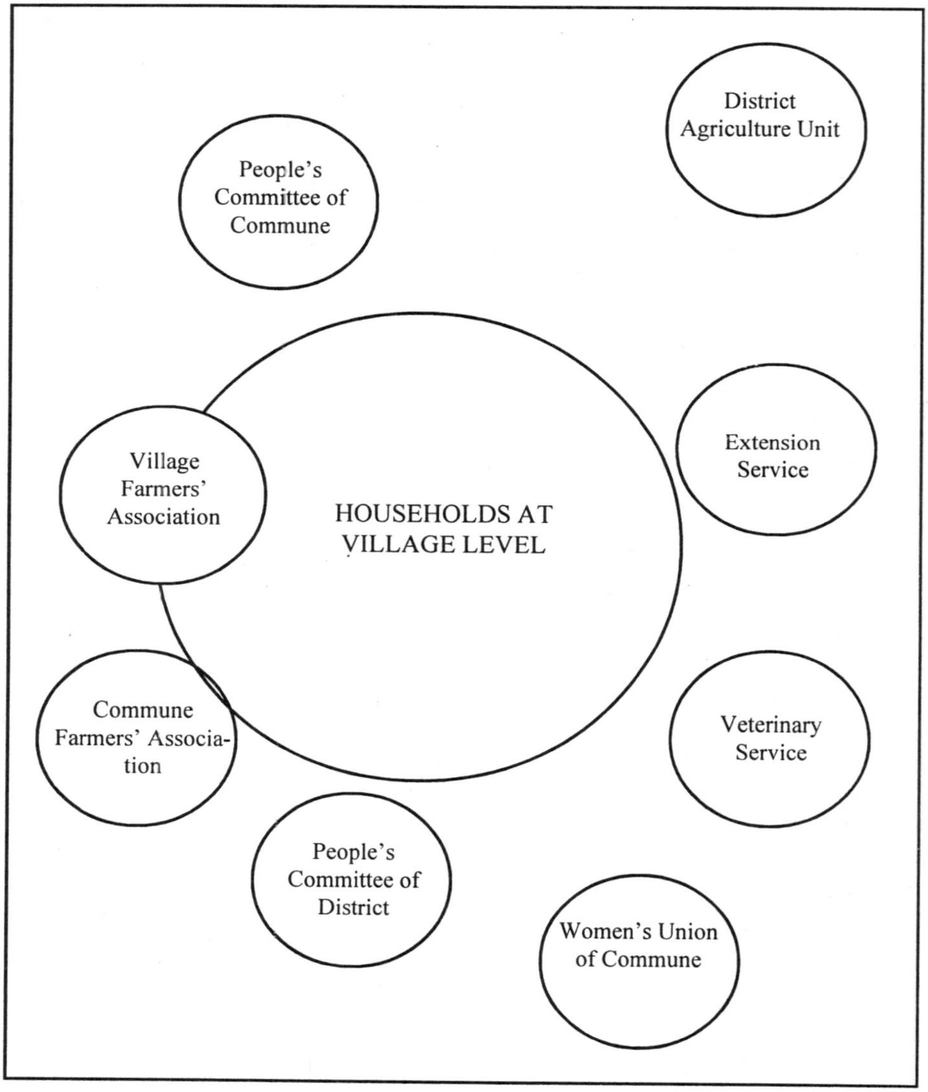

Source: Neela Mukherjee: *Participatory Learning and Action: With 100 Field Methods* (Concept, New Delhi), 2002

opposing forces, one favouring improvement (positive forces) and the other inhibiting them (negative forces). Ask participants to list one set of institutions first followed by the other.

11.4 Facilitate that participants write down or depict the institutions identified on Flash Cards in bold letters. Clarify that if a institution seems to be made of multiple elements, each element should be listed separately as a institutions. Different colour cards can be used for positive and negative forces, if the facilitator so desires.

11.5 Spread the cards with institutions releasing negative forces below the line and those releasing positive forces above the line.

11.6 Ask them to take a look at the cards and see if they would like to make any changes in their position.

11.7 Next the participants may be facilitated to assign weights to each of the institution denoting the strength of forces released. This can be done in two ways. One, the participants can use one of the scoring methods (discussed earlier such as free scoring, fixed scoring or vector scoring) *or* keep each force card at varying distance from the "present status line" in such a way that the distance denotes the strength of the force imparted by the institutions. Greater the distance, higher is the perceived strength of the force on the problem.

11.8 Check with the participants whether they are satisfied with the diagram and relative strength of the forces as depicted or would they like to make any modifications.

11.9 Once they are satisfied with the diagram, ask them to discuss on how they can bring changes in the situation. Which of the institutions releasing positive forces can be reinforced and which institutions releasing negative forces can be reformed, abolished or neutralised?

11.10 Interview the force field Analysis using the six helpers: why, what, where, whom, when and how.

11.11 In example of a Force Field Analysis is at *Figure* 32.

---

12. Visual Method for synthesising what we have learnt from this Session

---

In **Step 12**, the synthesis of the learning points is done by the trainer with the help of participants. The trainer should focus on the key elements of the sessions and help the participants to recall the inputs.

Figure 32: Force Field Analysis

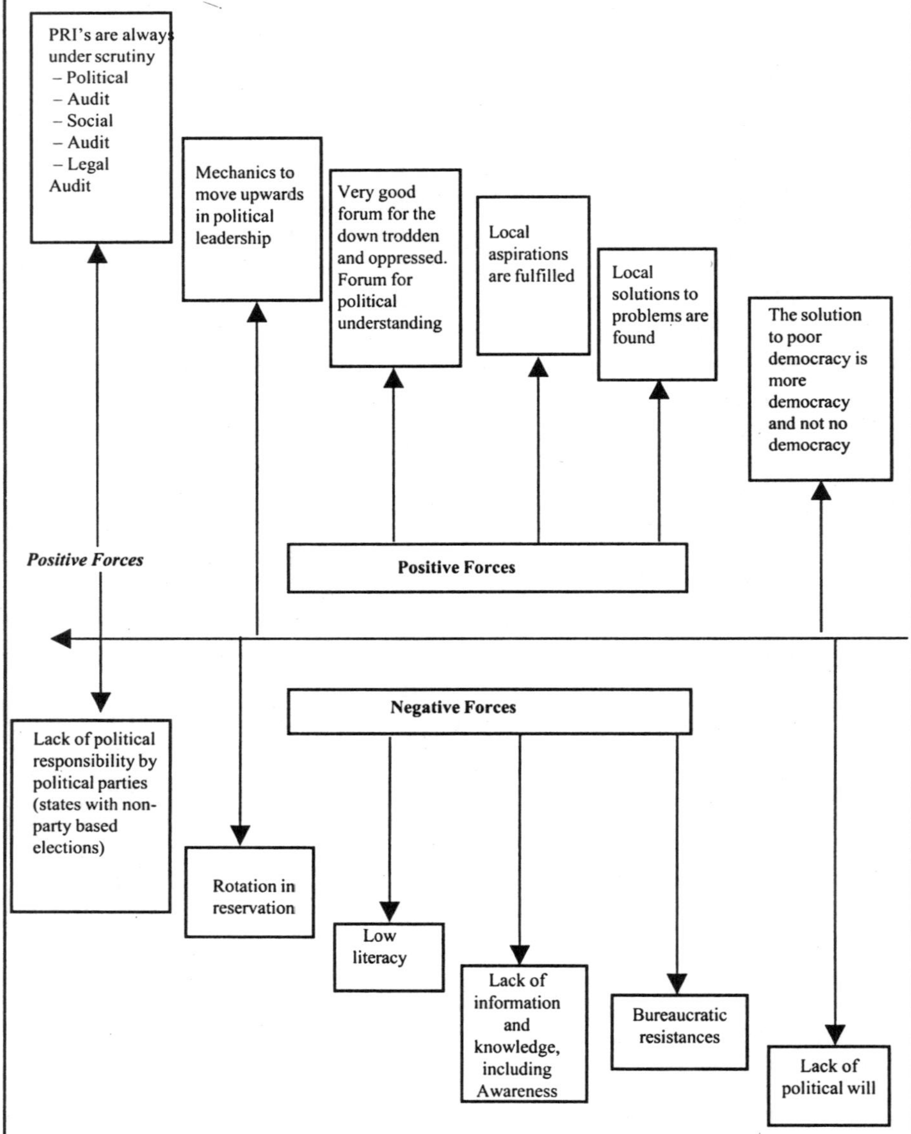

Participants: Yugandhar, Mani, Vasundhara Raje, George.
Facilitator: Amitava Mukherjee
Date: 6th July 2002, LBSNAA, Mussoorie

Base Module Section V
Session 16 Micro-Level Planning Orientation

Session Theme	PROBLEM IDENTIFICATION AND PRIORITIZATION
Duration	255 minutes
Venue	Village locale
Session Objectives	• *To enable the participants to comprehend and prioritise the problems contracting the village in micro-level planning for village development.* • *To impart the functional skills required for engaging in micro-level planning to the participants to overcome the problems.*

Expected Learning Outcomes

- The participants acquire functional skills for using PLA methods in identification of problems village development.
- They learn about prioritisation development problems using the acquired skills.

Content Flow and Training Methodology

Sr. No.	*Content*	*Training Methodology*	*Training Aids*	*Duration (in min.)*
1.	Energising Game	**Step 1** Dragon	None	15
2.	Problem Identification	**Step 2** Semi-Structured Interviews **Step 3** Key Informant Interviews **Step 4** Delphi Method	White paper, pens, flash cards, marker pens	45 45 45 Total: 135
3.	Problem Prioritisation	**Step 5** Scoring and Ranking **Step 6** Matrix Scoring	White paper, pens, seeds, marker pens	45 45 Total: 90
4.	Synthesis by Trainer/ Participant (s)	**Step 7** Visual Method	Notes, charts and matrices created by the participants	15

THE METHODOLOGICAL STEPS FOR SESSION 16

1. Play an energising game

In **Step 1**, all the participants play **"Dragon"**, an active game as follows:

1.1 The objective of the game is to energise the group before they begin the next phase of micro-level planning.
1.2 Find an open space outside and invite everyone to stand there.
1.3 Ask the group to form a line or a dragon and ask participants to run. And concurrently ask the front of the line to catch its tail. Then stop the dragon, turn the participants to face the other direction, and have the tail then catch the head.
1.4 This will result in a lot of smiling and laughing. This provides only a brief and energising break for the participants during the training. This fact should be told to the participants; otherwise, they would be expecting an underlying moral theme from the whole exercise.

2. Hold semi-structured interviews of some villagers

In **Step 2**, the trainer facilitates the participants in holding **Semi-Structured Interviews** of some of the villagers. The trainer should take care to include all sections from the village community, especially women for participating in the interviews. A series of interviews involving different groups of respondents may be held. These interviews may be conducted by different sub-groups from among the participants. **The focus of the interviews is to explore the development problems faced by the villagers, their sources and impact, the coping strategies, restraints and opportunities.** There can be pre-determined set of questions for this kind of interview. The questions asked are open-ended, probing and flexible. "For the local community, the semi-structured interview is conducted in an informal manner in a relaxed setting where queries emerge according to the responses received. It is a combination of outsiders initiating the interview followed by discussion by the local people on the topic concerned."[6]

2.1 The semi-structured interview are to be conducted in the context of the Analyses discussed in session 15. That is, the semi-structured

6. Mukherjee, 2003.

interview are to be conducted to identify the problems based on analysis of space, of time, of institution, of relationships and of priorities/preferences.

2.2 The problem identified are then recorded on cards. One problem is to be written on one card.

2.3 Semi-structured interview are to be held using open-ended questions. Never use leading questions or directive questions or closed ended questions. Examples of open-ended, leading questions, directive questions and closed-ended questions are given below:

Open Ended Question: What is the prospect of harvest this year?
Closed Ended Question: The prospect of harvest this year is bad. Yes/No?
Directive Question: Should you not say that the prospect of harvest is very good this year?
Leading Question: The prospect of a good harvest this year is very good. Isn't it so?

2.4 The trainer and the participants have to listen carefully to all the discussions being held and take notes about the problems being faced by the villagers and other relevant details.

2.5 While recording the outcomes of a semi-structured interview, the participants should distinguish between what are facts, what are opinions, what are rumours and what are hearsay.

---

3. Hold interviews of key-informants

In Step 3, the trainer facilitates the participants to identify some key-informants from among the villagers and then interviewing them. These key-informants may include the Sarpanch, Upa Sarpanch, the SHG leader, some extension workers, etc. The focus of the interviews is the same as in Step 2. Again, the interviewers take notes of all that is discussed.

3.1 The steps followed in step 2 has also to be followed in step 3.

3.2 If the findings of Semi-structured interview with key-informants generate new issues, as distinct from findings generated through Semi-structured interview with group(s), the difference has to be reconciled and/or reasons for the difference probed.

4. Use the Delphi Method to form problem clusters

After the interviews are over, then in **Step 4**, the trainer and the sub-groups of the participants can each make a brief presentation about the development problems faced by the villagers and compare their notes. The problems are made into clusters depending upon their affinity using the **Delphi Method**. The steps to be followed are reproduced below:

4.1 Use the information from the interviews to generate a set of village-level development problems.
4.2 Request volunteers to write each problem on a card/paper (only one per card/paper).
4.3 The cards/papers are then placed upon the ground or pinned upon the wall and grouped according to concept areas. One, some or all the participants can do either of these exercises. Cards showing the same problems are either removed or bunched together.
4.4 The participants must agree on the criteria for grouping or clustering, since this provides the theme areas.
4.5 Now discuss each theme with the participants.

5. Now score and rank the problem clusters

In **Step 5**, use the **Scoring and Ranking Methods** to prioritise the problem clusters. The steps are given below:

5.1 Ask the participants to write down each problem clusters on a flash card, recording only one problem on one card.
5.2 Participants so that the participants arrange the cards in one column.
5.3 Facilitate so that ask the participants identify the most important problem, based upon their discussions with the village community.
5.4 If you are using **Free Scoring**, ask the participants to place a large volume of seeds opposite the most important problem.
5.5 Then ask the participants to identify the next important problem. Encourage the participants to place some seeds against this problem, but lesser in quantity than that placed against the most important problem.
5.6 Proceed in this fashion, placing lesser and lesser quantities of seeds against the other problems according as the gravity of the problem diminishes, until all the problems have been scored.

5.7 Now request the participants to rank the problems. The problem which secured the largest quantity of seeds is the problem with the highest rank. The problem which has the smallest quantity of seeds against it is the lowest in rank. See *Figure 33* for an example of Scoring and Ranking.

5.8 Tree scoring or vector scoring can also be used. Follow steps essential for tree scoring we have discussed earlier.

---

6. Use the Matrix Scoring Method to prioritise the problem clusters

---

In **Step 6**, we use the **Matrix Scoring Method** to compare the different kinds of development problems that have been scored and ranked in the previous step. This method has been already described in Session 2 and *Figure 33* is illustrative. The essential steps are reproduced below:

6.1 Explain clearly the purpose of the exercise to the participants, namely, of finding out their priorities and the criteria against which they have expressed their priorities.

6.2 Initiate a discussion about the clusters of the development problems that have been scored and ranked in the previous step.

6.3 The next step is to facilitate a process which helps the participants to arrive at the criteria which have been used in the scoring and ranking process. Some practitioners find that one the simplest ways to determine the criteria is to do a quick comparison between pairs of problems discussed in the previous step. Arrive at the reasons why the participants find that a particular problem is more serious than the other. These reasons are actually nothing but the criteria. Alternatively a straight forward elucidation of the criteria against which priorities have been expressed can also lead to good results.

6.4 Ensure that the criteria are all positive and precise. Use of positive and negative criteria in the same exercise can be confusing. Write one criteria on one card.

6.5 Draw up a matrix with the problems appearing as the first column and criteria appearing as the first row. One can do it the other way round also. However, keep in mind that the comparisons are made criterion-wise and not problem-wise. It means that you take up a criterion and then do scoring for all the problems against that criterion. Once one criterion is over, move to the next, do the scoring for all the problems and record them until all criteria are covered for each of the problems.

Figure 33: Scoring from 10 Pebbles

Activities \ Involved Individuals	 Female	 Male	 Boy	 Girl	 Timing
Cleaning of cowshed	o o o o o o o o o o	—	—	o o o	1 Hour
Grazing	—	o o o o o o o o	o o o o o o	—	6 a.m. to 6 p.m.
Giving feed	o o o o	o o o o o	o o	o o	15 minutes
Milking	o o o o	o o o o o o	—	—	30 minutes
Taking animal to dispensary	—	o o o o o o o o	—	—	1 Day

Participants: Gokul Mahakud, Pabitra Loha, Kabir Tandi, Purindra, Hrushikesh, Nirjananada Mahakud

Figure 33A: Village – CHIKILI

Agriculture Constraints	Ranking	Solutions
Lack of availability of fertiliser	○ ○ ○	Fertilise department in the panchayat
Lack of knowledge in modern agriculture	○ ○ ○ ○	Gram sevak should visit regularly
Lack of water of irrigation	○	• Deep boaring well • Dug wells in the fields • Lift irrigation ponds • Motor for well
Lack of agriculture equipments (tractor, sprayer)	○ ○ ○ ○ ○	• Demonstration of equipment • Tools to be made • Supply of equipments
Lack of availability of pesticides	○ ○ ○ ○ ○ ○	Pesticide department in panchayat (Ghapuli)
Lack of credit facilities	○ ○	Easy term loan may be provided

Participants: Narupamani Loha, Chandra Kumbhar, Hemsugar kumbhar

6.6 Now interview the Matrix scoring using the six helpers: why, what, where, whom, when and how.

7. Visual Method for synthesising what we have learnt from this Session

In **Step 7**, the synthesis of the learning points is done by the trainer with the help of the participants. The trainer should focus the synthesis on the prioritized problems and the fact that this prioritization can be achieved through the use of participatory methods.

Base Module Section V
Session 17 Micro-Level Planning Orientation

Session Theme	SOLUTION IDENTIFICATION AND PRIORITIZATION
Duration	285 minutes
Venue	Village locale
Session Objectives	*To enable the finding solutions to the problems of the village.* *To impart the functional skills required for finding solutions and prioritising them, in micro-level planning to the participants.*

Expected Learning Outcomes

- The participants acquire functional skills for using PLA methods in finding solutions to problems for micro-level planning development.
- They can adopt a problem-solving approach for identifying solutions for development problems using the acquired skills.

Content Flow and Training Methodology

Sr. No.	*Content*	*Training Methodology*	*Training Aids*	*Duration (in minutes)*
1.	Finding the Objectives: Reversal of the Problem	**Step 1** Locating the objectives	Transparency, flip charts, markers etc.	15
2.	Finding Solutions or Development Interventions	**Step 2** Semi-Structured Interviews **Step 3** Group Discussions **Step 4** Delphi Method	White paper, pens, flash cards, marker pens	45 45 45 Total: 135

Sr. No.	*Content*	*Training Methodology*	*Training Aids*	*Duration (in minutes)*
3.	Prioritisation of Solutions or Development Interventions	**Step 5** Listing **Step 6** Problem-Activity Matrix	White paper, marker pens	15 45 Total: 60
4.	Setting up Activities: The Prioritised Solutions provide the Activities	**Step 7** Reorienting Activity and Aggregating wherever necessary	Do	45
5.	Injecting Gender Equity & Social Justice	**Step 8** Delphi Method **Step 9** Relational Matrix		45
6.	Synthesis by Trainer/ Participant(s)	**Step 10** Visual Method	Notes, charts and matrices created by the participants	15

THE METHODOLOGICAL STEPS FOR SESSION 17

1. Use the Method for the Reversal of the Problem

In Step 1:

1.1 The problems identified are all written down by the participants on flash cards and placed on the floor/ground as one column. The problems are all in the form of negative statements.

1.2 Now encourage the participants to write on card the opposite of the problems, and place them alongside the problem. For instance if the problem identified and prioritised by the community is "Lack of Education facilities for the girl children" then "the opposite of the problem will be Providing Facilities for Girl Children's Education".

1.3 Once all the "opposites" of the problems are worked out and written on cards, they "opposites" are placed alongside the "problem cards". Once the process is completed there will be two columns. One, of the problems and the second, of the "opposites". Now write activities necessary to achieve the "opposites", on separate cards. These cards are placed alongside the respective "opposites". Now there will be three columns. The column specifying the "opposites", is the column of solutions. The following table illustrates the point.

Problems	*Opposites*	*Solutions*
Unemployment	Employment for all	(i) Providing employment for all, (ii) Creating off farm employment, (iii) Making credit available.
Illiteracy amongst girls	Literacy amongst girls	Providing Education for girls
Lack of Drinking water in the villages	Drinking water available in village	(i) Providing drinking water by digging wells, (ii) Ensuring water supply by running water trains, (iii) Fitting a diesel pump in the river.

1.4 Now if there are more than one problem and there are more than one solution, we may need to prioritise the same. The facilitator should encourage people to rank or score the problems and/or the solutions using the method of dismissal earlier.

1.5 The participants now have a list of prioritised solutions of problems.

2. *Hold semi-structured interviews of some villagers*

In Step 2, the trainer can alternatively facilitate the participants in holding **Semi-Structured Interviews** of some of the villagers. The trainer should once again take care to include all sections from the village community, especially women for participating in the interviews. A series of interviews involving different groups of respondents are conducted by different sub-groups from among the participants. **The focus of the semi-structured interviews is to explore the solution or development interventions to the development problems which have been identified in the previous** session.

2.1 The trainer and the participants have to listen carefully to all the discussions being held and take notes about the solutions or development interventions for the problems suggested by the villagers and other relevant details.
2.2 See sections 2.1 to 2.5 session 16. Follow the same steps.
2.3 The same set of activities can also be done in focused group discussion.

---

3. *Use the Delphi Method to cluster the solutions or development interventions*

After the interviews are over, then in **Step 3**, the trainer and the sub-groups of the participants can each make a brief presentation about the solutions or development interventions suggested by the villagers and compare their notes. The solutions are clustered depending upon their affinity using the **Delphi Method**. The steps to be followed are reproduced below:

3.1 Use the information from the interviews to generate the solutions to the development problems.
3.2 Request volunteers to write each solution on a card or a piece of paper (only one per card/paper).
3.3 The card or a piece of paper are then placed upon the ground or pinned upon the wall and grouped according to concept areas. One, some or all the participants can do either this exercise. Exact duplicates are removed.
3.4 The participants must agree on the criteria for grouping or clustering, since this provides the theme areas.
3.5 Now discuss each theme area with the participants.

---

4. *Now list the solutions or the development interventions*

In **Step 4**, list the main solutions that flow from the previous step.

---

5. *Use the Problem-Activity Matrix Method to determine the relationship between the solutions and the problems*

In **Step 5**, we use the **Problem-Activity Matrix** to determine the relationship which the different solutions or development interventions have with the problems that have been identified, scored and ranked in the previous session. The following steps are suggested for this exercise:

5.1 Ask the participants to write the different identified problems on Flash Cards. Place the flash cards as items in the first column of a Matrix.

5.2 Ask the participants to write the planned development interventions (activities) on Flash Cards. Place this set of Flash Cards as items in the first row of the Matrix.

5.3 Now encourage the participants to ask whether there is a direct or an indirect connection between problem number 1 and development intervention number 1. It is possible that there is no connection between the intervention and the problem.

5.4 If there is a direct connection between the two, write 'D' in the square common to them; if there is an indirect connection, write 'I' and if there is no connection, put a cross.

5.5 Repeat the process for all development activities in relation to problem 1.

5.6 Repeat the process for all the development activities in relation to problem 2.

5.7 Repeat the process till all the planned activities have been pitted against all the identified problems.

5.8 Remember to always ask the question whether a particular activity has a direct or indirect or no relationship with the problems. Never do it the other way around.

5.9 Now ask the participants to count the number of direct and indirect connections that each activity has with the problems.

5.10 Ask the participants to record each count at the bottom of each column.

5.11 One may give a score of two for each direct connection, a score of 1 for each indirect connection and 0 for no connection. Then work out a total score for each activity.

5.12 The activities are now ranked according to the number of direct/indirect connections or the scores obtained. This ranked set of activities now become action points.

An example of a Problem Activity Matrix is at *Figure 34*.

---

6. *Draw a Relational Matrix of the Issue regarding gender and the prioritized activities*

In **Step 6**, the participants draw the **Relational Matrices** for the different Gender Issues and the activities. The steps for this exercise are similar to those that have been enumerated in Session 15. They are:

Figure 34: Problem Activity Matrix

	Activity 1	Activity 2	Activity 3		Activity n-1	Activity n
Problems of Widows	✓	✓	✗	✗	✓	✗
Female Headed Households	✗	✓	✗	✗	✗	✓
Disabled	✓	✗	✓	✓	✗	✗
Marginalisation of Scheduled Castes	✓	✓	✓	✗	✗	✓
Isolation of Scheduled Tribes	✓	✓	✓	✗	✗	✓
Social Exclusion of Especially Disadvantaged Groups (Scavengers etc.)	✓	✓	✗	✓	✗	✓

Note: A tick mark indicted the benefit of the activity to the relevant group. A cross mark indicates non-applicability of the activity to the relevant group.

Source: Amitava Mukherjee: *Participatory Rural Appraisal Methods and Applications in Rural Planning* (New Delhi: Vikas Publishing House 1995 and 2nd revised editon by New Delhi: Concept Publishing Company, 2003).

6.1 Ask the participants to write the issues on gender equity and social justice on Flash Cards and place them as items in the first column of a Matrix.

6.2 Ask the participants to write the activities prioritised in step 6 as items in the first row.

6.3 Now encourage the participants to ask whether there is a direct or an indirect connection between the Gender Issue on Gender equity and social justice number 1 and the activity number 1 *or* there is no connection.

6.4 If there is a direct connection between the two, write 'D' in the square common to them; if there is an indirect connection, write 'I' and if there is no connection, put a cross.

6.5 Repeat the process for all the Gender Issues in relation to activity number 1.

6.6 Repeat the process for all the Gender Issues in relation to activity number 2.

6.7 Repeat the process till all the Gender Issues have been pitted against all the activities.

6.8 Remember to always ask the question whether activity planned has a direct or indirect or no relationship with Issue Cluster. Never do it the other way around.

6.9 Now ask the participants to count the number of direct and indirect connections that each Gender Issue has with the activities.

6.10 Ask the participants to record each count at the bottom of each column.

6.11 If the activities address the activities, then the activities planned would meet the requirements for ensuring gender equity.

6.12 In case Issues are not, repeat not, addressed by the activities, then additional steps have to be taken to ensure that activities are generated to address the issue. For so doing all the steps for planning have to be repeated with specific focus on gender equity.

6.13 Repeat step 6 for Issues relating to social justice.

7. Visual Method for synthesising what we have learnt from this Session

In Step 7, the synthesis of the learning points is done by the trainer with the help of the participants. Trainer should refer to the visuals created repeatedly.

Base Module Section V
Session 18 Micro-Level Planning Orientation

Session Theme	ACTION PLANNING FOR MICRO-LEVEL PLANNING
Duration	195 minutes
Venue	Village locale
Session Objectives	*To enable the participants to comprehend the process of stakeholder participation in action planning for village development.* *To impart the functional skills required for engaging in action planning to the participants.*

Expected Learning Outcomes

- The participants acquire functional skills for using PLA methods in action planning for village development.
- They have a hands-on understanding of how to develop an Action Plan from a Tactical Plan.

Content Flow and Training Methodology

Sr. No.	*Content*	*Training Methodology*	*Training Aids*	*Duration (in minutes)*
1.	Injecting the Time Element	**Step 1**	Flash Cards, Flip Charts, Marker, Pens	60 minutes
2.	Determining the Allocations for Projects	**Step 2**	-Do-	60 minutes
3.	Budgeting	**Step 4**		60 minutes
4.	Synthesis by Trainer/ Participant(s)	**Step 10** Visual Method	Notes, charts and matrices created by the participants	15

THE METHODOLOGICAL STEPS FOR SESSION 18

1. *Use of Methods for Determining Allocation of Projects*

1.1 In **Step 1**, all the activities or development interventions are all written down by the participants on flash cards.

1.2 First, the participants identity the activities or development interventions which people themselves can execute without any external help, are classified as People's Sector.

1.3 Second, the participants classify the activities or development interven-tions which can be executed with credit, like a flour mill or an oil mill. These are classified as the Bank sector.

1.4 Third, the participants then identify the activities and development interventions which can be carried out, by funds from the Government only, like building bridges or constructing roads. These activities are clubbed under another sector called the Government sector.

1.5 Fourth, identify activities which can be carried out by mobilising funds from the donor agencies, like UNICEF or international non-government funding agencies like CARE, Oxfarm and Ford Foundation. Such activities can be child immunisation, or supplementary nutrition. These activities may be classified as Donor Sector Activities.

1.6 Seventh, now let the participants identify activities which requires contribution and combined effort of all, namely, the people, banks, donor and the Government. These activities are clustered under the Combined Sector.

1.7 Finally, facilitate so that the participants identify activities which cannot be executed by any of the above sectors. This is called the 'Residual Sector'.

1.8 Develop a Table such as at *Figure 35*, called Activity Sector-Classification Matrix.

1.9 The participants' attention should now be drawn to the importance of this Activity-Sector Matrix, viz., of locating sources of financing.

2. *Methods for using Time Element*

2.1 In **Step 2,** take the Table as at *Figure 35* (the Activity-Sector Classification).

Figure 35: Activity-Sector Classification Matrix

People Sector	*Bank Sector*	*Government Sector*	*Donor Sector*	*PRI Sector*	*Combined Sector*	*Residual Sector*
Activity -1p	Activity -1b	Activity -1g	Activity -1d	Activity -1pi	Activity -1c	Activity -1r
Activity -2p	Activity -2b	Activity -2g	Activity -2d	Activity -2pi	Activity -2c	Activity -2r
Activity -3p	Activity -3b	Activity -3g	Activity -3d	Activity -3pi	Activity -3c	Activity -3r
Activity -4p	Activity -4b	Activity -4g	Activity -4d	Activity -4pi	Activity -4c	Activity -4r
Activity -5p	Activity -5b	Activity -5g	Activity -5d	Activity -5pi	Activity -5c	Activity -5r
Activity -6p	Activity -6b	Activity -6g	Activity -6d	Activity -6pi	Activity -6c	Activity -6r

Note: p stands for people's sector; b for bank sector, g for government sector, d for donor sector, pi for PRI sector, c for combined sector and r for residual sector.

Source: Amitava Mukherjee: *Participatory Rural Appraisal Methods and Applications in Rural Planning* (New Delhi: Vikas Publishing House 1995 and 2nd revised editon by New Delhi: Concept Publishing Company, 2003).

2.2 Facilitate so that participants are able to identify activities in People's sector which "Must Be Done". Let the participants write 'M' against these activities. The participants then locate the activities which "should be done" and write 'S' on cards showing these activities. Finally the participants should identify the activities which "could be done" and write 'C' on cards bearing names of these activities.

2.3 The participants repeat the same process for the Bank Sector, Donor Sector, Combined sector and Residual Sector Activities.
2.4 The participants generate the MSC-Analysis Matrix as at *Figure 36.*

2.5 The facilitator is to draw attention of the participants to the fact that "Must Do" activities are mandatory, without which the intervention will collapse; "should activities" enhances the quality of the intervention and "could do" activities embellishes the interventions.

3. *Budgeting*

3.1 In **Step 3**, budgets are prepared.
3.2 For People sector, the costs of activities are estimated by the people themselves. The participants may facilitate the process.
3.3 For the Bank sector budget the costs of interventions are calculated by the participants according to unit cost norm of the Banks or NABARD.
3.4 For the Government sector, costs of activities are to be estimated by the participants according to norms specified by the Government. If the community facts that the costs are "under-estimates; a "difference of costs" charge may also be prepared.
3.5 In case of activities covered by the Donor sector, it may be necessary to arrive at cost estimated from different sources: people's estimate, Bank's/ NABARD's unit costs/Government prescribed cost, because Donor often do not often have fixed costs.
3.6 Cost estimates for combined sector may also be arrived at following the clues provided in 3.5.
3.7 The sub-totals are then added to arrive at the total.
3.8 *Figure 37* is a format for developing a budget.

4. *Synthesises*

In **Step 4**, the trainer synthesises the entire Micro-Planning Process through a visual or visuals. She/he may like to use *Figures 35, 38* and *Figure 39* to synthesise the learnings on micro-planning.

Figure 36: MSC Analysis-Time Matrix

		First Year	*Second Year*	*Third Year*	*Fourth Year*	*Fifth Year*
People's Sector Activities	Must Do	Activity 1p	Activity 1p	Activity 1p	Activity 1p	Activity 1p
	Should Do	Activity 1p	Activity 1p	Activity 1p	Activity 1p	Activity 1p
	Could Do	Activity 1p	Activity 1p	Activity 1p	Activity 1p	Activity 1p
Bank Sector Activities	Must Do	Activity 1b	Activity 2b	Activity 3b	Activity 4b	Activity 5b
	Should Do	Activity 1b	Activity 2b	Activity 3b	Activity 4b	Activity 5b
	Could Do	Activity 1b	Activity 2b	Activity 3b	Activity 4b	Activity 5b
Govern-ment Sector Activities	Must Do	Activity 1g	Activity 2g	Activity 3g	Activity 4g	Activity 5g
	Should Do	Activity 1g	Activity 2g	Activity 3g	Activity 4g	Activity 5g
	Could Do	Activity 1g	Activity 2g	Activity 3g	Activity 4g	Activity 5g
Donor Sector Activities	Must Do	Activity 1d	Activity 2d	Activity 3d	Activity 4d	Activity 5d
	Should Do	Activity 1d	Activity 2d	Activity 3d	Activity 4d	Activity 5d
	Could Do	Activity 1d	Activity 2d	Activity 3d	Activity 4d	Activity 5d
PRI Sector Activities	Must Do	Activity 1p	Activity 2g	Activity 3p	Activity 4p	Activity 5p
	Should Do	Activity 1p	Activity 2g	Activity 3p	Activity 4p	Activity 5p
	Could Do	Activity 1p	Activity 2g	Activity 3p	Activity 4p	Activity 5p
Combined Sector Activities	Must Do	Activity 1c	Activity 2c	Activity 3c	Activity 4c	Activity 5c
	Should Do	Activity 1c	Activity 2c	Activity 3c	Activity 4c	Activity 5c
	Could Do	Activity 1c	Activity 2c	Activity 3c	Activity 4c	Activity 5c
Residual Sector Activities	Must Do	Activity 1r	Activity 2r	Activity 3r	Activity 4r	Activity 5r
	Should Do	Activity 1r	Activity 2r	Activity 3r	Activity 4r	Activity 5r
	Could Do	Activity 1r	Activity 2r	Activity 3r	Activity 4r	Activity 5r
		1st Year	2nd Year	3rd Year	4th Year	5th Year
Total	Total Must Do					
	Total Should Do					
	Total Could Do					
	Grand Total					

Notes: Add up all the "must" activities of the year. Add up all the "should" activities of the year. Add up all the "Could" activities of the year. Add the total of the Must, Should and Could Do activities. P stands for people's sector; b for bank sector, g for government sector, d for donor sector, pi for PRI sector, c for combined sector and r for residual sector. The numerical stands for the year of implementation

Source: Amitava Mukherjee: *Participatory Rural Appraisal Methods and Applications in Rural Planning* (New Delhi: Vikas Publishing House 1995 and 2nd revised editon by New Delhi: Concept Publishing Company, 2003).

Figure 37: Year Wise Sector-Wise Budget Tables

	Quantity Required	Equipment	Infrastructure Required	Information Required	Person-Hours of labour required	Money Required	Risks Involved
Activity 1p							
Activity 2p							
Activity 3p							
Activity 4p							
Activity 5p							
Activity 6p							
Activity ...							
Activity N-1p							
Activity Np							
Grand Total for the year							

Notes: 'p' stands for people's sector. For other sectors, 'p' will be substituted by 'g' or 'b' for government and bank sector respectively or whatever as the case may be.

Figure 38: The Planning Cycle: Tactical Planning Stage: Stage-I (Mukherjee Methodology)

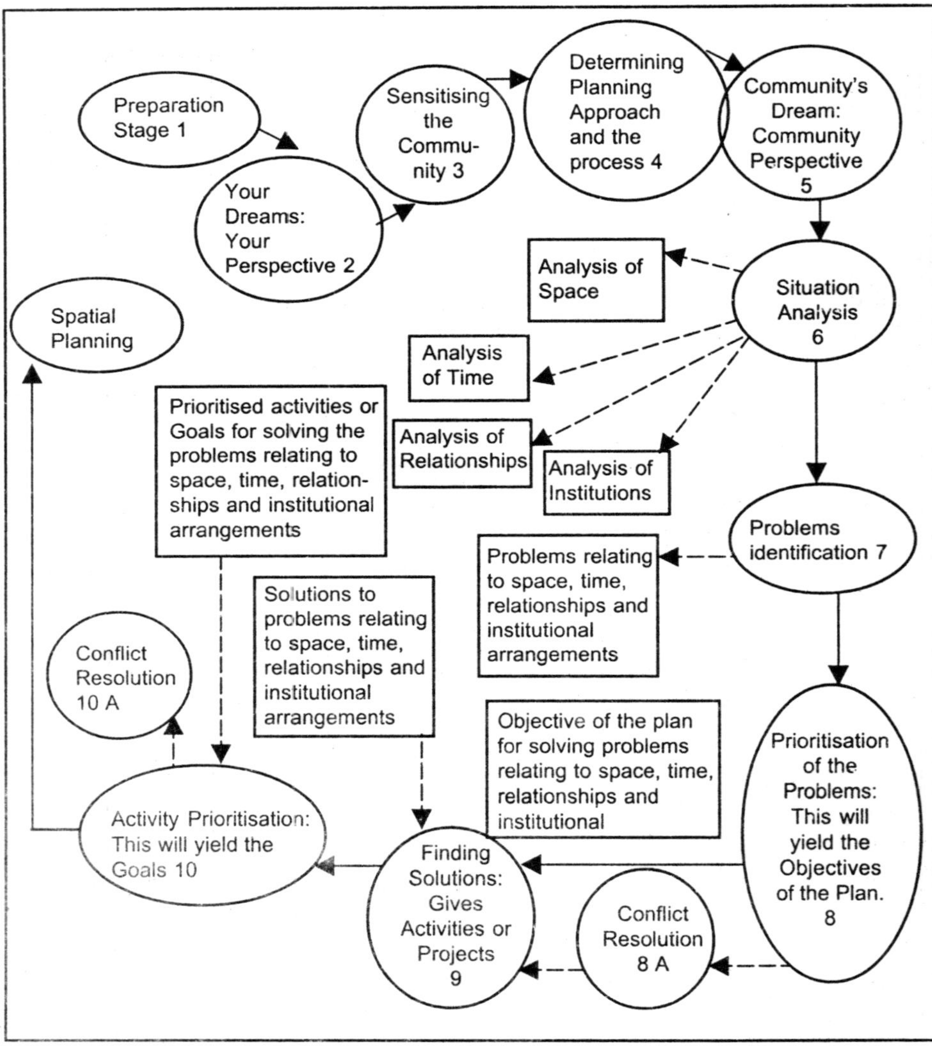

Source: Amitava Mukherjee, Development Tracks RTC, 2000.

Figure 39: Action Planning Stage

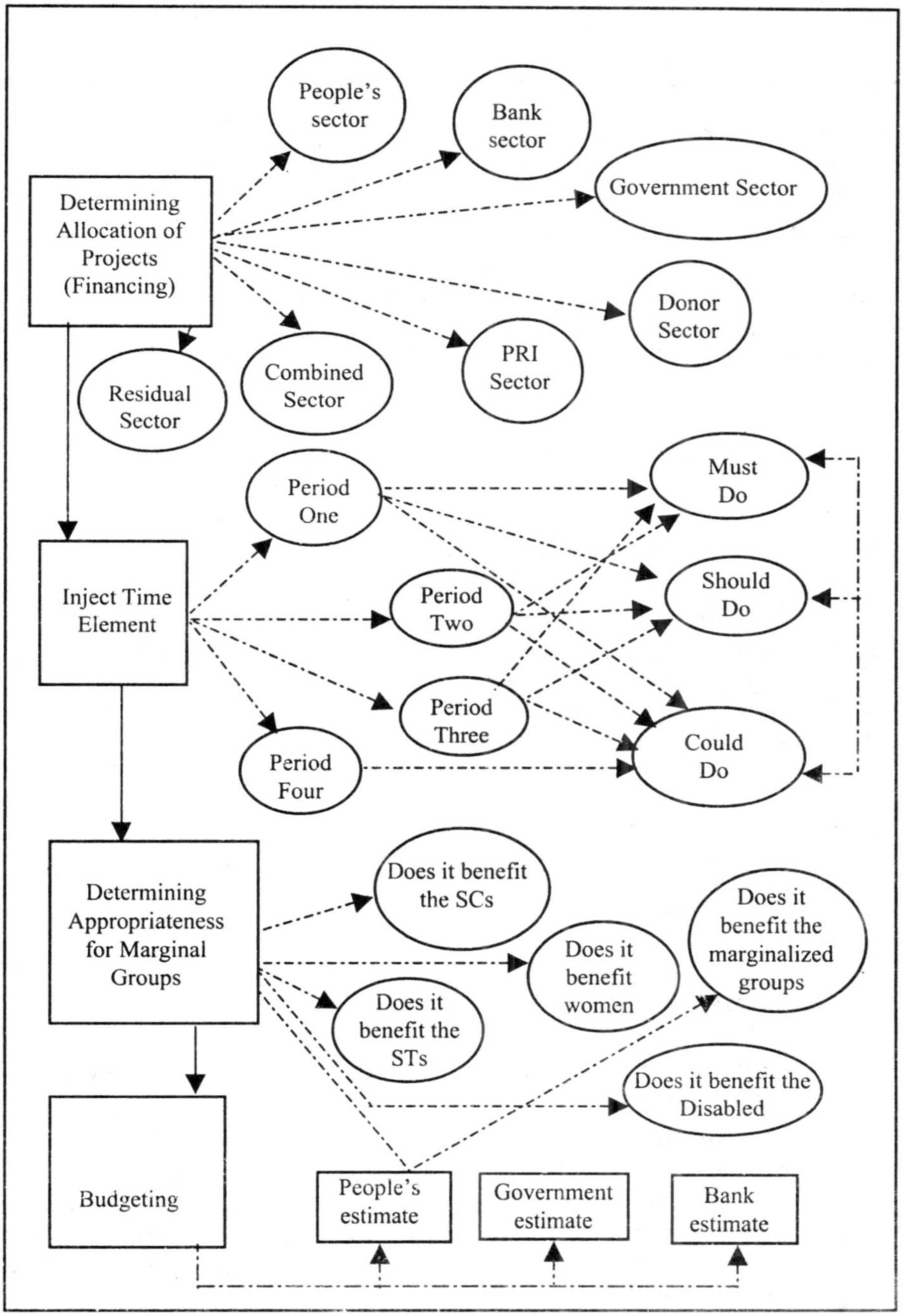

Base Module Section V
Last Session 19 **Micro-Level Planning Orientation**

Session Theme	ASSESSMENT OF TRAINING
Duration	75 minutes
Venue	Classroom without fixed furnitures
Seating	Sit/stand on the ground forming a circle; move around the room for the group work
Session Objective	*To assess the impact of the training process*

Expected Learning Outcomes

- The principal learnings that have flowed from the training are ascertained by the trainers.
- Each participant has prepared a proactive development agenda.

Content Flow and Training Methodology

Sr. No.	*Content*	*Training Methodology*	*Training Aids*	*Duration (in minutes)*
1.	Presentation by the Participants about the learning and action points	Step 1 Brainstorming Step 2 Delphi Method	Flip Charts, marker pens, flash cards	45
2.	Synthesis of Learning and Action Points by Trainer	Step 3 Visual Method	As desired by the trainer	30

THE METHODOLOGICAL STEPS FOR SESSION 5.3

1. In **Steps 1 & 2**, use **Brainstorming** and the **Delphi Technique** for enabling the participants to present the learning points and the corresponding action points for preparing their development agendas.
2. In **Step 3**, the trainer synthesising the learnings and the action points recalling the list of expectations from the training programme which the participants had prepared in Session No. 1.1 held on the very first day.

Chapter IV

A Suite of Training Modules

NOTE TO THE TRAINER FOR CHAPTER IV

INTRODUCTION

Chapter IV entitled "A Suite of Training Modules" is a collection of ten training modules designed in the overall training context of Panchayati Raj Governance for different audiences. The modules have been created by different combinations of the session plans of the Base Module, with suitable modifications wherever necessary. The modified session plans for Module Nos. 2, 3 and 4 have also been designed. The detailed content flow for Module Nos. 5-10 have been given and the trainer will be required to design the corresponding session plans from this information using the Base Module as a reference point.

The details of the ten training modules are given in **Table 1**.

Table 1

Module Description	*Module Objectives*	*Training Audience*	*Duration (in days)*	*Comments*
***Module 1*: Introductory Training for the Members and Government Functionaries of the Village Panchayat**	(a) To create an awareness amongst the participants about the basic principles of self government and people-centred community development and the rights and duties of the elected members and functionaries of the Village Panchayat. (b) To enhance the practical understanding of the participants about the basic structure and functioning of the Village Panchayat for meeting the goals of economic development, gender equity and social justice.	(a) The elected members and government functionaries of the Village Panchayat. (b) NGOs, Self-Help Groups, Mahila Mandals[1], Youth Mandals[2] (c)Bank Managers and their field officers.	5	There are 11 sessions and they have been drawn from the Base Module. The trainer will have to follow the corresponding session plans given in the Base Module.

1. Women's Groups
2. Groups of Young Men and Women formed at the village level. They participate in many activities like, community development and sports.

Module Description	*Module Objectives*	*Training Audience*	*Duration (in days)*	*Comments*
	(c) To orient the participants with the principles of good management of the Village Panchayat and the mechanisms for promoting them.			
***Module 2:* Introductory Training for the Members and Officers of the Intermediate Panchayat**	(a) To create an awareness amongst the participants about the basic principles of self government and people-centred community development and the rights and duties of the elected members and functionaries of the Intermediate Panchayat. (b) To enhance the practical understanding of the participants about the basic structure and functioning of the Intermediate Panchayat for meeting the goals of	(a) The elected members and government officials of the Intermediate Panchayat. (b) NGOs and other Voluntary Agencies and Groups. (c) Bank Branch Managers within the jurisdiction of the Intermediate Panchayat.	5	The same 11 sessions as in Module 1 have been included from the Base Module. But the focus of training being the Intermediate Panchayat, the session plans have been suitably modified and reproduced for the reference of the trainer.

Module Description	*Module Objectives*	*Training Audience*	*Duration (in days)*	*Comments*
	economic development, gender equity and social justice. (c) To orient the participants with the principles of good management of the Intermediate Panchayat and the mechanisms for promoting them.			
Module 3: **Training-cum- Awareness Camp for the Zilla Parishad Members and Officers**	(a) To create an awareness amongst the participants about the basic principles of self government and people-centred community development and the rights and duties of the elected members and functionaries of the Zilla Parishad. (b) To enhance the practical understanding of the participants about the basic structure and	(a) The members of the Zilla Parishad. (b) District Officers of the Zilla Parishad.	4	Eleven sessions have been included from the Base Module. But the focus of training being the Zilla Parishad, the session plans have been suitably modified and reproduced for the reference of the trainer.

Module Description	*Module Objectives*	*Training Audience*	*Duration (in days)*	*Comments*
	functioning of the Zilla Parishad for meeting the goals of economic development, gender equity and social justice. (c) To orient the participants with the principles of good management of the Zilla Parishad & the mechanisms for promoting them.			
***Module 4*: Training-cum-Awareness Camp for the Key Zilla Parishad Office Bearers**	(a) To create an awareness amongst the participants about the current state of the PRIs in India as institutions of self-government and the rights and duties of the Key Zilla Parishad Office Bearers. (b) To enhance the practical understanding of the participants about the basic structure and	(a) Chairpersons of the Zilla Parishads. (b) Chief Executive Officers of the Zilla Parishad.	3 ½	There are 10 sessions either drawn from Module 3 or the Base Module. For the session on the Person Power Management for the Zilla Parishad, some tips about the methodology to be followed have been given.

Module Description	*Module Objectives*	*Training Audience*	*Duration (in days)*	*Comments*
	functioning of the PRIs for meeting the goals of economic development, gender equity and social justice. (c) To orient the participants with the principles of good management of the PRIs and the mechanisms for promoting them.			
Module 5: **Operational Training for the Members and Officers of the Zilla Parishad**	(a) To help the participants to realize their potential and capacity to change the rural political, economic and social scenario especially in respect of economic development, gender equity and social justice. (b) To acquaint the elected representatives with the structure of	(a) Zilla Parishad Chairperson and Vice-Chairperson. (b) Officers and Heads of Departments of the Zilla Parishad. (c) Bank Officers from the District.		The content flow is same as the Base Module with suitable modifications. The thematic clusters have been given from which the trainer can prepare the session plans by referring to the Base Module. This was the

Module Description	*Module Objectives*	*Training Audience*	*Duration (in days)*	*Comments*
	Panchayati Raj bodies in the light of constitutional provisions, State Government Acts, Rules and Executive orders. (c) To appraise the elected representatives with the structure and functioning of Panchayati Raj bodies in the different States and make a comparison with their own State. (d) To orient the participants about knowledge and necessary skills in planning and implementation of rural development programmes with special reference to gender equity and social justice.			exercise which was followed for designing the session plans for the Base Module.

Module Description	*Module Objectives*	*Training Audience*	*Duration (in days)*	*Comments*
Module 6: **Operational Training for the Members and Officers of the Intermediate Panchayat**	(a) To help the participants to realize their potential and capacity to change the rural political, economic and social scenario. (b) To acquaint the elected representatives with the structure of Panchayati Raj bodies in the light of constitutional provisions, State Government Acts, Rules and Executive orders. (c) To appraise the elected representatives with the structure and functioning of Panchayati Raj bodies in the different States and make a comparison with their own State. (d) Appraise the participants about the state of development in	(a) Pramukh and Upa-Pramukh of the Panchayat Samity. (b) District Officers and Officers of the Panchayat Samity. (c) Bank Officers from the District.		The content flow is same as the Base Module with suitable modifications. The thematic clusters have been given from which the trainer can prepare the session plans by referring to the Base Module.

Module Description	*Module Objectives*	*Training Audience*	*Duration (in days)*	*Comments*
	the country and the State in the context of the different approaches to development, including the state of gender equity and social justice (e) To help the participants acquire attitudes, knowledge and skills necessary in for brining about social and economic development.			
Module 7: **Mass Awareness- cum-Motivation Camps for the Members and Officers of the Panchayat Raj Institutions**	(a) To refresh the understanding of the participants about the basic principles and objectives of establishing the PRIs in India and the rights and duties of PRI functionaries. (b) To assess how far the objectives have been met and why the PRI functionaries have not	(a) All Elected Panchayat functionaries including the Chairperson, Zilla Parishad; Pramukh, Panchayat Samity and the Sarpanch, Village Panchayat. (b) The key State officials like the Chief Secretary and departmental Secretaries and District officials.	1	The content flow has been suggested. The trainer will be required to design the corresponding session plans from these details, modifying those of the Base Module, wherever possible.

Module Description	*Module Objectives*	*Training Audience*	*Duration (in days)*	*Comments*
	achieved their full potential of changing the rural political, economic and social scenario.			
Module 8: Training-cum-Motivation Camps for the Members of the Gram Sabha	(a) To review the basic principles and objectives of establishing the PRIs in India and the rights and duties of the Gram Sabha. (b) To do a SWOT[3] analysis of how far the objectives have been met and why the PRI functionaries have not achieved their full potential.	(a) Members of the Gram Sabha. (b) The key government officers and staff at the village level.	4 hours	The content flow has been suggested. The trainer will be required to design the corresponding session plans from these details, modifying those of the Base Module, wherever possible.
Module 9: Mass Awareness Camps about Panchayati Raj	(a) To generate awareness about the basic principles and objectives of establishing the PRIs in India and the rights and duties of PRI	Members of the Public, NGOs and other interest groups.	4 hours	The content flow has been suggested. The trainer will be required to design the corresponding

3. Strengths, Weaknesses, Opportunities and Threats.

Module Description	*Module Objectives*	*Training Audience*	*Duration (in days)*	*Comments*
	functionaries. (b) To create public awareness of the expected role of the PRIs as institutions of self-government.			session plans from these details, modifying those of the Base Module, wherever possible.
Module 10: **Awareness Camps for the Media About Panchayati Raj**	(a) To provide an insight into the basic principles and objectives of establishing the PRIs in India and the rights and duties of PRI functionaries as enjoined in the letter and spirit of the Seventy Third Constitutional Amendment Act. (b) To enable the participants to make an assessment of how far the objectives have been met and why the PRIs have not achieved their full potential.	(a) Members of the National Press (Reporters/Chief Reporters) (b) The Chief of the News Bureau (c) The Editors of the Vernacular Press.	4 hours	The content flow has been suggested. The trainer will be required to design the corresponding session plans from these details, modifying those of the Base Module, wherever possible.

Module 1

Introductory Training for the Members and Government Functionaries of the Village Panchayat

PROFILE OF MODULE 1

INTRODUCTORY TRAINING FOR THE VILLAGE PANCHAYAT MEMBERS AND FUNCTIONARIES

Objectives

- To create an awareness amongst the participants about the basic principles of self government and people-centred community development and the rights and duties of the elected members and functionaries of the Village Panchayat and why these rights and duties are available to the Village Panchayat Members.
- To enhance the practical understanding of the participants about the basic structure and functioning of the Village Panchayat for meeting the goals of economic development, gender equity and social justice.
- To orient the participants with the principles of good management of the Village Panchayat and the mechanisms for promoting them.

Participants

- The elected members and government functionaries of the Village Panchayat.
- NGOs, Self-Help Groups, Mahila Mandals[4], Youth Mandals[5]
- Bank Managers and their field officers

Contents

1. Self-government and institutions of self government in the context of PRIs: Concepts, framework, implications and frame of action for economic and social development, for gender and social justice.
2. Concept and Principles of Democratic Decentralisation.
3. The Development Paradigm and its evolution.
4. Concept of Gender and Social Justice.

---

4. Women's Groups.
5. Groups of Young Men and Women formed at the village level. They participate in many activities like, community development and sports.

5. The role and structure of PRIs and the Gram Sabha.
6. The Seventy-Third Constitutional Amendment Act and the State Conformity Acts.
7. *De jure* Duties[6] and Responsibilities of the Gram Sabha and the Village Panchayat.
8. *De facto* Duties and responsibilities of the Gram Sabha and the Village Panchayat.
9. Gap between *de jure* and *de facto* functions of the Gram Sabha and the Village Panchayat and the reasons for this gap.
10. Ways and means to fill the gap between the *de jure* and *de facto* functions of the Gram Sabha and the Village Panchayat.
11. Role of line departments vis-à-vis the Village Panchayat and the obstacles for social and economic development and gender and social justice.
12. How to resolve the difficulties that affect the relationship between line departments and the Village Panchayat.
13. Emerging roles of MLAs, MLCs and MPs in the PRI set-up.
14. Management of Community Development Programmes.
15. People-centred Behaviours and Attitudes.
16. Autonomy and accountability of the Village Panchayat in both performance and finances.
17. Transparency in the affairs of the Village Panchayat: why and how?
18. Review and audit of development programmes.

Duration: Five Days

6. The generic functions of the Village Panchayat are listed in **Appendix A**.

CONTENT FLOW IN MODULE 1

Table 2
Introductory Training for Village Panchayat Members and Functionaries

Session No.	*Correspondence with Base Module*		*Session Theme*	*Time (in minutes)*
	Section	*Session No.*		
1.	General Orientation	1	Introductions and Icebreaking	80
2.	General Orientation	2	Principles of Panchayati Raj Governance	190
3.	General Orientation	3	Gender and Social Justice	165
4.	General Orientation	4	People-centred Community Development	240
5.	Politico-Legal Orientation	6	Role of Panchayati Raj Institutions	150
6.	Politico-Legal Orientation	7	Structure of Panchayati Raj Institutions	140
7.	Politico-Legal Orientation	8	Role of the Village Panchayat	180
8.	Management Orientation	10	Management of Community Development	405
9.	Management Orientation	12	Good Governance by a Village Panchayat	240
10.	Role Orientation	13	People-centred Behaviours and Attitudes	205
Total Duration of Training				1995 minutes 5 days

NOTE TO TRAINERS FOR USING MODULE 1

INTRODUCTORY TRAINING FOR THE VILLAGE PANCHAYAT MEMBERS AND FUNCTIONARIES

1. INTRODUCTION

Module 1 consists of a total of eleven sessions and its duration is five days. Out of these, ten sessions have been chosen from four different sections of the Base Module. The Module aims at creating an overall awareness and clarity about the fundamental concepts underlying Panchayati Raj Governance and the role of the Village Panchayat in this context. It is expected that this training event will enhance the degree of accountability and responsibility with which the different village-level individuals/institutions interface with each other. Greater bonding, increased coordination and an appreciation of each other's roles and constraints are some of the other likely training outcomes that would flow from this Module. In the end the Village Panchayat Members should seek their rights and carry out their duties.

2. MODULE CONTENTS

The *Content Flow for Module 1* is given at **Table 2**. Each session of Module 1 corresponds to a particular session of the Base Module. The trainer will be required to refer to the relevant session of the Base Module for conducting the training programme according to Module 1. Since each Session Plan is the exact replica of the corresponding one of the Base Module, the Plans have not been reproduced here. The information about the correspondence between the Sessions in Module 1 and those of the Base Module is also given in **Table 2**.

3. DURATION OF TRAINING

The Module requires about five training days. The total duration of training is estimated to be 34 hours and 30 minutes which is expected to extend over 5 days if training is held for 7 hours every day.

Module 1

Session 1 (1)*
General Orientation

Session Theme	INTRODUCTIONS AND ICEBREAKING
Duration	80 minutes
Venue	Classroom without fixed furnitures
Seating	Sit and/or stand on the floor forming a circle; move around the room for the game; sit in two or more circles for the Ranking Method. The participants can also be seated on chairs if they so desire.
Session Objective	*To create a feeling of comradeship amongst participants and trainers*

Expected Learning Outcomes

- The participants and trainers are acquainted with each other and begin to form a sympathetic group.
- The participants understand the training design, purpose and methodology.
- The trainer becomes aware of the expectations of the participants from the training programme.

Content Flow and Training Methodology

Sr. No.	*Content*	*Training Methodology*	*Training Aids*	*Duration (in min)*
1.	Welcoming the Participants	**Step 1** Talk by the President, Zilla Parishad	—	10
2.	Game for Introductions and Icebreaking	**Step 2** Seed Game	Seeds of various kinds	20
3.	Overview of training goal, content, methodology and scope	**Step 3** Visual Method	Posters and Slides	20
4.	Expectations of participants from the training	**Step 4** Ranking Method	Flash cards, flip charts and marker pens, seeds/ pebbles	30

* The number in the parenthesis refers to the Session of Base Module of Chapter 3.

Module 1

Session 2 (2)*
General Orientation

Session Theme PRINCIPLES OF PANCHAYATI RAJ GOVERNANCE

Duration *190 minutes*

Venue Classroom without fixed furnitures

Seating Sit/stand on the floor forming a circle for the group work; move around the room for the games. The participants can also sit on chairs if they wish to.

Session Objective *To expand the conceptual understanding of the participants about the basic principles of Panchayati Raj Governance.*

Expected Learning Outcomes

- The participants have an increased understanding of the philosophy of self government, the concept and principles underlying PRIs.

Content Flow and Training Methodology

Sr. No.	*Content*	*Training Methodology*	*Training Aids*	*Duration (in min.)*
1.	Game for Introductions and Icebreaking	**Step 1** Name Game	None	15
2.	(a) To emphasise that what the participants know about the value of Panchayati Raj Institutions. (b) History of the evolution of Panchayati Raj Institutions.	**Step 2** Johari's Window **Step 3** Timeline to trace the Evolution of the PRIs and the underlying motive for setting up the PRI system.	Flip charts, flash cards and marker pens	70[7]

* The number in the parenthesis refers to the Session of Base Module of Chapter 3.

7. It is suggested that the duration indicated for the sessions that use PLA based training methods may be factored thus:
Preparation time: 50; Presentation and Discussion time: 20; Total: 70

Sr. No.	*Content*	*Training Methodology*	*Training Aids*	*Duration (in min.)*
3.	Democratic Decentralization (a) Its true meaning; underlying concepts and philosophy. (b) Factors that make democratic decentralisation work. (c) The fundamental basis of PRIs: self government with the attendant responsibilities, transparency and accountability.	**Step 4** Brainstorming **Step 5** Delphi Technique **Step 6** Listing, Sorting and Matrix Scoring	Cards, marker pens, Flip charts and seeds of different varieties for the scoring/ sorting exercise	45
4.	Synthesis of learning points by Trainer/Participants	**Step 7** Visual Method	Overhead slides, Flip Charts, cards prepared by the participants	15

Module 1 Session 3 (3)*

General Orientation

Session Theme	GENDER AND SOCIAL JUSTICE
Duration	165 minutes
Venue	Classroom without fixed furnitures
Seating	Sit or stand on the floor forming a circle for the group work, move around the room for the games. They can also sit on chairs.
Session Objective	*To conscientise the participants about the social concerns related to gender, social justice and social exclusion.*

Expected Learning Outcomes

- The participants understand the issues related to gender and social exclusion that are prevalent in village-level society.
- They become aware of the duties of the Intermediate Panchayat for promoting social justice through both its governance and development related functions.

Content Flow and Training Methodology

Sr. No.	*Content*	*Training Methodology*	*Training Aids*	*Duration (in min.)*
1.	Energising Game	**Step 1** Who are We?	None	15
2.	Concept of Gender, Differences between sexuality and gender	**Step 2** Gender Analysis through Pictures	Flip Charts and marker pens	45[8]
3.	Neglect of gender and social justice	**Step 3** Gendered Resource Mapping	Flip Charts and marker pens	45
4.	Explore ways and means to rectify the situation	**Step 4** Access Social Mapping **Step 5** Solution Tree	Flip Charts and marker pens	45
5.	Synthesis of learning points	**Step 6** Visual Method	Overhead slides/maps, pictures	15

* The number in the parenthesis refers to the Session of Base Module of Chapter 3.

8. It is suggested that the duration be factored thus:
   Preparation time: 30; Presentation and Discussion time: 15; Total: 45

Module 1 Session 4(4)*
General Orientation

Session Theme	PEOPLE-CENTRED COMMUNITY DEVELOPMENT
Duration	240 minutes
Venue	Classroom without fixed furnitures
Seating	Sit or stand on the floor forming a circle for group work; move around the room for the game and picture/poster sessions. They can also sit on chairs.
Session Objective	*To impart to the participant a conceptual understanding of people-centered community development.*

Expected Learning Outcomes

- The participants get acquainted with the different approaches and programmes for village development.
- They are able to appreciate the philosophy of people-centered community development.

Content Flow and Training Methodology

Sr. No.	*Content*	*Training Methodology*	*Training Aids*	*Duration (in minutes)*
1.	(a) Changes in the development paradigm. (b) The consistency of the status of decentralisation in India with the changing development paradigm.	**Step 1** Historical Transect **Step 2** Lecture Method	Flip charts, marker pens, overhead slides, cards	60[9]
2.	Different approaches to development and the approach most appropriate for village level development.	**Step 3** Matching Game	Cards, marker pens, seeds or pebbles	45

* The number in the parenthesis refers to the Session of Base Module of Chapter 3.

9. Preparation time: 25, Presentation and Discussion time: 20; Lecture: 15

Sr. No.	*Content*	*Training Methodology*	*Training Aids*	*Duration (in minutes)*
3.	(a) Status of village development in India in the context of the different development approaches. (b) Status of gender equity and social justice in this context.	**Step 4** Pictures	Slides, drawings of cartoons	30
4.	Ways and means to improve the status of village development in India.	**Step 5** Ranking and Scoring	Cards, marker pens, seeds or pebbles	45
5.	Development Programmes and ways and means to improve their efficiency.	**Step 6** Pie Charts **Step 7** Ranking and Scoring	Flip Charts, marker pens, cards, coins of different denominations adding to a rupee, seeds or pebbles	45
6.	Synthesis of learning points by Trainer/ Participant(s)	**Step 8** Visual Method	Overhead slides/ Flip Charts prepared by the participants.	15

Module 1

Session 5(6)*
Politico-Legal Orientation

Session Theme	ROLE OF PANCHAYATI RAJ INSTITUTIONS
Duration	150 minutes
Venue	Classroom without fixed furnitures
Seating	Sit or stand on the ground forming a circle; move around the room for the Force Field Analysis and picture-based discussions. They can also sit on chairs if they so wish.
Session Objective	*To expand the practical understanding of the participants about the social mandate of the Panchayati Raj Institutions.*

Expected Learning Outcomes

Enlarged the comprehension of the participants about:

- The social mandate of the PRIs for meeting the ends of gender equity and social justice.
- The extent of the fulfilment of the social mandate.

Content Flow and Training Methodology

Sr. No.	*Content*	*Training Methodology*	*Training Aids*	*Duration (in minutes)*
1.	Self-government and PRIs: Implications and frame of action for economic development, gender equity and social justice.	**Step 1** Visual Method using a Cartoon show and picture based discussions	Cartoons and pictures	45[10]

* The number in the parenthesis refers to the Session of Base Module of Chapter 3.

10. It is suggested that the duration indicated for the sessions may be factored thus:
Cartoon Show and Display of Pictures: 30
Discussion time: 15
Total: 45

Sr. No.	*Content*	*Training Methodology*	*Training Aids*	*Duration (in minutes)*
2.	What were the original intentions of legislation and protagonists for the movement for self-government?	**Step 2** Lecture Method	Flash cards/ slides/ transparencies	30
3.	What happened to the original ideas and justifications for the PRIs?	**Step 3** Force Field Analysis **Step 4** Brainstorming	Different coloured cards, flip charts, marker pens	60
4.	Synthesis of learning points	**Step 5** Visual Method	As desired by trainer	15

Module 1

Session 6 (7)*
Politico-Legal Orientation

Session Theme	STRUCTURE OF PANCHAYATI RAJ INSTITUTIONS
Duration	140 minutes
Venue	Classroom without fixed furnitures
Seating	Sit or stand on the ground forming a circle. They can also sit on chairs if they so wish.
Session Objective	*To expand the knowledge of the participants about the legal premise and structure of Panchayati Raj Institutions.*

Expected Learning Outcome

- Increased acquaintance with the mandate and features of the Seventy Third Constitutional Amendment Act, the State Conformity Act for PRIs and the structure of PRIs

Content Flow and Training Methodology

Sr. No.	*Content*	*Training Methodology*	*Training Aids*	*Duration (in minutes)*
1.	Game for Enhancing Group Dynamics	**Step 1** Saboteur	None	20
2.	The Seventy Third Constitutional Amendment Act and the State Conformity Act: Mandate and Salient Features	**Step 1** Lecture Method	As desired by the trainer	60
3.	Structure of Panchayati Raj Institutions -Gram Sabha, Village Panchayat, Panchayat Samity and Zilla Parishad	**Step 2** Lecture Method **Step 3** Role Play/Drama of a Gram Sabha	As desired by the trainer	45
4.	Synthesis of learning points by Trainer/ Participant(s)	**Step 4** Visual Method	Overhead slides, Flip Charts	15

* The number in the parenthesis refers to the Session of Base Module of Chapter 3.

Module 1 — Session 7 (8)*

Politico-Legal Orientation

Session Theme	ROLE OF THE VILLAGE PANCHAYAT
Duration	180 minutes
Venue	Classroom without any fixed furnitures
Seating	Sit or stand on the floor forming a circle. They can also sit on chairs if they wish.
Session Objective	*To conscientise the participants about their rights and duties as members of the Intermediate Panchayat and generate an urge in them to seek their rights.*

Expected Learning Outcomes

Increased awareness about:

- Their own rights and duties.
- The rightful place of the Intermediate Panchayat in grassroots governance.
- Its role, responsibilities and functions.
- What is necessary for having those rights, responsibilities and functions.

Content Flow and Training Methodology

Sr. No.	*Content*	*Training Methodology*	*Training Aids*	*Duration (in minutes)*
1.	*De jure* Functions of the Intermediate Panchayat	**Step 1** Brainstorming **Step 2** Delphi Method	Flip charts, flash cards, marker pens	15 45
2.	*De facto* functions of the Intermediate Panchayat	**Step 3** Brainstorming **Step 4** Delphi Method	Flip charts, flash cards, marker pens	15 45
3.	How empowered is the Intermediate Panchayat?	**Step 5** Empowerment Circle	Large sheets of paper, flip charts, several	45

* The number in the parenthesis refers to the Session of Base Module of Chapter 3.

Sr. No.	*Content*	*Training Methodology*	*Training Aids*	*Duration (in minutes)*
	Panchayat?		coloured marker pens, flash cards, seeds, Post-It stickers, bindis	
4.	Synthesis of learning points by Trainer/ Participant(s)	**Step 6** Visual Method	Overhead slides, Flip Charts	15

Module 1

Session 8 (10)*
Management Orientation

Session Theme	MANAGEMENT OF COMMUNITY DEVELOPMENT
Duration	225 minutes
Venue	Village Locale for the Social and Resource Mapping Classroom without fixed furnitures for the remaining session.
Seating	Sit or stand on the floor or ground forming a circle; move around the room for the role play and group work.
Session Objective	*To empower the participants to function as agents of community development.*

Expected Learning Outcomes

The participants know about:

- The fundamentals of managing community development.
- The role of the Intermediate Panchayat in this context.
- The role of different development institutions and agencies and their linkages with the Intermediate Panchayat.

Content Flow and Training Methodology

Sr. No.	*Content*	*Training Methodology*	*Training Aids*	*Duration (in minutes)*
1.	Role of the Intermediate Panchayat in Community Development	Step 1 Social Mapping	Flip Charts, marker pens	60
2.	Protection and Management of Common Property Resources	Step 2 Resource Mapping	Flip Charts, marker pens	60

* The number in the parenthesis refers to the Session of Base Module of Chapter 3.

Sr. No.	*Content*	*Training Methodology*	*Training Aids*	*Duration (in minutes)*
Return to Classroom from Village Locale				
3.	The Intermediate Panchayat and the Community Development Network in the District level	**Step 3** Venn Diagramming	Flip Charts, marker pens, white paper, cards, scissors, glue	45
4.	The Quality of the Relationship of the Intermediate Panchayat with other institutions/ individuals operating within the District	**Step 4** Communication Linkage Matrix	Flip Charts, marker pens, white paper, cards, scissors, glue, seeds and as desired by trainer and participants	45
5.	Synthesis of Learning Points by Trainer/ Participants	**Step 5** Visual Method	Overhead slides/Flip Charts	15

Module 1

Session 9 (12)*
Management Orientation

Session Theme	GOOD GOVERNANCE BY THE VILLAGE PANCHAYAT
Duration	240 minutes
Venue	Classroom without fixed furnitures
Seating	Sit or stand on the floor forming a circle; move around the room for the role play and group work. They can also sit on chairs.
Session Objective	*To orient the participants with the principles of good governance and the mechanisms for promoting them.*

Expected Learning Outcomes

The participants understand the basic values related to good governance of transparency, responsiveness, participation and accountability; understand the role of the Gram Sabha in this context and acquire skills for using the instruments of social and gender audit for promoting these values.

Content Flow and Training Methodology

Sr. No.	*Content*	*Training Methodology*	*Training Aids*	*Duration (in min.)*
1.	Citizens' Charter for the Intermediate Panchayat	**Step 1** Case Study Method **Step 2** Brainstorming **Step 3** Delphi Method **Step 4** Ranking Method	Flip Charts, marker pens, cards and Citizens' Charter of some Intermediate Panchayats as case studies	90
2.	Role and Responsibilities of the Village Gram Sabha	**Step 5** Drama/Role Play	As desired by the trainer	30

* The number in the parenthesis refers to the Session of Base Module of Chapter 3.

Sr. No.	*Content*	*Training Methodology*	*Training Aids*	*Duration (in min.)*
3.	Financial Transparency-Rationale and Practices: Gram Sabha, Publicity of Accounts and expenditure, monthly meetings, inspection of registers, financial audit	**Step 6** Case Study Method **Step 7** Lecture Method	As desired by the trainer	45
4.	Social and Gender Audit of Community Development Initiatives	**Step 8** Brainstorming **Step 9** Delphi Method **Step 10** Matrix Scoring Method	Flip Charts, marker pens, cards, different varieties of seeds for the scoring	60
5.	Synthesis of Learning Points by Trainer/. Participants	**Step 11** Visual Method	Overhead slides/ Flip Charts	15

Module 1

Session 10 (13)*
Role Orientation

Session Theme	PEOPLE-CENTRED BEHAVIOURS AND ATTITUDES
Duration	205 minutes
Venue	Classroom without fixed furnitures
Seating	Sit or stand on the floor forming a circle; move around the room for the role play and group work. They can also sit on chairs if they wish.
Session Objective	*To enable the participants to comprehend the different kinds of people-centred behaviours and attitudes.*

Expected Learning Outcomes

The participants are conscientised about the desired pro-people and pro-poor behaviours and attitudes that are expected of an Intermediate Panchayat member and learn to emulate them

Content Flow and Training Methodology

Sr. No.	*Content*	*Training Methodology*	*Training Aids*	*Duration (in minutes)*
1.	(a) How does an Intermediate Panchayat member/ development official usually behave? (b) What are the appropriate behaviours for a member/official?	**Step 1** Game "As a Zilla Parishad member, I mainly..."[11] **Step 2** Brainstorming	Flash cards, marker pens, flip charts, slides, transparencies	45 30
2.	Non-Verbal Behaviour	**Step 3** Game: Non-Verbal Circles	Chairs, sticks to improvise	25

* The number in the parenthesis refers to the Session of Base Module of Chapter 3.

11. Adapted from Chambers 2002.

Sr. No.	*Content*	*Training Methodology*	*Training Aids*	*Duration (in minutes)*
3.	Role of a Intermediate Panchayat Member	**Step 4** Role Play/ Drama		30
4.	Game for Enhancing Group Dynamics	**Step 5** Chairs	Chairs	30
5.	Modelling of People-Centred Attitudes	**Step 6** Johari's Window **Step 7** Slide Show	Slides, sketches	30
6.	Synthesis of Learning Points	**Step 8** Visual Method	Flip Charts, marker pens	15

Module 2

Introductory Training for the Members and Officers of the Intermediate Panchayat

PROFILE OF MODULE 2

INTRODUCTORY TRAINING FOR THE MEMBERS AND OFFICERS OF INTERMEDIATE PANCHAYAT

Objectives

- To create an awareness amongst the participants about the basic principles of self government and people-centred community development and the rights and duties of the elected members and functionaries of the Intermediate Panchayat and why they are unable to exercise their rights and discharge their duties.
- To enhance the practical understanding of the participants about the basic structure and functioning of the Intermediate Panchayat for meeting the goals of economic development, gender equity and social justice.
- To orient the participants with the principles of good management of the Intermediate Panchayat and the mechanisms for promoting them.

Participants

- The elected members and government officials of the Intermediate Panchayat.
- NGOs and other Voluntary Agencies and Groups.
- Bank Branch Managers within the jurisdiction of the Intermediate Panchayat.

Chaired by: President, Zilla Parishad.

Conducted by: Chief Executive Officer, Zilla Parishad and other Heads of Departments of the Zilla Parishad.

Contents

1. Self government and institutions of self government in the context of PRIs: Concepts, framework and the implications and frame of action for economic and social development, for gender and social justice.

2. Concept and Principles of Democratic Decentralisation.
3. The Development Paradigm and its evolution.
4. Concept of Gender and Social Justice.
5. Role and structure of the PRIs and the Gram Sabha.
6. The Seventy-Third Constitutional Amendment Act and the State Conformity Acts.
7. *De jure* Duties[12] and Responsibilities of the Intermediate Panchayat, the Gram Sabha and the Village Panchayat.
8. *De facto* Duties and responsibilities of the Intermediate Panchayat, the Gram Sabha and the Village Panchayat.
9. Gap between *de jure* and *de facto* functions of the Intermediate Panchayat, the Gram Sabha and the Village Panchayat and the reasons for this gap.
10. Ways and means to fill the gap between *de jure* and *de facto* functions of the Intermediate Panchayat, the Gram Sabha and the Village Panchayat.
11. Role of the Zilla Parishad Officials vis-à-vis the Intermediate Panchayat.
12. How to resolve the difficulties that affect the relationship between line departments and the Intermediate Panchayat.
13. Emerging roles of MLAs, MLCs and MPs in the PRI set-up.
14. Management of Community Development Programmes.
15. People-centred Behaviours and Attitudes.
16. Autonomy and accountability of the Intermediate Panchayat in both performance and finances.
17. Transparency in the affairs of the Intermediate Panchayat: why and how?
18. Review and audit of development programmes.

Duration: Five Days

12. The generic functions of the Intermediate Panchayat are listed in Appendix B.

CONTENT FLOW IN MODULE 2

Table 3
Introductory Training for the Members and Officers of the Intermediate Panchayat

Session No.	*Correspondence with Base Module*		*Session Theme*	*Time (in minutes)*
	Section	*Session No.*		
1.	General Orientation	1	Introductions and Icebreaking	80
2.	General Orientation	2	Principles of Panchayati Raj Governance	190
3.	General Orientation	3	Gender and Social Justice	165
4.	General Orientation	4	People-centred Community Development	240
5.	Politico-Legal Orientation	6	Role of Panchayati Raj Institutions	150
6.	Politico-Legal Orientation	7	Structure of Panchayati Raj Institutions	140
7.	Politico-Legal Orientation	8	Role of the Intermediate Panchayat	180
8.	Management Orientation	10	Management of Community Development	405
9.	Management Orientation	12	Good Governance by a Intermediate Panchayat	240
10.	Role Orientation	13.	People-centred Behaviours and Attitudes	205
Total Duration of Training				1995 (33 hours 150 minutes)

NOTE TO TRAINERS FOR USING MODULE 2

INTRODUCTORY TRAINING FOR THE MEMBERS AND OFFICERS OF THE INTERMEDIATE PANCHAYAT

1. INTRODUCTION

Module 2 aims at creating an overall awareness and clarity about the fundamental concepts underlying Panchayati Raj Governance and the role of the Intermediate Panchayat amongst its elected members and the Block/Taluka level officers. Module 2 consists of 11 sessions from the Base Module. The duration of Module 2 is 5 days.

Module 2 is similar to Module 1, ***only the focus of training is the institution of the Intermediate Panchayat instead of the Village Panchayat***. The content flow and the training methodology to be used are similar for both Modules, except for the fact that in Module 2, the trainer focuses on the Intermediate Panchayat. For example, in Session No.7 of Module 2, for discussing the role of the Intermediate Panchayat, the trainer follows the same sequence of training methods as suggested in Session 8 of the Base Module. The discussions about the *de facto* and *de jure* functions will now be held with reference to the Intermediate Panchayat, with cross-references, wherever necessary to the functions of the Village Panchayat. The modified Session Plans are given for the ready reference of the trainer. The corresponding session number of the Base Module is given in parentheses, for example 7(8).

It is suggested that Module 2 be conducted by the Chief Executive Officer, Zilla Parishad and other senior officials of the Zilla Parishad. The programme can be chaired by the President, Zilla Parishad.

2. MODULE CONTENTS

The *Content Flow for Module 2* is given at **Table 3**. Each session of Module 2 corresponds to a particular session of the Base Module. The trainer will be required to refer to the relevant session of the Base Module for following the methodological sequence for conducting the training according to Module 2.

3. DURATION OF TRAINING

The Module requires about five training days, if training is conducted for 7 hours daily. The total duration of training is estimated to be 2070 minutes, which is 34 hours and 30 minutes.

Module 2 Session 1(1)*
General Orientation

Session Theme	INTRODUCTIONS AND ICEBREAKING
Duration	80 minutes
Venue	Classroom without fixed furnitures
Seating	Sit or stand on the floor forming a circle; move around the room for the game; sit in two or more circles for the Ranking Method.
Session Objective	*To create a feeling of comradeship amongst participants and trainers.*

Expected Learning Outcomes

- The participants and trainers are acquainted with each other and begin to form a sympathetic group.
- The participants understand the training design, purpose and methodology.
- The trainer becomes aware of the expectations of the participants from the training programme.

Content Flow and Training Methodology

Sr. No.†	*Content*	*Training Methodology*	*Training Aids*	*Duration (in min.)*
1.	Welcoming the Participants	**Step 1** Talk by the President, Zilla Parishad	Public Address system	10
2.	Game for Introductions and Icebreaking	**Step 2** Seed Game	Seeds of various kinds	20
3.	Overview of training goal, content, methodology and scope	**Step 3** Visual Method	Posters and Slides	20
4.	Expectations of participants from the training	**Step 4** Ranking Method	Flash cards, flip charts and marker pens, seeds/pebbles	30

* The number in the parenthesis refers to the Session of Base Module of Chapter 3.

† *Note:* These Serial Number continuous in this module 2.

Module 2 — Session 2(2)* General Orientation

Session Theme	**PRINCIPLES OF PANCHAYATI RAJ GOVERNANCE**
Duration	190 minutes
Venue	Classroom without fixed furnitures
Seating	Sit/stand on the ground forming a circle for the group work; move around the room for the games.
Session Objective	*To expand the conceptual understanding of the participants about the basic principles of Panchayati Raj Governance.*

Expected Learning Outcomes

- The participants have an increased understanding of the philosophy of self government, the concept and principles underlying PRIs.

Content Flow and Training Methodology

Sr. No.	*Content*	*Training Methodology*	*Training Aids*	*Duration (in minutes)*
5.	Game for Introductions and Icebreaking	**Step 1** Name Game	None	15
6.	(a) To emphasise that what the participants know about the value of Panchayati Raj Institutions. (b) History of the evolution of Panchayati Raj Institutions	**Step 2** Johari's Window **Step 3** Time-line to trace the Evolution of the PRIs and the underlying motive for setting up the PRI system	Flip charts, flash cards and marker pens	70[13]

* The number in the parenthesis refers to the Session of Base Module of Chapter 3.

13. It is suggested that the duration indicated for the sessions that use PLA based training methods may be factored thus:
Preparation time: 50; Presentation and Discussion time: 20; Total: 70

Sr. No.	*Content*	*Training Methodology*	*Training Aids*	*Duration (in minutes)*
7.	Democratic Decentralization (d) Its true meaning; underlying concepts and philosophy. (e) Factors that make democratic decentralisation work. (f) The fundamental basis of PRIs: self-government with the attendant responsibilities, transparency and accountability	**Step 4** Brainstorming **Step 5** Delphi Technique **Step 6** Listing, Sorting and Matrix Scoring	Cards, marker pens, Flip charts and seeds of different varieties for the scoring/ sorting exercise	45
8.	Synthesis of learning points by Trainer/Participants	**Step 7** Visual Method	Overhead slides, Flip Charts, cards prepared by the participants	15

Module 2 Session 3 (3)*
General Orientation

Session Theme	GENDER AND SOCIAL JUSTICE
Duration	165 minutes
Venue	Classroom without fixed furnitures
Seating	Sit or stand on the floor forming a circle for the group work, move around the room for the games. They can also sit on chairs.
Session Objective	*To conscientise the participants about the social concerns related to gender, social justice and social exclusion.*

Expected Learning Outcomes

- The participants understand the issues related to gender and social exclusion that are prevalent in village-level society.
- They become aware of the duties of the Intermediate Panchayat for promoting social justice through both its governance and development related functions.

Content Flow and Training Methodology

Sr. No.	*Content*	*Training Methodology*	*Training Aids*	*Duration (in minutes)*
9.	Energising Game	**Step 1** Who are We?	None	15
10.	Concept of Gender, Differences between sex-uality and gender	**Step 2** Gender Analysis through Pictures	Flip Charts and marker pens	45[14]
11.	Neglect of gender and social justice	**Step 3** Gendered Resource Mapping	Flip Charts and marker pens	45

* The number in the parenthesis refers to the Session of Base Module of Chapter 3.

14. It is suggested that the duration be factored thus:
Preparation time: 30; Presentation and Discussion time: 15; Total: 45

Sr. No.	*Content*	*Training Methodology*	*Training Aids*	*Duration (in minutes)*
12.	Explore ways and means to rectify the situation	**Step 4** Access Social Mapping **Step 5** Solution Tree	Flip Charts and marker pens	45
13.	Synthesis of learning points	**Step 6** Visual Method	Overhead slides/ maps, pictures	15

Module 2 — Session 4 (4)*

General Orientation

Session Theme PEOPLE-CENTRED COMMUNITY DEVELOPMENT

Duration 240 minutes

Venue Classroom without fixed furnitures.

Seating Sit or stand on the floor forming a circle for group work; move around the room for the game and picture/poster sessions. Participants can also sit on chairs.

Session Objective *To impart to the participant a conceptual understanding of people-centred community development.*

Expected Learning Outcomes

- The participants get acquainted with the different approaches and programmes for village development
- They are able to appreciate the philosophy of people-centred community development.

Content Flow and Training Methodology

Sr. No.	*Content*	*Training Methodology*	*Training Aids*	*Duration (in min.)*
14.	(a) Changes in the development paradigm (b) The consistency of the status of decentralisation in India with the changing development paradigm	**Step 1** Historical Transect **Step 2** Lecture Method	Flip charts, marker pens, overhead slides, cards	60[15]
15.	Different approaches to development and the approach most appropriate for village level development	**Step 3** Matching Game	Cards, marker pens, seeds or pebbles	45

* The number in the parenthesis refers to the Session of Base Module of Chapter 3.

15. Preparation time: 25, Presentation and Discussion time: 20; Lecture: 15

Sr. No.	*Content*	*Training Methodology*	*Training Aids*	*Duration (in min.)*
16.	(c) Status of village development in India in the context of the different development approaches (d) Status of gender equity and social justice in this context	**Step 4** Pictures	Slides, drawings of cartoons	30
17.	Ways and means to improve the status of village development in India	**Step 5** Ranking and Scoring	Cards, marker pens, seeds or pebbles	45
18.	Development Programmes and ways and means to improve their efficiency	**Step 6** Pie Charts **Step 7** Ranking and Scoring	Flip Charts, marker pens, cards, coins of different denominations adding to a rupee, seeds or pebbles	45
19.	Synthesis of learning points by Trainer/ Participant(s)	**Step 8** Visual Method	Overhead slides/Flip Charts prepared by the participants	15

Module 2 Session 5(6)*
Politico-Legal Orientation

Session Theme	ROLE OF PANCHAYATI RAJ INSTITUTIONS
Duration	150 minutes
Venue	Classroom without fixed furnitures
Seating	Sit or stand on the ground forming a circle; move around the room for the Force Field Analysis and picture-based discussions. They can also sit on chairs if they so wish.
Session Objective	*To expand the practical understanding of the participants about the social mandate of the Panchayati Raj Institutions.*

Expected Learning Outcomes

Enlarged the comprehension of the participants about:

- The social mandate of the PRIs for meeting the ends of gender equity and social justice.
- The extent of the fulfilment of the social mandate.

Content Flow and Training Methodology

Sr. No.	*Content*	*Training Methodology*	*Training Aids*	*Duration (in min.)*
20.	Self-government and PRIs: Implications and frame of action for economic development, gender equity and social justice	**Step 1** Visual Method using a Cartoon show and picture based discussions	Cartoons and pictures	45[16]
21.	What were the original intentions of legislation and protagonists for the movement for self-government?	**Step 2** Lecture Method	Flash cards/ slides/ transparencies	30

* The number in the parenthesis refers to the Session of Base Module of Chapter 3.

16. It is suggested that the duration indicated for the sessions may be factored thus: Cartoon Show and Display of Pictures: 30; Discussion time: 15; Total: 45

Sr. No.	*Content*	*Training Methodology*	*Training Aids*	*Duration (in min.)*
22.	What happened to the original ideas and justifications for the PRIs?	**Step 3** Force Field Analysis **Step 4** Brainstorming	Different coloured cards, flip charts, marker pens	60
23.	Synthesis of learning points	**Step 5** Visual Method	As desired by trainer	15

Module 2 Session 6 (7)*
Politico-Legal Orientation

Session Theme	STRUCTURE OF PANCHAYATI RAJ INSTITUTIONS
Duration	140 minutes
Venue	Classroom without fixed furnitures
Seating	Sit or stand on the ground forming a circle. They can also sit on chairs if they so wish.
Session Objective	*To expand the knowledge of the participants about the legal premise and structure of Panchayati Raj Institutions.*

Expected Learning Outcome

- Increased acquaintance with the mandate and features of the Seventy Third Constitutional Amendment Act, the State Conformity Act for PRIs and the structure of PRIs

Content Flow and Training Methodology

Sr. No.	*Content*	*Training Methodology*	*Training Aids*	*Duration (in min.)*
24.	Game for Enhancing Group Dynamics	**Step 1** Saboteur	None	20
25.	The Seventy Third Constitutional Amendment Act and the State Conformity Act: Mandate and Salient Features	**Step 1** Lecture Method	As desired by the trainer	60
26.	Structure of Panchayati Raj Institutions — Gram Sabha, Village Panchayat, Panchayat Samity and Zilla Parishad	**Step 2** Lecture Method **Step 3** Role Play/ Drama of a Gram Sabha	As desired by the trainer	45
27.	Synthesis of learning points by Trainer/ Participant(s)	**Step 4** Visual Method	Overhead slides, Flip Charts	15

* The number in the parenthesis refers to the Session of Base Module of Chapter 3.

Module 2 Session 7 (8)*
Politico-Legal Orientation

Session Theme	ROLE OF THE INTERMEDIATE PANCHAYAT
Duration	180 minutes
Venue	Classroom without any fixed furnitures
Seating	Sit or stand on the floor forming a circle. They can also sit on chairs if they wish.
Session Objective	*To conscientise the participants about their rights and duties as members of the Intermediate Panchayat and generate an urge in them to seek their rights.*

Expected Learning Outcomes : Increased awareness about:

- Their own rights and duties.
- The rightful place of the Intermediate Panchayat in grassroots governance.
- Its role, responsibilities and functions.
- What is necessary for having those rights, responsibilities and functions.

Content Flow and Training Methodology

Sr. No.	*Content*	*Training Methodology*	*Training Aids*	*Duration (in min.)*
28.	*De jure* Functions of the Intermediate Panchayat	**Step 1** Brainstorming **Step 2** Delphi Method	Flip charts, flash cards, marker pens	15 45
29.	*De facto* functions of the Intermediate Panchayat	**Step 3** Brainstorming **Step 4** Delphi Method	Flip charts, flash cards, marker pens	15 45
30.	How empowered is the Intermediate Panchayat?	**Step 5** Empowerment Circle	Large sheets of paper, flip charts, several coloured	45

* The number in the parenthesis refers to the Session of Base Module of Chapter 3.

Sr. No.	*Content*	*Training Methodology*	*Training Aids*	*Duration (in min.)*
			marker pens, flash cards, seeds, Post-It stickers, bindis	
31.	Synthesis of learning points by Trainer/ Participant(s)	**Step 6** Visual Method	Overhead slides, Flip Charts	15

Module 2

Session 8 (10)*
Management Orientation

Session Theme	MANAGEMENT OF COMMUNITY DEVELOPMENT
Duration	225 minutes
Venue	Village Locale for the Social and Resource Mapping Classroom without fixed furnitures for the remaining session.
Seating	Sit or stand on the floor or ground forming a circle; move around the room for the role play and group work.
Session Objective	*To empower the participants to function as agents of community development.*

Expected Learning Outcomes: The participants know about:

- The fundamentals of managing community development.
- The role of the Intermediate Panchayat in this context.
- The role of different development institutions and agencies and their linkages with the Intermediate Panchayat.

Content Flow and Training Methodology

Sr. No.	*Content*	*Training Methodology*	*Training Aids*	*Duration (in min.)*
32.	Role of the Intermediate Panchayat in Community Development	**Step 1** Social Mapping	Flip Charts, marker pens	60
33.	Protection and Management of Common Property Resources	**Step 2** Resource Mapping	Flip Charts, marker pens	60
	Return to Classroom from Village Locale			
34.	The Intermediate Panchayat and the Community Development Network in the District level	**Step 3** Venn Diagramming	Flip Charts, marker pens, white paper, cards, scissors, glue	45

* The number in the parenthesis refers to the Session of Base Module of Chapter 3.

Sr. No.	*Content*	*Training Methodology*	*Training Aids*	*Duration (in min.)*
35.	The Quality of the Relationship of the Intermediate Panchayat with other institutions/ individuals operating within the District	**Step 4** Communication Linkage Matrix	Flip Charts, marker pens, white paper, cards, scissors, glue, seeds and as desired by trainer and participants	45
36.	Synthesis of Learning Points by Trainer/ Participants	**Step 5** Visual Method	Overhead slides/Flip Charts	15

Module 2 Session 9 (12)*
Management Orientation

Session Theme	GOOD GOVERNANCE BY THE INTERMEDIATE PANCHAYAT
Duration	240 minutes
Venue	Classroom without fixed furnitures
Seating	Sit or stand on the floor forming a circle; move around the room for the role play and group work. They can also sit on chairs.
Session Objective	*To orient the participants with the principles of good governance and the mechanisms for promoting them.*

Expected Learning Outcomes

- The participants understand the basic values related to good governance of transparency, responsiveness, participation and accountability; understand the role of the Gram Sabha in this context and acquire skills for using the instruments of social and gender audit for promoting these values.

Content Flow and Training Methodology

Sr. No.	*Content*	*Training Methodology*	*Training Aids*	*Duration (in min.)*
37.	Citizens' Charter for the Intermediate Panchayat	**Step 1** Case Study Method **Step 2** Brainstorming **Step 3** Delphi Method **Step 4** Ranking Method	Flip Charts, marker pens, cards and Citizens' Charter of some Intermediate Panchayats as case studies	90
38.	Role and Responsibilities of the Village Gram Sabha	**Step 5** Drama/Role Play	As desired by the trainer	30

* The number in the parenthesis refers to the Session of Base Module of Chapter 3.

Sr. No.	*Content*	*Training Methodology*	*Training Aids*	*Duration (in min.)*
39.	Financial Transparency-Rationale and Practices: Gram Sabha, Publicity of Accounts and expenditure, monthly meetings, inspection of registers, financial audit	**Step 6** Case Study Method **Step 7** Lecture Method	As desired by the trainer	45
40.	Social and Gender Audit of Community Development Initiatives	**Step 8** Brainstorming **Step 9** Delphi Method **Step 10** Matrix Scoring Method	Flip Charts, marker pens, cards, different varieties of seeds for the scoring	60
41.	Synthesis of Learning Points by Trainer/ Participants	**Step 11** Visual Method	Overhead slides/Flip Charts	15

Module 2 Session 10 (13)*

Role Orientation

Session Theme	PEOPLE-CENTRED BEHAVIOURS AND ATTITUDES
Duration	205 minutes
Venue	Classroom without fixed furnitures
Seating	Sit or stand on the floor forming a circle; move around the room for the role play and group work. They can also sit on chairs if they wish.
Session Objective	*To enable the participants to comprehend the different kinds of people-centred behaviours and attitudes.*

Expected Learning Outcomes

- The participants are conscientised about the desired pro-people and pro-poor behaviours and attitudes that are expected of an Intermediate Panchayat member and learn to emulate them.

Content Flow and Training Methodology

Sr. No.	*Content*	*Training Methodology*	*Training Aids*	*Duration (in minutes)*
42.	(a) How does an Intermediate Panchayat member/development official usually behave? (b) What are the appropriate behaviours for a member/official?	**Step 1** Game "As a Zilla Parishad member, I mainly..."[17] **Step 2** Brainstorming	Flash cards, marker pens, flip charts, slides, transparencies	45 30
43.	Non-Verbal Behaviour	**Step 3** Game: Non-Verbal Circles	Chairs, sticks to improvise	25

* The number in the parenthesis refers to the Session of Base Module of Chapter 3.

17 Adapted from Chambers 2002.

Sr. No.	*Content*	*Training Methodology*	*Training Aids*	*Duration (in minutes)*
44.	Role of a Intermediate Panchayat Member	**Step 4** Role Play/ Drama		30
45.	Game for Enhancing Group Dynamics	**Step 5** Chairs	Chairs	30
46.	Modelling of People-Centred Attitudes	**Step 6** Johari's Window **Step 7** Slide Show	Slides, sketches	30
47.	Synthesis of Learning Points	**Step 8** Visual Method	Flip Charts, marker pens	15

Module 3
Training-cum-Awareness Camp for the Zilla Parishad Members and Officers

PROFILE OF MODULE 3

TRAINING-CUM-AWARENESS CAMP FOR THE ZILLA PARISHAD MEMBERS AND OFFICERS

Objectives

- To create an awareness amongst the participants about the basic principles of self government and people-centred community development and the rights and duties of the elected members and functionaries of the Zilla Parishad and analyse why they are unable to exercise their rights and discharge their duties fully.
- To enhance the practical understanding of the participants about the basic structure and functioning of the Zilla Parishad for meeting the goals of economic development, gender equity and social justice.
- To orient the participants with the principles of good management of the Zilla Parishad and the mechanisms for promoting them.

Participants

- The members of the Zilla Parishad.
- District Officers of the Zilla Parishad.

Special Invitees

1. Officials from the State Government.
2. All MLAs, MLCs, MPs.
3. Academicians from educational institutions.
4. A Minister from the State Government.
5. Lead Bank Officer and other District Coordinators of Banks.

Contents

1. Self government and institutions of self government in the context of PRIs: Concepts, framework and the implications and frame of action for economic and social development, for gender and social justice.

2. Concept and Principles of Democratic Decentralisation.
3. The Development Paradigm and its evolution.
4. Concept of Gender and Social Justice.
5. Role and structure of the PRIs and the Gram Sabha.
6. The Seventy-Third Constitutional Amendment Act and the State Conformity Acts.
7. *De jure* Duties and Responsibilities of the Zilla Parishad and the Gram Sabha.
8. *De facto* Duties and responsibilities of the PRIs and the Gram Sabha.
9. Gap between *de jure* and *de facto* functions of the Zilla Parishad and the Gram Sabha.
10. Ways and means to fill the gap between *de jure* and *de facto* functions.
11. Role of the Zilla Parishad Officials vis-à-vis the PRIs for functioning as institutions of self-government.
12. How to resolve the difficulties that affect the relationship between the Heads of Departments the PRIs.
13. Emerging roles of MLAs, MLCs and MPs in making the PRIs autonomous institutions.
14. How to manage inter-relationships among the three tiers of the PRIs?
15. People-centred Behaviours and Attitudes.
16. Autonomy and accountability of the Zilla Parishad in both performance and finances.
17. Transparency in the affairs of the Zilla Parishad: why and how?
18. Review and audit of development programmes.

Duration: Two and a Half Days (@ 7 hours of training daily).

CONTENT FLOW IN MODULE 3

Table 4
Training-cum-Awareness Camp for the Zilla Parishad Members and Officers

Session No.	*Correspondence with Base Module*		*Session Theme*	*Time (in minutes)*
	Section	*Session No.*		
1.	General Orientation	1	Introductions and Icebreaking	80
2.	Politico-Legal Orientation	5	Panchayati Raj Governance	90
3.	General Orientation	4	People-centred Community Development	240
4.	General Orientation	3	Gender and Social Justice	165
5.	Politico-Legal Orientation	6	Role of Panchayati Raj Institutions	150
6.	Politico-Legal Orientation	7	Structure of Panchayati Raj Institutions	140
7.	Politico-Legal Orientation	8	Role of the Zilla Parishad	180
8.	Management Orientation	10	Management of Community Development	225
9.	Management Orientation	12	Good Governance by the Zilla Parishad	240
10.	Role Orientation	13	People-centred Behaviours and Attitudes	205
Total Duration of Training				1715 (28 hours 15 minutes)

NOTE TO TRAINERS FOR USING MODULE 3

TRAINING-CUM-AWARENESS CAMP FOR THE ZILLA PARISHAD MEMBERS AND OFFICERS

1. INTRODUCTION

Module 3 aims at creating an overall awareness and clarity about the fundamental concepts underlying Panchayati Raj Governance and the role of the Zilla Parishad amongst its members and district level officers. It consists of the 11 sessions including the session on *Assessment of Training*. The duration of the Module is estimated to be about two and a half days if training is conducted for about 7 hours daily.

Module 3 is similar to Module 2, ***only the focus of training is the institution of the Zilla Parishad instead of the Intermediate Panchayat***. It has been suggested that some special invitees be present in the training programme for expanding the cross-learning process. The programme can be chaired by a Minister of the State Government, to impart due importance to the subject.

2. MODULE CONTENTS

The ***Content Flow for Module 3*** is given at **Table 4**. Each session of Module 3 corresponds to a particular session of the Base Module which is mentioned in parentheses. For example, Session 4 of Module 3 corresponds to Session 3 of the Base Module. This is indicated in the relevant Session Plan by Session No. 4(3). The trainer will be required to refer to the relevant session of the Base Module for the methodological steps to be followed for conducting the training programme according to Module 3.

3. DURATION OF TRAINING

The Module requires about four training days. The total duration of training is estimated to be 1790 (29 hours 30 minutes).

Module 3

Session 1 (1)*
General Orientation

Session Theme	INTRODUCTIONS AND ICEBREAKING
Duration	80 minutes
Venue	Classroom without fixed furnitures
Seating	Sit/stand on the ground forming a circle; move around the room for the game; sit in two or more circles for the Ranking Method.
Session Objective	*To create a feeling of comradeship amongst participants and trainers.*

Expected Learning Outcomes

- The participants and trainers are acquainted with each other and begin to form a sympathetic group.
- The participants understand the training design, purpose and methodology.
- The trainer becomes aware of the expectations of the participants from the training programme.

Content Flow and Training Methodology

Sr. No.†	*Content*	*Training Methodology*	*Training Aids*	*Duration (in min.)*
1.	Welcoming the Participants	**Step 1** Talk by the Hon'ble Minister	As desired	10
2.	Game for Introductions and Icebreaking	**Step 2** Seed Game	Seeds of various kinds	20
3.	Overview of training goal, content, methodology and scope	**Step 3** Visual Method	Posters and Slides	20
4.	Expectations of participants from the training	**Step 4** Ranking Method	Flash cards, flip charts and marker pens, seeds /pebbles	30

* The number in the parenthesis refers to the Session of Base Module of Chapter 3.

† The Serial numbers are continuous in this module.

Module 3 Session 2 (5)*
Politico-Legal Orientation

Session Theme	PANCHAYATI RAJ GOVERNANCE
Duration	90 minutes
Venue	Classroom without fixed furnitures
Seating	Sit/stand on the ground forming a circle; move around the room for the game and picture/poster sessions.
Session Objective	*To expand the practical understanding of the participants about the concept of self government and its institutions.*

Expected Learning Outcomes

- Increased understanding of the principles underlying the concept of self government, the role and functions of PRIs as institutions for self government at the grassroots level.

Content Flow and Training Methodology

Sr. No.	*Content*	*Training Methodology*	*Training Aids*	*Duration (in minutes)*
5.	Game for Experience sharing among the Participants about Village Panchayat Governance	**Step 1** Stepping Stones	None	30
6.	Self -government and the Panchayat Raj Institutions : Concept and Status	**Step 2** Poster and Picture based discussions and Lecture Method	Posters/Pictures and any other aids as desired by the trainer	45
7.	Synthesis of Learning Points by Trainer/ Participants	**Step 3** Visual Method	Overhead slides, Flip Charts	15

* The number in the parenthesis refers to the Session of Base Module of Chapter 3.

Module 3 Session 3 (4)*

General Orientation

Session Theme	PEOPLE-CENTRED COMMUNITY DEVELOPMENT
Duration	240 minutes
Venue	Classroom without fixed furnitures
Seating	Sit/stand on the ground forming a circle for group work; move around the room for the game and picture/poster sessions.
Session Objective	*To impart to the participant a conceptual understanding of people-centred community development.*

Expected Learning Outcomes

- The participants get acquainted with the different approaches and programmes for village development.
- They are able to appreciate the philosophy of people-centred community development.

Content Flow and Training Methodology

Sr. No.	*Content*	*Training Methodology*	*Training Aids*	*Duration (in min.)*
8.	(a) Changes in the development paradigm (b) The consistency of the status of decentralisation in India with the changing development paradigm	**Step 1** Historical Transect **Step 2** Lecture Method	Flip charts, marker pens, overhead slides, cards	60[18]
9.	Different approaches to development and the approach most appropriate for village level development	**Step 3** Matching Game	Cards, marker pens, seeds or pebbles	45

* The number in the parenthesis refers to the Session of Base Module of Chapter 3.

18. Preparation time: 25, Presentation and Discussion time: 20; Lecture: 15

Sr. No.	*Content*	*Training Methodology*	*Training Aids*	*Duration (in min.)*
10.	(c) Status of village development in India in the context of the different development approaches (d) Status of gender equity and social justice in this context	**Step 4** Pictures	Slides, drawings of cartoons	30
11.	Ways and means to improve the status of village development in India	**Step 5** Ranking and Scoring	Cards, marker pens, seeds or pebbles	45
12.	Development Programmes and ways and means to improve their efficiency	**Step 6** Pie Charts **Step 7** Ranking and Scoring	Flip Charts, marker pens, cards, coins of different denominations adding to a rupee, seeds or pebbles	45
13.	Synthesis of learning points by Trainer/ Participant(s)	**Step 8** Visual Method	Overhead slides/Flip Charts prepared by the participants	15

Module 3 Session 4 (3)*
General Orientation

Session Theme	**GENDER AND SOCIAL JUSTICE**
Duration	165 minutes
Venue	Classroom without fixed furnitures
Seating	Sit/stand on the ground forming a circle for the group work, move around the room for the games.
Session Objective	*To conscientise the participants about the social concerns related to gender, social justice and social exclusion.*

Expected Learning Outcomes

- The participants understand the issues related to gender and social exclusion that are prevalent in village-level society.
- They become aware of the duties of the Zilla Parishad for promoting social justice through both its governance and development related functions.

Content Flow and Training Methodology

Sr. No.	*Content*	*Training Methodology*	*Training Aids*	*Duration (in minutes)*
14.	Energising Game	**Step 1** Who are We?	None	15
15.	Concept of Gender, Differences between sexuality and gender	**Step 2** Gender Analysis through Pictures	Flip Charts and marker pens	45[15]
16.	Neglect of gender and social justice	**Step 3** Gendered Resource Mapping	Flip Charts and marker pens	45

* The number in the parenthesis refers to the Session of Base Module of Chapter 3.

19. It is suggested that the duration be factored thus:
Preparation time: 30; Presentation and Discussion time: 15; Total: 45

Sr. No.	*Content*	*Training Methodology*	*Training Aids*	*Duration (in minutes)*
17.	Explore ways and means to rectify the situation	**Step 4** Access Social Mapping **Step 5** Solution Tree	Flip Charts and marker pens	45
18.	Synthesis of learning points	**Step 6** Visual Method	Overhead slides/maps, pictures	15

Module 3

Session 5(6)*
Politico-Legal Orientation

Session Theme	**ROLE OF PANCHAYATI RAJ INSTITUTIONS**
Duration	150 minutes
Venue	Classroom without fixed furnitures
Seating	Sit/stand on the ground forming a circle; move around the room for the Force Field Analysis and picture-based discussions.
Session Objective	*To expand the practical understanding of the participants about the social mandate of the Panchayati Raj Institutions.*

Expected Learning Outcomes

Enlarged the comprehension of the participants about:

- The social mandate of the PRIs for meeting the ends of gender equity and social justice.
- The extent of the fulfilment of the social mandate.

Content Flow and Training Methodology

Sr. No.	*Content*	*Training Methodology*	*Training Aids*	*Duration (in min.)*
19.	Self-government and PRIs: Implications and frame of action for economic development, gender equity and social justice	**Step 1** Visual Method using a Cartoon show and picture based discussions	Cartoons and pictures	45[20]
20.	What were the original intentions of legislation and protagonists for the movement for self-government?	**Step 2** Lecture Method	Flash cards/ slides/ transparencies	30

* The number in the parenthesis refers to the Session of Base Module of Chapter 3.

20. It is suggested that the duration indicated for the sessions may be factored thus: Cartoon Show and Display of Pictures: 30; Discussion time: 15; Total: 45

Sr. No.	*Content*	*Training Methodology*	*Training Aids*	*Duration (in min.)*
21.	What happened to the original ideas and justifications for the PRIs?	**Step 3** Force Field Analysis **Step 4** Brainstorming	Different coloured cards, flip charts, marker pens	60
22.	Synthesis of learning points	**Step 5** Visual Method	As desired by trainer	15

Module 3

Session 6 (7)*
Politico-Legal Orientation

Session Theme	STRUCTURE OF PANCHAYATI RAJ INSTITUTIONS
Duration	140 minutes
Venue	Classroom without fixed furnitures
Seating	Sit/stand on the ground forming a circle
Session Objective	*To expand the knowledge of the participants about the legal premise and structure of Panchayati Raj Institutions.*

Expected Learning Outcome

- Increased acquaintance with the mandate and features of the Seventy Third Constitutional Amendment Act, the State Conformity Act for PRIs and the structure of PRIs.

Content Flow and Training Methodology

Sr. No.	*Content*	*Training Methodology*	*Training Aids*	*Duration (in minutes)*
23.	Game for Enhancing Group Dynamics	**Step 1** Saboteur	none	20
24.	The Seventy Third Constitutional Amendment Act and the State Conformity Act: Mandate and Salient Features	**Step 1** Lecture Method	As desired by the trainer	60
25.	Structure of Panchayati Raj Institutions — Gram Sabha, Village Panchayat, Panchayat Samity and Zilla Parishad	**Step 2** Lecture Method **Step 3** Role Play/ Drama of a Gram Sabha	As desired by the trainer	45
26.	Synthesis of learning points by Trainer/Participant(s)	Step 4 **Visual Method**	Overhead slides, Flip Charts	15

* The number in the parenthesis refers to the Session of Base Module of Chapter 3.

Module 3

Session 7 (8)*
Politico-Legal Orientation

Session Theme	ROLE OF THE ZILLA PARISHAD
Duration	180 minutes
Venue	Classroom without any fixed furnitures
Seating	Sit/stand on the ground forming a circle
Session Objective	*To conscientise the participants about their rights and duties as members of the Zilla Parishad and generate an urge in them to seek their rights.*

Expected Learning Outcomes: Increased awareness about:

- Their own rights and duties.
- The rightful place of the Zilla Parishad in grassroots governance.
- Its role, responsibilities and functions.
- What is necessary for having those rights, responsibilities and functions.

Content Flow and Training Methodology

Sr. No.	*Content*	*Training Methodology*	*Training Aids*	*Duration (in min.)*
27.	*De jure* Functions of the Zilla Parishad	**Step 1** Brainstorming **Step 2** Delphi Method	Flip charts, flash cards, marker pens	15 45
28.	*De facto* functions of the Zilla Parishad	**Step 3** Brain-storming **Step 4** Delphi Method	Flip charts, flash cards, marker pens	15 45
29.	How empowered is the Zilla Parishad?	**Step 5** Empowerment Circle	Large sheets of paper, flip charts, several coloured marker pens, flash cards, seeds, Post-It stickers, bindis	45
30.	Synthesis of learning points by Trainer/ Participant(s)	**Step 6** Visual Method	Overhead slides, Flip Charts	15

* The number in the parenthesis refers to the Session of Base Module of Chapter 3.

Module 3 Session 8 (10)*

Management Orientation

Session Theme	MANAGEMENT OF COMMUNITY DEVELOPMENT
Duration	225 minutes
Venue	Village Locale for the Social and Resource Mapping Classroom without fixed furnitures for the remaining session.
Seating	Sit/stand on the ground forming a circle; move around the room for the role play and group work.
Session Objective	*To empower the participants to function as agents of community development.*

Expected Learning Outcomes : The participants know about:

- The fundamentals of managing community development.
- The role of the Zilla Parishad in this context.
- The role of different development institutions and agencies and their linkages with the Zilla Parishad.

Content Flow and Training Methodology

Sr. No.	*Content*	*Training Methodology*	*Training Aids*	*Duration (in minutes)*
31.	Role of the Zilla Parishad in Community Development	**Step 1** Social Mapping	Flip Charts, marker pens	60
32.	Protection and Management of Common Property Resources	**Step 2** Resource Mapping	Flip Charts, marker pens	60
	Return to Classroom from Village Locale			
33.	The Zilla Parishad and the Community Development Network in the District level	**Step 3** Venn Diagramming	Flip Charts, marker pens, white paper, cards, scissors, glue	45

* The number in the parenthesis refers to the Session of Base Module of Chapter 3.

Sr. No.	*Content*	*Training Methodology*	*Training Aids*	*Duration (in minutes)*
34.	Quality of Relationship of the Zilla Parishad with other institutions/ individuals operating within the District	**Step 4** Communication Linkage Matrix	Flip Charts, marker pens, white paper, cards, scissors, glue, seeds and as desired by trainer and participants	45
35.	Synthesis of Learning Points by Trainer/ Participants	**Step 5** Visual Method	Overhead slides/Flip Charts	15

Module 3

Session 9 (12)*
Management Orientation

Session Theme	GOOD GOVERNANCE BY THE ZILLA PARISHAD
Duration	240 minutes
Venue	Classroom without fixed furnitures
Seating	Sit/stand on the ground forming a circle; move around the room for the role play and group work.
Session Objective	*To orient the participants with the principles of good governance and the mechanisms for promoting them.*

Expected Learning Outcomes

- The participants understand the basic values related to good governance of transparency, responsiveness, participation and accountability; understand the role of the Gram Sabha in this context and acquire skills for using the instruments of social and gender audit for promoting these values.

Content Flow and Training Methodology

Sr. No.	*Content*	*Training Methodology*	*Training Aids*	*Duration (in minutes)*
36.	Citizens' Charter for the Zilla Parishad	**Step 1** Case Study Method **Step 2** Brainstorming **Step 3** Delphi Method **Step 4** Ranking Method	Flip Charts, marker pens, cards and Citizens' Charter of some Zilla Parishads as case studies	90
37.	Role and Responsibilities of the Village Gram Sabha	**Step 5** Drama/Role Play	As desired by the trainer	30

* The number in the parenthesis refers to the Session of Base Module of Chapter 3.

Sr. No.	*Content*	*Training Methodology*	*Training Aids*	*Duration (in minutes)*
38.	Financial Transparency — Rationale and Practices: Gram Sabha, Publicity of Accounts and expenditure, monthly meetings, inspection of registers, financial audit	**Step 6** Case Study Method **Step 7** Lecture Method	As desired by the trainer	45
39.	Social and Gender Audit of Community Development Initiatives	**Step 8** Brainstorming **Step 9** Delphi Method **Step 10** Matrix Scoring Method	Flip Charts, marker pens, cards, different varieties of seeds for the scoring	60
40.	Synthesis of Learning Points by Trainer/ Participants	**Step 11** Visual Method	Overhead slides/Flip Charts	15

Module 3 Session 10 (13)*
Role Orientation

Session Theme PEOPLE-CENTRED BEHAVIOURS AND ATTITUDES

Duration 205 minutes

Venue Classroom without fixed furnitures

Seating Sit/stand on the ground forming a circle; move around the room for the role play and group work.

Session Objective *To enable the participants to comprehend the different kinds of people-centred behaviours and attitudes.*

Expected Learning Outcomes

- The participants are conscientised about the desired pro-people and pro-poor behaviours and attitudes that are expected of a Zilla Parishad member and learn to emulate them.

Content Flow and Training Methodology

Sr. No.	*Content*	*Training Methodology*	*Training Aids*	*Duration (in min.)*
41.	(a) How does a Zilla Parishad member/ development official usually behave? (b) What are the appropriate behaviours for a member/official?	**Step 1** Game "As a Zilla Parishad member, I mainly..."[21] **Step 2** Brainstorming	Flash cards, marker pens, flip charts, slides, transparencies	45 30
42.	Non-Verbal Behaviour	**Step 3** Game: Non-Verbal Circles	Chairs, sticks to improvise	25
43.	Role of a Zilla Parishad Member	**Step 4** Role Play/ Drama		30
44.	Game for Enhancing Group Dynamics	**Step 5** Chairs	Chairs	30

* The number in the parenthesis refers to the Session of Base Module of Chapter 3.

21. Adapted from Chambers 2002.

Sr. No.	*Content*	*Training Methodology*	*Training Aids*	*Duration (in min.)*
45.	Modelling of People-Centred Attitudes	**Step 6** Johari's Window **Step 7** Slide Show	Slides, sketches	30
46.	Synthesis of Learning Points	**Step 8** Visual Method	Flip Charts, marker pens,	15

Module 4

Training-cum-Awareness Camp for the Key Zilla Parishad Office Bearers

PROFILE OF MODULE 4

TRAINING-CUM-AWARENESS CAMP FOR THE KEY ZILLA PARISHAD OFFICE BEARERS

Objectives

- To create an awareness amongst the participants about the current state of the PRIs in India as institutions of self-government and the rights and duties of the Key Zilla Parishad Office Bearers.
- To enhance the practical understanding of the participants about the basic structure and functioning of the PRIs for meeting the goals of economic development, gender equity and social justice.
- To orient the participants with the principles of good management of the Zilla Parishad and the mechanisms for promoting them.

Participants

- Chairpersons, Zilla Parishad.
- Chief Executive Officers of the Zilla Parishad.

Addressed By

- Preferably a Cabinet Minister of the State Government.

Contents

1. *Panchayati Raj Governance*
   (a) The basic ethos of Panchayati Raj Institutions.
   (b) Self government and institutions of self government in the context of PRIs: Concepts, framework and the implications and frame of action for economic and social development, for gender and social justice.
2. *Gender and Social Justice*
   (a) Concept of Gender and Social Justice.
   (b) The unfulfilled tasks before the three tiers of PRIs with regard to making the PRIs institutions of self government for social and gender justice.

3. *Empowerment of the PRIs*
    (a) The Seventy-Third Constitutional Amendment Act and the State Conformity Acts.
    (b) Divergence between the intent of the Conformity Acts and the actual reality and the causes for this situation.
    (c) Powers and functions exercised by PRIs in the context of Eleventh Schedule of the Constitution, with special reference to planning for social and economic development and social and gender justice.
    (d) *De jure* Duties and Responsibilities of the PRIs and the Gram Sabha.
    (e) *De facto* Duties and responsibilities of the PRIs and the Gram Sabha.
    (f) Gap between *de jure* and *de facto* functions of the PRIs and the Gram Sabha.
    (g) Ways and means to fill the gap between *de jure* and *de facto* functions with reference to the expected and actual role of government vis-à-vis the PRIs in making them institutions of self government.
4. *Person Power Management of the PRIs*
    (a) Personnel policies for the PRIs including the creation of a PRI Cadre of Officers and extension staff.
5. *The PRI Network*
    (a) How to manage the inter-relationships between the three tiers of the PRIs?
    (b) Role of the Zilla Parishad Officials vis-à-vis the PRIs for functioning as institutions of self-government.
    (c) How to resolve the difficulties that affect the relationship between the Heads of Departments and the PRIs.
    (d) How to manage inter-relationships among the three tiers of the PRIs?
6. *Good Governance by the PRIs*
    (a) Degrees of freedom and accountability of the PRIs, both financial and performance related.
    (b) Why and how to improve transparency in functioning.
    (c) Review and audit of development programmes.
7. *People-centred Behaviours and Attitudes*

Duration: Three and a Half Days (@ 7 hours of training daily)

CONTENT FLOW IN MODULE 4

Table 5
Training-cum-Awareness Camp for the Key Zilla Parishad Office Bearers

Thematic Clusters and Ideas	*Session No.*	*Session No. of Base Module/ Module 3*	*Time (in minutes)*
Address by Cabinet Minister on "The basic ethos of Panchayati Raj Institutions"	1	—	30
Panchayati Raj Governance (a) Self government and institutions of self government in the context of PRIs: Concepts, framework and the implications and frame of action for economic and social development, for gender and social justice.	2	6 Base Module	150
Gender and Social Justice (a) Concept of Gender and Social Justice. (b) The unfulfilled tasks before the three tiers of PRIs with regard to making the PRIs institutions of self government for social and gender justice.	3	3 Base Module Note: Include discussion on the unfulfilled tasks before the PRIs in this context	165
Empowerment of the PRIs (a) The Seventy-Third Constitutional Amendment Act and the State Conformity Acts. (b) Divergence between the intent of the Conformity Acts and the actual reality and the causes for this situation.	4 and 5	7 and 8 Base Module	140 180

Thematic Clusters and Ideas	*Session No.*	*Session No. of Base Module/ Module 3*	*Time (in minutes)*
(c) Powers and functions exercised by PRIs in the context of Eleventh Schedule of the Constitution, with special reference to planning for social and economic development and social and gender justice. (d) *De jure* Duties and Responsibilities of the PRIs and the Gram Sabha. (e) *De facto* Duties and responsibilities of the PRIs and the Gram Sabha. (f) Gap between *de jure* and *de facto* functions of the PRIs and the Gram Sabha. (g) Ways and means to fill the gap between *de jure* and *de facto* functions with reference to the expected and actual role of government vis-à-vis the PRIs in making them institutions of self government.			
Person Power Management of the PRIs	6.	— *Note*: The session can begin by Brainstorming about the possible reforms in this context and the ideas clustered by the Delphi Technique, followed by	90

Thematic Clusters and Ideas	*Session No.*	*Session No. of Base Module/ Module 3*	*Time (in minutes)*
		Ranking the clusters. Next use case studies from other Zilla Parishads as illustrations.	
The PRI Network (a) How to manage the inter-relationships between the three tiers of the PRIs? (b) Role of the Zilla Parishad Officials vis-à-vis the PRIs for functioning as insti-tutions of self-govern-ment. (c) How to resolve the difficulties that affect the relationship between the Heads of Departments the PRIs. (d) How to manage inter-relationships among the three tiers of the PRIs?	7.	8 Module 3	225
Good Governance by the PRIs (a) Degrees of freedom and accountability of the PRIs, both financial and performance related. (b) Why and how to improve transparency in functioning. (c) Review and audit of development programmes.	8.	9 Module 3	240
People Centred Behaviours and Attitudes	9.	13 Base Module	205
Total Duration of Training			1425 (24 hours & 45 minutes)

NOTE TO TRAINERS FOR USING MODULE 4

TRAINING-CUM-AWARENESS CAMP FOR THE KEY ZILLA PARISHAD OFFICE BEARERS

1. INTRODUCTION

Module 4 brings together the Chairperson and the Chief Executive Officer of the Zilla Parishad for a process of experience sharing and collaborative learning. The Module creates an overall awareness and clarity about the fundamental concepts underlying Panchayati Raj Governance and the role of the PRIs in the highest hierarchical level of the PRIs. It is suggested that the programme should begin with an address about basic ethos of Panchayati Raj Institutions by a Cabinet Minister of the State Government.

2. MODULE CONTENTS

The Module contents are organized into seven thematic clusters consisting of different ideas. It has 10 sessions. Each thematic cluster of Module 4 corresponds to one or more sessions of the Base Module. The trainer will have to focus on the ideas within each thematic cluster while using the training methodology suggested in the corresponding sessions of the Base Module. Modifications similar to those made for Module 3 in the Session Plans of the Base Module will have to be also made by the trainer for Module 4. The *Content Flow for Module 4* is given in **Table 5**.

3. DURATION OF TRAINING

The Module requires about three and a half training days. The total duration of training is estimated to be 1500 minutes (25 hours).

Module 5

Operational Training for the Members and Officers of the Zilla Parishad

PROFILE OF MODULE 5

OPERATIONAL TRAINING FOR THE MEMBERS AND OFFICERS OF THE ZILLA PARISHAD

Objectives

- To help the participants to realize their potential and capacity to change the rural political, economic and social scenario especially in respect of economic development, gender equity and social justice and induce them to seek their rights and duties.
- To acquaint the elected representatives with the structure of Panchayati Raj bodies in the light of constitutional provisions, State Government Acts, Rules and Executive orders.
- To appraise the elected representatives with the structure and functioning of Panchayati Raj bodies in the different States and make a comparison with their own State.
- To orient the participants about knowledge and necessary skills in planning and implementation of rural development programmes with special reference to gender equity and social justice.

Participants

- Zilla Parishad Chairperson and Vice- Chairperson.
- Officers and Heads of Departments of the Zilla Parishad.
- Bank Officers from the District.

Contents

- Section 1: General Orientation
- Section 2: Politico-Legal Orientation
- Section 3: Management Orientation
- Section 4: Role Orientation
- Section 5: Micro-Level Planning Orientation
- Section 6: Field Immersion

Duration: Variable depending on the needs.

DETAILED CONTENT FLOW IN MODULE 5

Operational Training for the Members and Officers of the Zilla Parishad

SECTION 1: GENERAL ORIENTATION

(a) Democratic and political decentralization.
(b) What factors contribute to making democratic decentralization work.
(c) Changes in development paradigm and the consistency of current state of decentralisation in India with the changing paradigm.
(d) Different approaches to development (such as rights approach, empowerment approach, etc.) and the approach most appropriate for development for India at its current juncture in its development history.
(e) State of development in the country and the state in the context of the different approaches to development, including the state of gender equity and social justice.
(f) Ways and means to improve the state of development of the country, especially of the marginalised groups like women, Scheduled Castes/Scheduled Tribes and Other Backward Castes.
(g) Development Programmes and ways and means to improve their efficiency.
(h) How to ensure that the rule of law prevails in case a conflict arises between the "Rule of Law" *vs.* the "Rule of the Majority".

SECTION 2: POLITICO-LEGAL ORIENTATION

(a) Panchayati Raj:
- Historical background of why the present system of PRI was adopted?
- Concepts underlying PRIs: Units of Self government.
- Concepts of democratic decentralisation: Political and economic.
- Philosophy behind the democratic decentralisation: Social justice, gender equity and giving voice to the silent majority.
- The current status of the PRIs and the reasons for the state.

(b) Salient Features of Panchayati Raj structure in the concerned

State: Gram Sabha, Village Panchayat, Panchayat Samity, and Zilla Parishad.

(c) Self government and institution of self government in the context of PRIs: Concepts and framework.

(d) Self government and institution of self government in the context of PRIs: Implications and frame of action for economic development, gender equity and social justice.

(e) *De jure and de facto* functions of Zilla Parishads with particular reference to:
- Formation of the Standing Committee.
- Planning and Implementation of District Level plans.
- Ensuring gender equity.
- Securing social justice.
- Management of rural development schemes.
- Monitoring and evaluation having special regard for community participation, gender equity and social justice.
- *De jure* and *de facto* resources of Zilla Parishad.

(f) Personnel Management of the Zilla Parishad.

SECTION 3: MANAGEMENT ORIENTATION

(a) Administrative coordination with different Panchayat Samities.

(b) Role of Zilla Parishad in planning and development.

(c) Role of District level officials.

(d) Decentralized Planning:
- Creation of Data Base
- Preparation of Plans
- Mobilisation of Resources

(e) Implementation of Special Programmes.

(f) Budget of Zilla Parishad.

(g) Powers and Functions of Zilla Parishad.

(h) Resource Mobilization.

(i) Conduct of Business:
- Meetings of the Zilla Parishad
- Agenda
- Vote of No Confidence
- Disqualification of Members
- Quorum
- Minutes of Meeting

(j) Training of elected members and officials.

(k) Maintenance of the property of the Zilla Parishads.

(l) Management of Primary schools.

SECTION 4: ROLE ORIENTATION

A. Behavioural Aspects

(a) Roles and responsibilities of elected representatives as facilitators of the process of development.
(b) Roles and responsibilities of elected representatives as planners and implementers of plans for engendering gender equity and social justice.
(c) Roles and responsibilities of elected representatives as regulators being units of self government.
(d) Roles and responsibilities of elected representatives as custodians of public property being units of self government.
(e) Roles and responsibilities of Officials as facilitators of the process of development, as regulators and as custodians of public property, being part of units of self government.
(f) Roles and responsibilities of elected representatives as facilitators of the process of bringing about social justice with special reference to management of conflict and conflict resolution.
(g) Relationship between officials and elected representatives of the PRIs with the State Government within the framework of the district administration.

B. Attitudes and Behaviour

(a) Eschewing Dominance
(b) Shedding Arrogance
(c) Embracing Errors
(d) Fostering accountability (both performance and financial) and transparency.
(e) Team Building
(f) Eliminating errors of biases
(g) Seeking Diversity
(h) Respecting other's views
(i) Believing that people know their problems and are capable of suggesting solutions.
(j) The reality of the people count. People's analysis, people's criteria, people's monitoring, people's evaluation, people's views and people's knowledge counts. Not ours.

SECTION 5: MICRO-LEVEL PLANNING ORIENTATION

A. Planning for Development: On-Farm Livelihoods

(a) Agriculture, including agricultural extension.
(b) Land improvement, implementation of agrarian-reforms and soil conservation, minor irrigation, management of water resources including water harvesting.

B. Planning for Development: Off Farm Livelihoods

(a) Animal husbandry, dairying and poultry, fisheries etc.
(b) Small scale industries, including agro processing industries.
(c) Khadi, village and cottage industries.

C. Planning for Development of Physical Capital

(a) Rural housing and drinking water.
(b) Roads, culverts, bridges, ferries, waterways and other means of communication.
(c) Markets and fairs.
(d) Social forestry and farm forestry.
(e) Management of common property resources.
(f) Maintenance of community assets.
(g) Rural electrification and non-conventional energy sources.
(h) Poverty alleviation programmes.

D. Planning for Development of Human Capital

(a) Education, including primary and secondary schools.
(b) Technical training and vocational education.
(c) Adult and non-formal education, libraries and cultural activities.
(d) Family welfare, Health and sanitation, including hospitals, primary health centres and dispensaries.
(e) Women and child development.
(f) Social welfare, including welfare of the physically and mentally challenged people.
(g) Welfare of the weaker sections, and in particular, of women, Scheduled Castes and Scheduled Tribes.
(h) Public distribution system.
(i) Immediate and mid-term response to natural disaster/calamity.

SECTION 6: FIELD IMMERSION

The objectives of the field immersion are primarily to expose the participants to successful projects and help them internalise the lessons from this experience. Visits may be arranged to model Panchayats, individuals/social workers who have helped bring about social change, Cooperative Banks and Non-Governmental Organisations who have done innovative work. Visits may also be arranged to an agricultural research programme like a seed multiplication farm, dairy farm, cattle and poultry farms, afforestation sites, etc. In all cases the visit will be structured and there will be facilitators to help the participants process the information that they assimilate. This will help the participants to internalise the experience so that they can use it when they return to their Zilla Parishads.

NOTE TO TRAINERS FOR USING MODULE 5

OPERATIONAL TRAINING FOR THE MEMBERS AND OFFICERS OF THE ZILLA PARISHAD

1. INTRODUCTION

Module 5 follows the pattern of the Base Module in suggesting an operational or foundational training programme for the members and officers of the Zilla Parishad. The flow of contents is similar to that in the Base Module with the focus shifted from the Gram Panchayat to the Zilla Parishad. The trainer can replicate the methodology suggested in the Base Module for conducting training according to Module 5 with focus on Zilla Parishad. The thematic clusters for the Module contents have been specified and the trainer can design the corresponding session plans from them. This exercise was done for the Base Module and its session plans are indicative.

The Content flows of Module 5 will be the same as in the Base Module and hence are not repeated here.

Module 6

Operational Training for the Members and Officers of the Intermediate Panchayat

PROFILE OF MODULE 6

OPERATIONAL TRAINING FOR THE MEMBERS AND OFFICERS OF THE INTERMEDIATE PANCHAYAT

Objectives

- To help the participants to realize their potential and capacity to change the rural political, economic and social scenario.
- To acquaint the elected representatives with the structure of Panchayati Raj bodies in the light of constitutional provisions, State Government Acts, Rules and Executive orders.
- To appraise the elected representatives with the structure and functioning of Panchayati Raj bodies in the different States and make a comparison with their own State.
- Appraise the participants about the state of development in the country and the state in the context of the different approaches to development, including the state of gender equity and social justice.
- To help the participants acquire attitudes, knowledge and skills necessary for bringing about social and economic development.

Participants

- Pramukh and Upa-Pramukh of the Panchayat Samity.
- District Officers and Officers of the Panchayat Samity.
- Bank Officers from the District.

Contents

- Section 1: General Orientation
- Section 2: Politico-Legal Orientation
- Section 3: Management Orientation
- Section 4: Role Orientation
- Section 5: Micro-Level Planning Orientation
- Section 6: Field Immersion

Duration: Variable depending upon the training needs.

DETAILED CONTENT FLOW IN MODULE 6

Operational Training for the Members and Officers of the Intermediate Panchayat

SECTION 1: GENERAL ORIENTATION

(a) Concepts of development and shifts in development paradigm.
(b) Concept of democratic decentralization and factors that contribute to making democratic decentralization work.
(c) Different approaches to development.
(d) State of development in the country and the state in the context of the different approaches to development, including the state of gender equity and social justice.
(e) Democratic Decentralization and people's participation in political and economic governance.
(f) Rural Development Programmes.
(g) How to ensure that the rule of law prevails in case a conflict arises between the "Rule of Law" *vs.* the "Rule of the Majority".

SECTION 2: POLITICO-LEGAL ORIENTATION

(a) Decentralisation: Concepts and principles in historical context.
(b) Panchayati Raj: Concept and Status as institutions of self government for social justice and gender equity.
(c) Self government and institution of self government in the context of PRIs: Concepts and framework.
(d) Self government and institution of self government in the context of PRIs: Implications and frame of action.
(e) Salient Features of Panchayati Raj structure in the concerned State-Gram Sabha, Gram Panchayat, Panchayat Samity, and Zilla Parishad.
(f) De jure and de facto functions of Panchayat Samities with particular reference to nurturing the village level institutions of self government:
- The Village Panchayats.
- Planning and implementation of Block Level plans and programmes.
- Ensuring gender justice.
- Securing social justice.
- Management of rural development schemes.

- Monitoring and evaluation, having special regard for community participation, gender equity and social justice.

(g) *De jure and de facto* resources of the Panchayat Samities.
(h) Roles and responsibilities of Staff of Panchayat Samity.
(i) Supervision of Village Panchayats.

SECTION 3: MANAGEMENT ORIENTATION

(a) Team work.
(b) Administrative coordination with Zilla Parishad and different Panchayats.
(c) Emerging role of Panchayat Samity in Planning and Development.
(d) Role of block level officials.
(e) Maintenance of Records, accounts, audit and budgets.
(e) Preparation of Block 1evel plans.
(f) Coordination of preparation of Village-level Plans.
(g) Implementation of Special Programmes.
(h) Panchayat Samity.
(i) Resource Mobilization.
(j) Building relationship with State Government agencies operating at State/District/Block Level Agencies operating within District such as Banks/Cooperatives and Voluntary Organisations.
(k) Management of common property resources.
(l) Management of Public utility services.
(m) Managing the relationship between officials and elected representatives.
(n) Governance of the Panchayat Samity:
- Conduct of Business.
- Transparency in conduct of business.
- Resolution.
- No Confidence in Pramukh or Up-Pramukh.
- Administration of Affairs of Panchayat Samity.
- Establishment and general administration of Panchayat Samity.
- Imposition of Taxes etc. by Panchayat Samity.
- Fees for Inspection of Records and for obtaining Certified Copies.
- Panchayat Samity fund, accounts, audit and budgeting.
- Budgeting for the Panchayat Samity.
- Supervision of Village Panchayats .
- Immovable Properties.

- Administrative Report on Panchayat Administration.
- Registers and records of Panchayat Samities.

SECTION 4: ROLE ORIENTATION

A. Role and Responsibilities

(a) Roles and responsibilities of elected representatives as facilitators of the process of development.
(b) Roles and responsibilities of elected representatives as regulators being units of self government.
(c) Roles and responsibilities of elected representatives as custodians of public property being units of self government.
(d) Roles and responsibilities of Officials as facilitators of the process of development; as regulators and as custodians of public property, being part of units of self government.
(e) Roles and responsibilities of elected representatives as facilitators of the process of bringing about social justice with special reference to management of conflict and conflict resolution.
(f) Role of Panchayat functionaries as Community Contacts.
(g) Role of Panchayat functionaries in fostering a transparent and accountable system of governance.

B. Attitudes and Behaviour

(a) Eschewing Dominance
(b) Shedding Arrogance
(c) Embracing Errors
(d) Transparent behaviour
(e) Eliminating biases
(f) Seeking Diversity
(g) Respecting other's views
(h) Believing that people know their problems and are capable of suggesting solutions.
(i) The reality of the people count
(j) People's analysis, people's criteria, people's monitoring, people's evaluation, people's views and people's knowledge counts. Not ours.

SECTION 5: MICRO-LEVEL PLANNING ORIENTATION

- Agriculture, including agricultural extension

- Land improvement, implementation of agrarian reforms, land consolidation and soil conservation.
- Minor irrigation, water management and watershed development.
- Animal husbandry, dairying and poultry
- Fisheries
- Social forestry and farm forestry
- Minor forest produce
- Small scale industries, including food processing industries
- Khadi, village and cottage industries
- Rural housing
- Drinking water
- Fuel and fodder
- Roads, culverts, bridges, ferries, waterways and other means of communication.
- Rural electrification, including distribution of electricity
- Non-conventional energy sources.
- Poverty alleviation programme
- Education, including primary and secondary schools
- Technical training and vocational education
- Adult and non-formal education and Libraries
- Markets and fairs
- Family welfare, health and sanitation, including hospitals, primary health centres and dispensaries.
- Women and child development
- Social welfare, including welfare of the physically and mentally challenged.
- Welfare of the weaker sections of society, and in particular, of women and those belonging to Scheduled Castes and Scheduled Tribes.
- Immediate and mid-term response to natural disaster/calamity
- Management of common property resources
- Maintenance of community assets

SECTION 6: FIELD IMMERSION

The objectives of the field immersion are primarily to expose the participants to successful projects and help them internalise the lessons from this experience. Visits may be arranged to model Panchayats, individuals/social workers who have helped bring about social change, Cooperative Banks and Non-Governmental Organisations who have done innovative work. Visits may also be arranged to an agricultural research programme like a seed multiplication farm, dairy farm, cattle and poultry farms, afforestation sites, etc. In all cases the visit will be structured and there will be facilitators to help the participants process the information that they assimilate. This will help the participants to internalise the experience so that they can use it when they return to their Panchayat Samities.

NOTE TO TRAINERS FOR USING MODULE 6

OPERATIONAL TRAINING FOR THE MEMBERS AND OFFICERS OF THE INTERMEDIATE PANCHAYAT

1. INTRODUCTION

Module 6 follows the pattern of the Base Module in suggesting an operational or foundation training programme for the members and officers of the Intermediate Panchayat. The flow of contents is similar to that in the Base Module with focus of Intermediate Panchayats in place of Gram Panchayats. The trainer can draw from the methodology suggested in the Base Module for extensive use in Module 6. The thematic clusters have been given in detail from which the corresponding session plans can be designed. This is the exercise which has already been done for the Base Module and is indicative.

The Content flows of Module 6 will be the same as in the Base Module and hence are not repeated here.

Module 7

Mass Awareness-cum-Motivation Camps for the Members and Officers of the Panchayat Raj Institutions

PROFILE OF MODULE 7

MASS AWARENESS-CUM-MOTIVATION CAMPS FOR THE MEMBERS AND OFFICERS OF THE PANCHAYAT RAJ INSTITUTIONS

OBJECTIVES

- To refresh the understanding of the participants about the basic principles and objectives of establishing the PRIs in India and the rights and duties of PRI functionaries.
- To assess how far the objectives have been met and why the PRI functionaries have not achieved their full potential of changing the rural political, economic and social scenario.

PARTICIPANTS

- All Elected Panchayat functionaries including the Chairperson, Zilla Parishad; Pramukh, Panchayat Samity and the Sarpanch, Village Panchayat.
- The key State officials like the Chief Secretary and departmental Secretaries and District officials.

ADDRESS BY

The Chief Minister. However, since the number of such programmes in a State will be very large, the CM may be able to spare time for a few of them. In the others, the message from the CM can be disseminated either through a video recording or audio cassettes or printed leaflets.

CHAIRED BY

Minister for Rural Development and Panchayati Raj of the State Government.

CONTENTS

1. Basic Principles behind Panchayati Raj Governance.

2. Self government and institutions of self government in the context of PRIs: Concepts and framework, implications and frame of action.
3. Self Government for social and gender justice.
4. Rights and duties of the PRIs.
5. Reasons for the shortfall in realising the full potential of the PRIs.
6. Duties and responsibilities of the elected members and government officers in respect of making the Panchayats true units of self-government, for social and gender justice.
7. Inter-relationships between elected members and government officers of the PRIs for making the Panchayats units of self-government, for social and gender justice.
8. Autonomy, accountability both financial and performance related and transparency: how are they achieved?

Duration: One day 8 a.m. to 5 p.m., with breakfast and lunch.

NOTE TO TRAINERS FOR USING MODULE 7

MASS AWARENESS-CUM-MOTIVATION CAMPS FOR THE MEMBERS AND OFFICERS OF THE PANCHAYAT RAJ INSTITUTIONS

1. INTRODUCTION

Module 7 is in the nature of a one-day awareness raising and motivation camp which brings the elected members from the three tiers of the PRIs and the State and District level officers together for a process of self-introspection and group learning. Their understanding of the basic principles underlying the establishment of the PRIs is refreshed. They recall the rights and duties of the PRI members. Based on this, they assess the fulfilment of the objectives of the PRIs and the reasons for the PRIs not realizing their full potential. It is expected that the whole exercise will throw up an *agenda of actions* for both proactive policy-making and better field-level programme implementation. This kind of camp will also facilitate information flows among different stakeholder-groups like State-level Secretaries, district officers and PRI elected members whose combined efforts are necessary for enabling the PRIs to achieve their goals of economic and social development with gender and social justice.

2. MODULE CONTENTS

The theme areas for the Module Contents have been specified. The trainer can draw from the session plans and methodology given in the Base Module for covering the suggested areas.

Module 8

Training-cum-Motivation Camps for the Members of the Gram Sabha

PROFILE OF MODULE 8

TRAINING-CUM-MOTIVATION CAMPS FOR THE MEMBERS OF THE GRAM SABHA

Objectives

- To review the basic principles and objectives of establishing the PRIs in India and the rights and duties of the Gram Sabha.
- To do a SWOT[22] analysis of how far the objectives have been met and why the PRI functionaries have not achieved their full potential.

Participants

- Members of the Gram Sabha.
- The key government officers and staff at the village level.

Contents

1. Basic Principles behind the establishment of the PRIs.
2. Self government and institutions of self government in the context of the PRIs for social and gender justice.
3. Rights and duties of the Gram Sabha.
4. Reasons for the shortfall in realising the full potential of the Gram Sabha in making the PRIs the true units of self-government for social and gender justice.
5. Role of the Gram Sabha in the functioning of the different village level committees.
6. How would the Gram Sabha ensure autonomy, accountability both financial and performance related and transparency of the Village Panchayat and social audit?

Duration: Four Hours

22. Strengths, Weaknesses, Opportunities and Threats.

NOTE TO TRAINERS FOR USING MODULE 8

TRAINING-CUM-MOTIVATION CAMPS FOR MEMBERS OF THE GRAM SABHA

1. INTRODUCTION

Module 8 is in the nature of half a day awareness raising session for the members of the Gram Sabha. The module is intended to galvanise the members of the Gram Sabha to actively participate in the meetings of Gram Sabha, being aware of their roles, roles of the Gram Panchayats and of the rights and duties of the PRI functionaries. It is expected that members of the Gram Sabha would realise the reasons for which the PRIs have not really been able to acquit themselves creditably. Such realisation would help the members of the Gram Sabha to support the PRI functionaries to seek their rights to govern and convert the PRIs as truly units of local self-governance.

2. MODULE CONTENT AND METHODOLOGY

Since the participants are likely to be large, the Trainer has to adopt a training methodology appropriate for large groups. Poster sessions, group-activity and lecture — Video demonstration can be fruit fully used.

Module 9
Mass Awareness Camps about Panchayati Raj

PROFILE OF MODULE 9

MASS AWARENESS CAMPS ABOUT PANCHAYATI RAJ INSTITUTIONS

Objectives

- To generate awareness about the basic principles and objectives of establishing the PRIs in India and the rights and duties of PRI functionaries.
- To create public awareness of the expected role of the PRIs as institutions of self-government.

Participants

- Members of the Public, NGOs and other interest groups.

Address By

- Public figures/opinion leaders.

Chaired By

- Opinion leaders wherever warranted.

Contents

1. Basic Principles behind Panchayati Raj Governance.
2. Self government and institutions of self government in the context of PRIs: Concepts and framework, implications and frame of action.
3. Self Government for social and gender justice.
4. Rights and duties of the PRIs.
5. Reasons for the shortfall in realising the full potential of the PRIs as institutions of self-government for social justice and gender equity.
6. Role of the public in securing autonomy, accountability both financial and performance related and transparency of the PRIs.

***Duration:** Four Hours*

NOTE TO TRAINERS FOR USING MODULE 9

MASS AWARENESS CAMP ABOUT PANCHAYATI RAJ INSTITUTIONS

1. INTRODUCTION

Module 9 is in the nature of a campaign. The campaign is expected to inform public opinion about the rights and duties of PRI functionaries and about the reasons that have been instrumental in preventing PRIs from discharging their responsibilities as enjoined by the spirit and letter of the Constitution. It is expected that an informed public opinion will create an enabling environment for the PRI functionaries to seek their rights and duties.

2. TRAINING METHODOLOGY

Since Module 9 is expected to be administered to large audiences, it is important that the Trainer uses methods for delivery of inputs appropriate for large gatherings. Exhibition, Cinema and public lectures are some of the suggested methods.

Module 10

Awareness Camps for the Media About Panchayati Raj

PROFILE OF MODULE 10

AWARENESS CAMPS FOR THE MEDIA ABOUT PANCHAYATI RAJ

Objectives

- To provide an insight into the basic principles and objectives of establishing the PRIs in India and the rights and duties of PRI functionaries as enjoined in the letter and spirit of the Seventy Third Constitutional Amendment Act.
- To enable the participants to make an assessment of how far the objectives have been met and why the PRIs have not achieved their full potential.

Participants

- Members of the National Press (Reporters/Chief Reporters), the Chief of the News Bureau, the Editors of the Vernacular Press.

Address By

- The Chief Minister and/or the Minister-in-charge of Panchayati Raj and Rural Development.

Chaired By

- The Editor of a newspaper.

Contents

1. Basic Principles behind the establishment of the PRIs.
2. Self government and institutions of self government in the context of PRIs: implications and frame of action.
3. Potential role of PRIs for social and gender justice.
4. Reasons for the shortfall in realising the full potential of the PRIs as institutions of self-government.
5. Duties and responsibilities of the elected members and officials of the PRIs for making the PRIs true units of self-government, for social and gender justice.
6. Role of the media in creating a demand for the transformation of the PRIs.

Duration: 4 hours

NOTE TO TRAINERS FOR USING MODULE 10

1. INTRODUCTION

Module 10 is in the nature of a campaign to do advocacy work with the media. The awareness generation of the media should help in harnessing its support to make the PRIs true institutions of local self-governance, by acting as pressure prints to allow PRI functionaries seek their rights and responsibilities.

2. TRAINING METHODOLOGY

Since the Trainers will be dealing with a highly sensitive and informed audience in module 10, it would be necessary to prepare well and invite guest speakers who are well informed. The role of good handouts of different dimensions of training will be critical as they may be used for the participants as copy material for their reporting.

APPENDICES

APPENDIX A

Functions of the Village Panchayat

I. **Preparation of annual plans for the development of the Panchayat area**
   1. Preparation of annual budget
   2. Providing relief in natural calamities
   3. Removal of encroachments on public properties
   4. Organising voluntary labour and contribution for community works
   5. Maintenance of essential statistics of the villages

II. **Agriculture, including Agricultural Extension**
   1. Promotion and development of agricultural extension
   2. Promotion and development of agriculture and horticulture
   3. Development of wastelands
   4. Development and maintenance of grazing lands and preventing their unauthorised alienation and use.

III. **Animal Husbandry, Dairying and Poultry**
   1. Improvement of breed of cattle, poultry and other livestock
   2. Promotion of dairy farming, poultry and piggery
   3. Grassland development

IV. **Fisheries**
   Development of fisheries in the villages

V. **Social and Farm Forestry, Minor Forest Produce, Fuel and Fodder**
   1. Planting and preservation of trees on the sides of roads and other public lands under its control.
   2. Fuel plantations and fodder development
   3. Promotion of farm forestry
   4. Development of social forestry

VI. **Khadi, Village and Cottage Industries**
   1. Promotion of rural and cottage industries
   2. Organisation of conferences, seminars and training programmes, agricultural and industrial exhibitions for the benefit of the rural areas.

VII. **Rural Housing**

1. Distribution of house sites within village/police station limits
2. Maintenance of records relating to the houses, sites and other private and public properties.

VIII. **Drinking Water**

1. Construction, repair and maintenance of drinking water wells, tanks and ponds.
2. Prevention and control of water pollution
3. Maintenance of rural water supply schemes

IX. **Roads, Buildings, Culverts, Bridges, Ferries, Waterways and Other Means of Communication**

1. Construction and maintenance of village roads, drains and culverts.
2. Maintenance of boats, ferries and waterways.

X. **Rural Electrification including Distribution of Electricity**

1. Providing for the maintenance of lighting of public streets and other places.

XI. **Non-Conventional Energy Sources**

1. Promotion and development of non-conventional energy schemes.
2. Maintenance of community non-conventional energy schemes.
3. Propagation of improved chulhas/cooking ovens and other efficient energy devices.

XII. **Poverty Alleviation Programmes**

1. Promotion of public awareness and participants in poverty alleviation programmes for fuller employment and creation of productive assets, etc.
2. Selection of beneficiaries under various programmes through the Gram Sabha.
3. Participation in effective implementation and monitoring.

XIII. **Education, including Primary and Secondary Schools**

1. Promotion of public awareness and participation in primary and secondary education.
2. Ensuring full enrolment and attendance in primary schools.

XIV. **Adult and Non-formal Education**
Promotion of Adult Literacy

XV. **Libraries**
Village libraries and Reading Rooms

XVI. **Cultural Activities**
Promotion of social and cultural Activities

XVII. **Markets and Fairs**
1. Maintenance of general sanitation
2. Cleaning of public roads, drains, tanks wells and other public places
3. Maintenance and regulation of burning and burial grounds
4. Construction and maintenance of public latrines
5. Disposal of unclaimed corpses and carcasses
6. Management and control of washing and bathing ghats/sites

XVIII. **Public Health and Family Welfare**
1. Implementation of Family Welfare Programmes
2. Prevention and remedial measures against epidemics
3. Regulation of sale of meat, fish and other perishable food articles
4. Participation in programmes of human and animal vaccination
5. Licensing of eating and entertainment establishments
6. Destruction of stray dogs
7. Regulation of curing, tanning and dyeing of skins and hides
8. Regulation of offensive and dangerous trades

XIX. **Women and Child Development**
1. Participation in the implementation of the social welfare programmes, including welfare of the handicapped, mentally retarded and destitute
2. Participation in the implementation of the specific programmes for the welfare of the weaker sections

XX. **Public Distribution System**
1. Promotion of public, awareness with regard to the distribution of essential commodities.
2. Monitoring the public distribution system

XXI. **Maintenance of Community Assets**

1. Maintenance of community assets
2. Preservation and maintenance of other community assets

XXIII. **Construction and Maintenance of Dharmashalas/Shelters and Similar Institutions**

XXIV. **Construction and Maintenance of Cattle Sheds Ponds and Cart Stands**

XXV. **Construction and Maintenance of Slaughter Houses**

XXVI. **Maintenance of public parks, playgrounds, etc.**

XXVII. **Regulation of manure pits in public places**

XXVIII. **Establishment and Control of Shanties**

XXIX. **Any other Functions that may be entrusted**

APPENDIX B

Functions of the Intermediate Panchayat

I. **General Functions**

1. Preparation of the Annual Plans in respect of the schemes entrusted to it by virtue of the Act and those assigned to it by the Government or the Zilla Panchayat and submission thereof to the Zilla Panchayat within the prescribed time for integration with the District Plan.
2. Consideration and consolidation of the Annual Plans of all Gram Panchayats in the taluka and submission of the consolidated plan to the Zilla Panchayat.
3. Preparation of annual budget of the taluka and its submission within the prescribed time to the Zilla Panchayat.
4. Performing such functions and executing such works as may be entrusted to it by the Government or the Zilla Panchayat.
5. Providing relief in natural calamities.

II. **Agriculture, including Agricultural Extension**

1. Promotion and development of agriculture and horticulture
2. Maintenance of agricultural seed farms
3. Storing and distribution of insecticides and pesticides
4. Promotion of improved methods of cultivation
5. Promotion of cultivation and marketing of vegetables, fruits and flowers
6. Training of farmers and extension activities

III. **Land Improvement and Soil Conservation**

1. Assisting the government and Zilla Panchayat in implementation of land improvement and soil conservation programmes of the government.

IV. **Minor Irrigation, Water Management and Watershed Development**

1. Assisting the government and Zilla Panchayat in the construction and maintenance of Minor Irrigation works.
2. Implementation of community and individual irrigation works.

V. **Animal Husbandry, Dairying and Poultry**

1. Maintenance of veterinary and animal husbandry services
2. Improvement of breed of cattle, poultry and other livestock
3. Promotion of dairy farming, poultry and piggery
4. Prevention of epidemics and contagious diseases

VI. **Fisheries**

1. Promotion of fisheries development

VII. **Khadi, Village and Cottage Industries**

1. Promotion of rural and cottage industries
2. Organisation of conferences, seminars and training programmes, agricultural and industrial exhibitions.

VIII. **Rural Housing**

1. Implementation of housing schemes and distribution of house sites in villages outside Village/Police Station limits.

IX. **Drinking Water**

1. Establishment, repairs and maintenance of rural water supply schemes.
2. Prevention and control of water pollution.
3. Implementation of rural sanitation schemes.

X. **Social and Farm Forestry, Minor Forest Product, Fuel and Fodder**

1. Planting and preservation of trees on the sides of roads and other public lands under its control.
2. Fuel plantation and fodder development.
3. Promotion of farm forestry.

XI. **Roads, Buildings, Bridges, Ferries, Waterways and other means of Communication**

1. Construction and maintenance of public roads, drains, culverts and other means of communications which are not under the control of any other authority or the government.
2. Maintenance of any building or other property vested in the Intermediate Panchayat.
3. Maintenance of boats, ferries and waterways.

XII. **Non-conventional Energy sources**

1. Promotion and development of non-conventional energy sources.

XIII. **Poverty Alleviation Programmes**

1. Implementation of poverty alleviation programmes.

XIV. **Education including Primary and Secondary Schools**

1. Promotion of primary and secondary education.
2. Construction, repair and maintenance of primary school buildings.
3. Promotion of social education through youth clubs and Mahila Mandals[1].

XV. **Technical Training and Vocational Education**

1. Promotion of rural artisan and vocational training.

XVI. **Adult and Non-formal Education**

1. Implementation of adult literacy.

XVII. **Cultural Activities**

1. Promotion of social and cultural activities.

XVIII. **Market and Fairs**

1. Regulation of fairs and festivals.

XIX. **Health and Family Welfare**

1. Promotion of health and family welfare programmes.
2. Promotion of immunisation and vaccination programmes.
3. Health and sanitation at fairs and festivals.

XX. **Women and Child Development**

1. Promotion of programmes relating to development of women and children.
2. Promotion of school, health and nutrition programmes.
3. Promotion of participation of voluntary organisations in women and child development programmes.

XXI. **Social Welfare including Welfare of the Handicapped and Mentally Retarded**

1. Social welfare programmes including welfare of the handicapped, mentally retarded and destitute.
2. Monitoring the old age and widow's pensions and pensions for the handicapped.

---

1. Women's Groups.

XXII. Welfare of the Weaker Sections and in particular of the Scheduled Castes and Scheduled Tribes

1. Promotion of welfare of Scheduled Castes, Scheduled Tribes and other weaker sections.
2. Protecting such castes and classes from social injustice and exploitation.

XXII. Rural Electrification

1. Promotion of rural electrification.

XXIV. Co-operation

Promotion of co-operative activities.

XXV. Libraries

1. Promotion of libraries.

XXVI. Such other functions as may be entrusted

APPENDIX C

Functions of Zilla Parishad

I. General Functions

Overall supervision, co-ordination and integration of development schemes at taluka and district levels and preparing the plan for the development of the district.

II. Agriculture (including Agricultural Extension) and Horticulture

1. Promotion of measures to increase agricultural production and to popularise the use of improved agricultural implements and the adoption of improved agricultural practices.
2. Opening and maintenance of agricultural and horticultural farms and commercial farms.
3. Establishment and maintenance of godowns.
4. Conducting agricultural fairs and exhibitions.
5. Management of agricultural and horticultural extension and training centres.
6. Training of farmers.

III. Land Improvement and Soil Conservation

Planning and implementation of land improvement and soil conservation programmes entrusted by the Government.

IV. Minor Irrigation, Water Management and Watershed Development

1. Construction, renovation and maintenance of minor irrigation works.
2. Providing for the timely and equitable distribution and full use of water irrigation schemes under the control of the Zilla Panchayat.
3. Watershed development programmes.
4. Development of groundwater resources.

V. **Animal Husbandry, Dairying and Poultry**

1. Establishment and maintenance of taluka and village veterinary hospitals, first-aid centres and mobile veterinary dispensaries.
2. Improvement of breed of cattle, poultry and other livestock.
3. Promotion of dairy farming, poultry and piggery.
4. Prevention of epidemics and contagious diseases.

VI. **Fisheries**

1. Development of fisheries in irrigation works vested in the Zilla Panchayat.
2. Promotion of inland, brackish water and marine fish culture.
3. Implementation of fishermen's welfare programmes.

VII. **Khadi, Village and Cottage Industries**

1. Promotion of rural and cottage industries.
2. Establishment and management of training-cum-production centres.
3. Organisation of marketing facilities for products of cottage and village industries.
4. Implementation of schemes of State Boards and All India Boards and Commissions for development of rural and cottage industries.

VIII. **Small Scale Industries including Food Processing Industries**

1. Promotion of small-scale industries.

IX. **Rural Housing**

1. Promotion of rural housing programme.

X. **Drinking Water**

1. Promotion of drinking water and rural sanitation programmes.

XI. **Minor Forest Produce and Fuel and Fodder**

1. Promotion of social and farm forestry, fuel plantation and fodder development.
2. Management of minor forest produce of the forests raised in community lands.
3. Development of wasteland.

XII. Roads, Building, Bridges, Ferries, Waterways and other Means of Communications

1. Construction of maintenance of district roads and culverts, causeways and bridges (excluding State highways and village roads).
2. Construction of administrative and other buildings in connection with requirements of the Zilla Panchayat.

XIII. Non-conventional Energy Sources

1. Promotion and development of non-conventional energy sources.

XIV. Poverty-alleviation Programmes

1. Planning, supervision and monitoring and implementation of poverty alleviation programmes.

XV. Education including Primary and Secondary Schools

1. Promotion of educational activities in the district including the establishment and maintenance of primary and secondary schools.
2. Establishment and maintenance of *ashrams*, schools and orphanages.
3. Survey and evaluation of educational activities.

XVI. Technical Training and Vocational Education

1. Establishment and maintenance of rural artisan and vocational training centres.
2. Encouraging and assisting rural vocational training centres.

XVII. Adult and Non-formal Education

1. Planning and implementation of programmes of adult literacy and non-formal education programme.

XVIII. Markets and Fairs

1. Regulation of important fairs and festivals in the district.

XIX. Health and Family Welfare

1. Management of hospitals and dispensaries excluding those under the management of government or any other authority.
2. Implementation of maternity and child health programmes.
3. Implementation of family welfare programmes.

4. Implementation of immunisation and vaccination programme.

XX. Women and Child Development

1. Promotion of programmes relating to development of women and children.
2. Promotion of school health and nutrition programmes.
3. Promotion of participation of voluntary organisations in women and child development programmes.

XXI. Social Welfare, including welfare of the Handicapped and Mentally Retarded

1. Promotion of social welfare programmes, including welfare of the handicapped, mentally retarded and destitute.

XXII. Welfare of the Weaker Sections and in particular of the Scheduled Castes and Scheduled Tribes

1. Promotion of educational, economic, social, cultural and other interests of the Scheduled Castes, Scheduled Tribes and Backward Classes.

Bibliography

Bradley, Sarah Murray (1995): *How People Use Pictures* (London: International Institute for Environment and Development).

Chambers, Robert (1997): *Whose Reality Counts* (London: Intermediate Technology Press).

Chambers, Robert (2002): *Participatory Workshops* (London: Earthscan).

Institute of Social Sciences (2000): *Status of Panchayati Raj in the State, and Union Territories of India* (New Delhi: Concept Publishing Company).

Kapur, S. (2002): *Planning and Conducting a Training Programme* (New Delhi: Infinity Books).

Mukherjee, Amitava (1995): *Participatory Rural Appraisal: Methods and Applications in Rural Planning* (New Delhi: Vikas Publishing House 1995 and 2nd revised edition by New Delhi: Concept Publishing Company, 2003).

Mukherjee, Neela (2002): *Participatory Learning and Action: With 100 Field Methods* (New Delhi: Concept Publishing Company).

National Institute of Rural Development (2001): *India: Panchayati Raj Report* (Hyderabad: National Institute of Rural Development) Volume I and II.

Palanithurai, G. (2002): *Capacity Building for Local Body Leaders* (New Delhi: Concept Publishing Company).

Pretty, Jules N., Guijt Irene, Thompson, John and Scoones (1995): *Participatory Learning and Action, A Trainer's Guide* (London: International Institute for Environment and Development).

Towin Shend, John (2001): *The Trainer's Pocketbook* (New Delhi: Research Press).

Vidya Bhawan Society (2001): *Panchayati Raj Janpratinidhi Sandarshika (Handbook for People-Representative)* (Udaipur: School of Local Self-Government and Responsible Citizenship).

Index